The ANIMAL DRAWING Primer

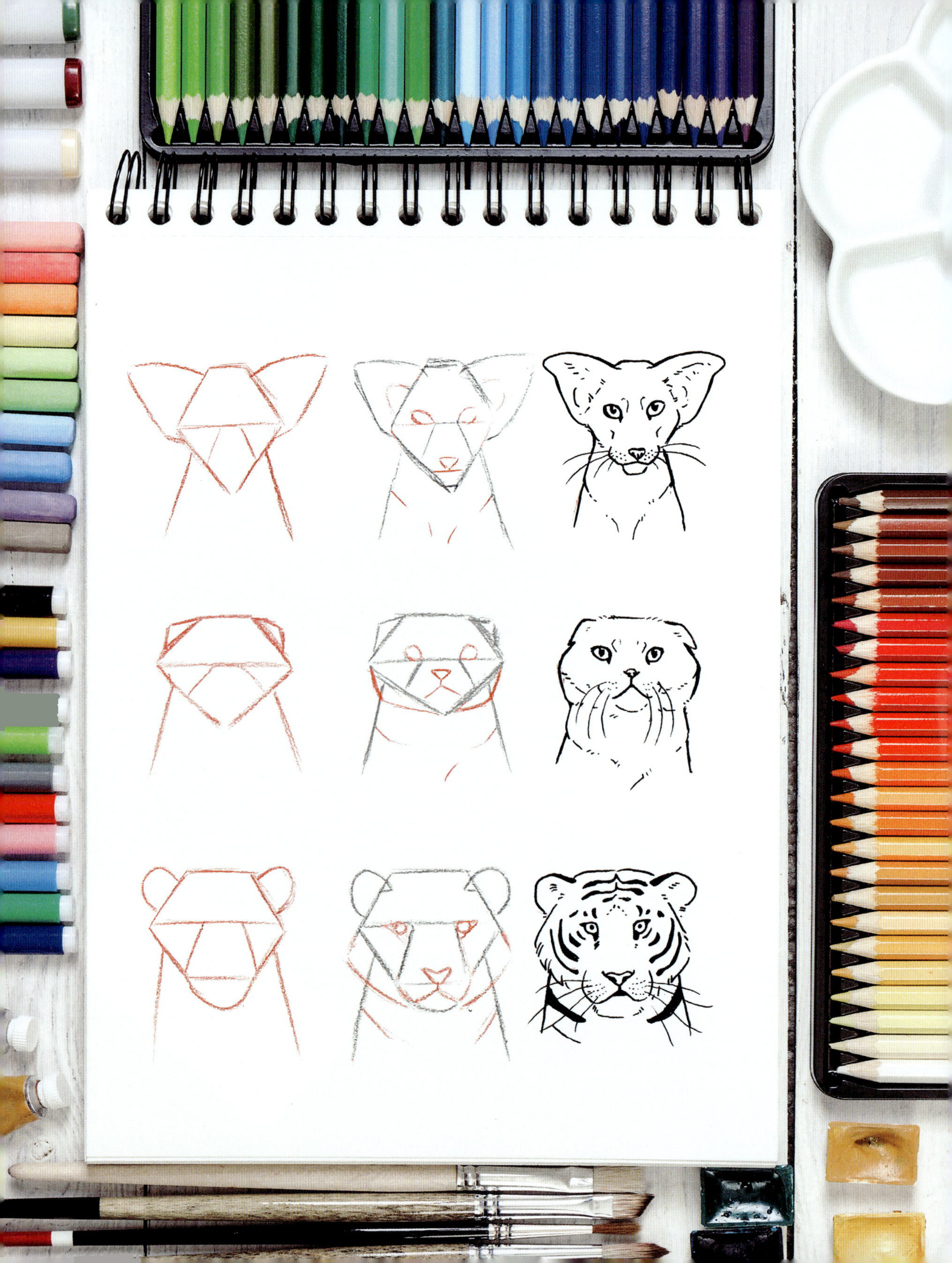

Fundamental Tutorials for Illustrating
Dogs, Cats, Horses ***and More***

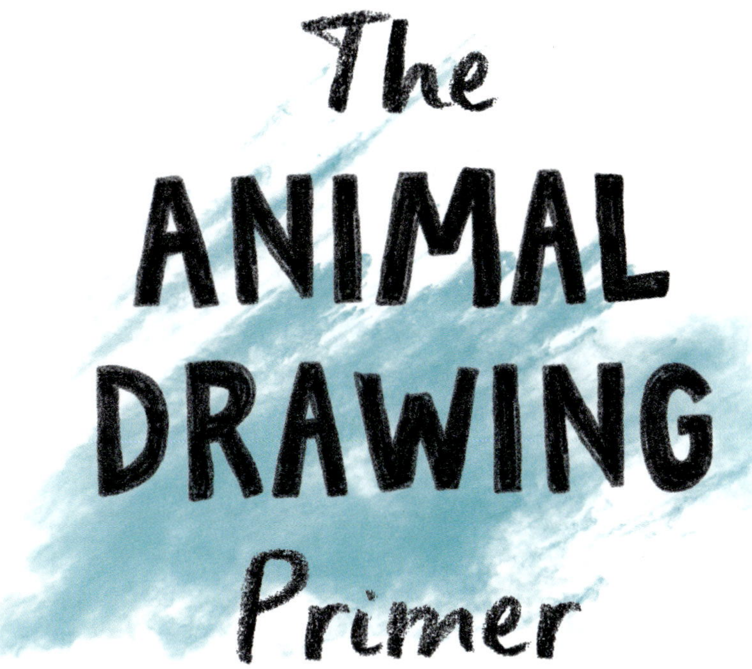

Jennifer Rae Phillips
Creator of Jen Rae Art

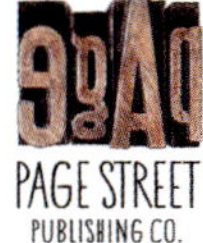

FOR JOHN AND GRAHAM, TWO ARTISTS WHO WERE TAKEN TOO SOON BUT I'VE NOT GONE A DAY WITHOUT.

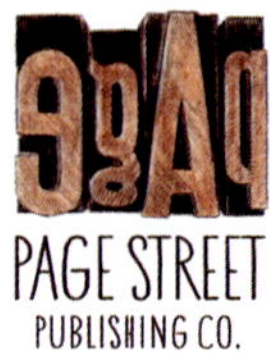

First published in 2023 by
Page Street Publishing Co.
27 Congress Street, Suite 1511
Salem, MA 01970
www.pagestreetpublishing.com

Distributed by Macmillan, sales in Canada by The Canadian Manda Group.

27 26 25 24 23 1 2 3 4 5

ISBN-13: 978-1-64567-937-0
ISBN-10: 1-64567-937-3

Library of Congress Control Number: 2022952239

Cover and book design by Rosie Stewart for Page Street Publishing Co.
Artwork by Jennifer Rae Phillips

Printed and bound in the United States

Page Street Publishing protects our planet by donating to nonprofits like The Trustees, which focuses on local land conservation.

Contents

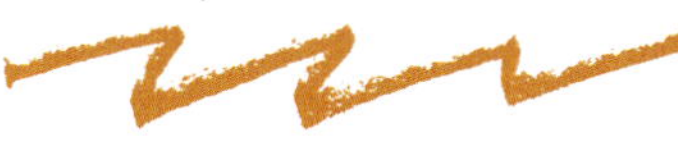

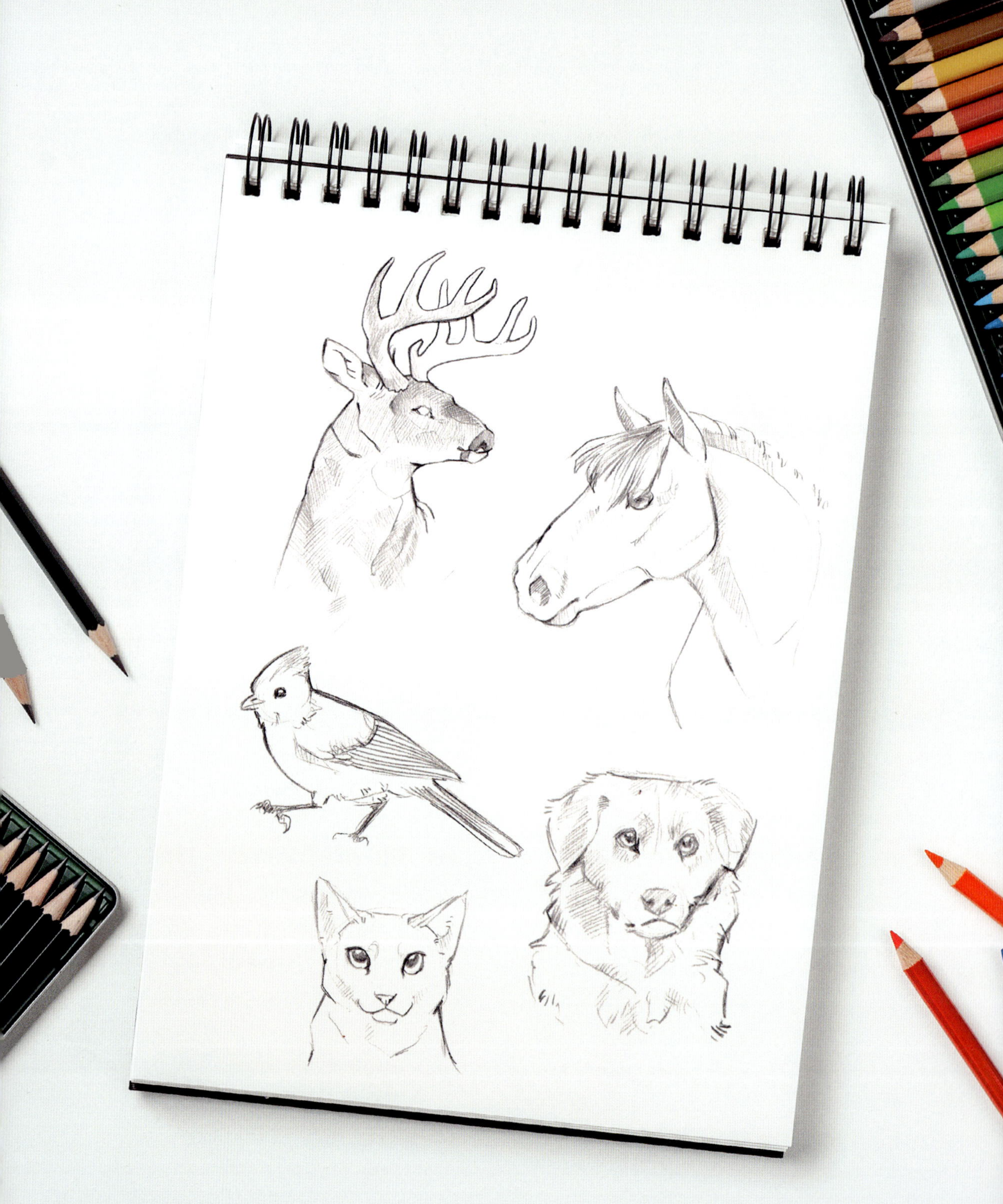

Introduction

There's just something about animals that intrigues so many people, especially artists.

Is it the way they move? Perhaps it's the way they see and experience the world, which reminds us to slow down and tune into something primal. Alas, maybe it's their innocence that we creative people want to capture and celebrate through art.

Whatever the reason, it can often feel challenging and even intimidating for us artists to bring animals to the page. They're made up of so many moving parts, shapes and volumes.

I've been drawing animals my entire life. I find them captivating and inspirational. Along my creative journey, I've been through countless moments of finding animals difficult to portray. So, I've learned a whole host of tricks to make the animals less complicated and therefore easy to draw. I teach people online and have created courses to help make animals exciting and accessible.

What I aim to do with this book is to show you how you can draw animals, even if you've never felt confident enough to try before. Here, you will find tutorials on drawing common creatures that you may see in your day-to-day life, from dogs and cats to horses and deer. The reason for this, and we will explore this later, is that drawing from life is an incredibly useful skill that can help you build upon the lessons you find in this book. So, if these animals are common and easy to see in person, then there are more opportunities to learn and explore as you develop your drawing skills.

Each tutorial is broken down into steps and detailed in a way to make the process as easy as possible. And, at the end of each tutorial, you will have your very own animal drawing. What's more, there are bonus mini-tutorials tucked in at the end of several chapters to show you how you can use what you've learned to create different animals. For example, you may draw the Labrador Side View (page 14) with one tutorial, but then decide you'd like to draw a collie instead.

While much of this book focuses on common animals that you are likely to encounter, I've made sure to include tutorials on how you can turn the understanding of domestic creatures into drawings or illustrations of wild animals. For example, wolves are just large domestic dogs with similar proportions. So, once you know how to draw a dog, you can transfer that knowledge to their wild counterparts. Again, I'll show you how.

First, I'm going to discuss a bit about media, sketching and how to see shapes in the animals you're going to draw. I'll also talk about tools you'll need for the tutorials. I'll see you on the inside.

Jenny Rae

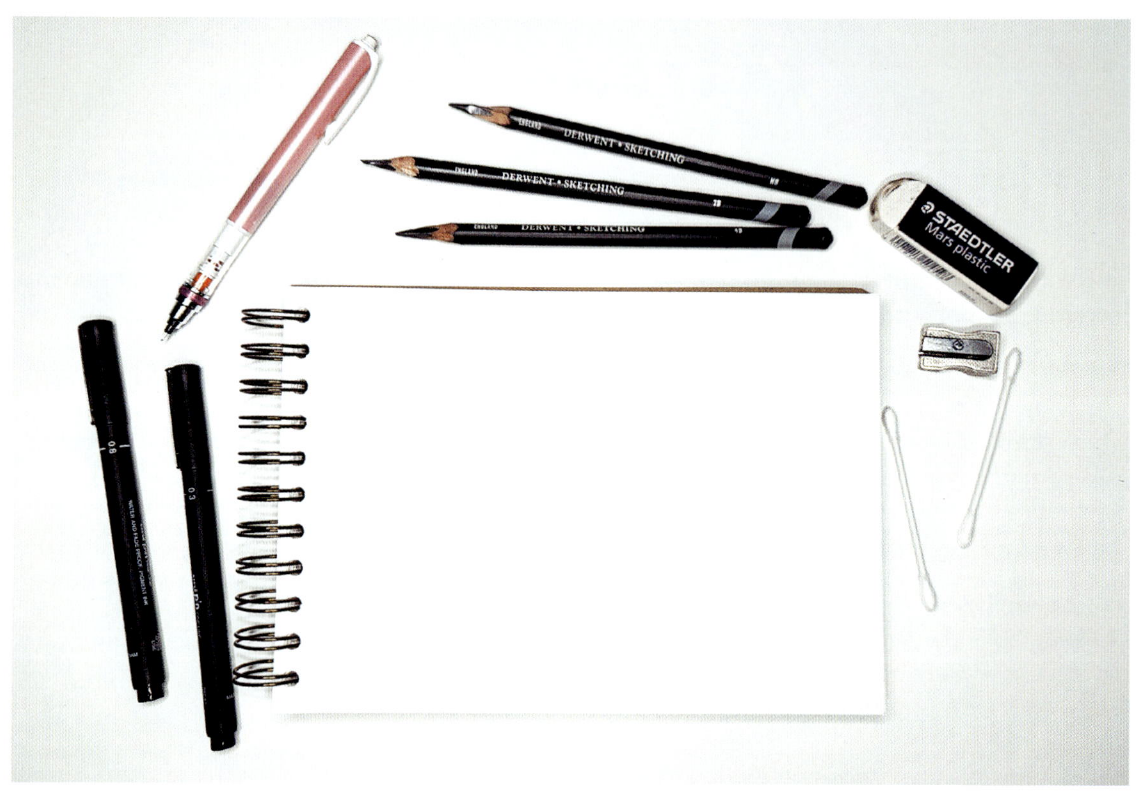

First Things First

USEFUL TOOLS

It's time to dispel the myth that you need to buy the best of the best materials in order to draw or enjoy this book.

I'm a firm believer that art can be made with anything, and if you're a complete beginner, you can start with things you have laying around. Perhaps that's a few sheets of printer paper and colored pencils. Even that old ballpoint pen that's been stowed in a kitchen drawer may be useful.

You can start to branch out (if you choose to) as you grow and your understanding of drawing improves. One thing I will say, however, is that there is some substance to material quality and how that can affect your enjoyment of the process. For example, investing in a nice sketchbook with smooth and thick paper has benefits that are worth considering for seasoned artists. Their pages may be more resilient to erasing and resketching, or they might take lighter lines because the grain of the paper isn't textured like more budget-friendly books.

Another aspect is that some higher-quality materials may last longer. The nib of a branded fineliner is likely to resist wear and tear more than a discounted brand, or the lead of a high-end colored pencil may break less often than its more affordable counterpart.

My suggested strategy is this: To start, stick with the tools you have laying around. At minimum, I recommend the following:

- **One HB pencil:** "H" stands for "hard," so this will be your lighter pencil.
- **One 2B or 4B Pencil:** "B" refers to how "black" the lead is with higher numbers being darker. This will be your darker pencil.
- **Two black pens, one thick and one thin:** These can be any type that you have. Just bear in mind that some pens, like those with gel ink, will need to dry before you erase so that it doesn't smudge.
- **Paper**
- **Eraser**
- **Pencil sharpener**
- **Blender:** This can be your fingertip or, if you don't want to get dirty, a piece of tissue or cotton ball will work well.
- **Ruler (optional)***

* The tutorials include measurements to help you get proportions and placements of shapes as accurate as possible. I encourage you to eyeball these measurements as much as you can. This may be challenging at first, but it will definitely get easier the more you do it. Once you've gotten used to eyeballing it, you'll be able to draw these animals any size you want. However, feel free to use a ruler if you find it helpful!

For the tutorials, I'll write under the assumption that you'll be using an HB pencil, a 2B pencil, two different thicknesses of pens and a tissue or your finger for blending.

See how you get on with those. If you wish to buy new materials, here is a list of some of my preferred supplies. I'll mention my favorite brands, but what's available to you may depend on your location:

- **Mechanical pencils and lead in sizes 0.3, 0.5 and 0.7 with a weight of H, 2B and 4B:** These negate the need for a sharpener but can be prone to lead breakage when used under pressure. My favorite brand is Pentel®, but most are pretty great. You can also just buy the different lead weights matching these sizes and switch them around in the same pencil until you get more pencils to accommodate your leads.
- **Waterproof black fineliner pens in sizes 0.05, 0.3 and 0.8:** Uni® Pin produces my favorite fineliners.
- **Eraser:** My go-to is a Staedtler® Mars® Plastic eraser.
- **Paper blending stump:** These are really tightly compressed sticks of paper that you can sharpen. They are great if you don't want to get pencil on your fingers but want a smoother finish for your shading.

- **Hardbound sketchbook with smooth paper designed for drawing:** Oftentimes sketchbooks come with symbols to state what the paper is good for. Look for a symbol that shows a pencil, and aim for a paperweight of between 140 and 180gsm. Illo sketchbook™ is a very popular mixed media sketchbook in a pleasant square shape. Otherwise, I like Seawhite of Brighton and Talens Art Creation sketchbooks. Paper is fundamentally personal though, so do explore what you like.

The next few materials are my favorites for adding color, and we will explore using them at the end of the book.

- **Watercolor paints:** I like having a portable set with half pans in a selection of colors. A good option is Winsor & Newton. The sets come in a variety of sizes. A set of 24 colors is a nice place to start.
- **Alcohol markers:** My favorite is Ohuhu®. These are a great blend of affordable and durable.
- **Wax core colored pencils:** I use Arteza® Expert Colored Pencils. They're affordable and come in great ranges of colors.

SEEING SHAPES

Animals are made up of so many intricate moving parts that genuinely make them look intimidating and complicated. But fear not, everything can be made much simpler. What I've done is broken down all of the animals into simple shapes. All you have to do is draw the shapes shown and mimic what I've laid out for you.

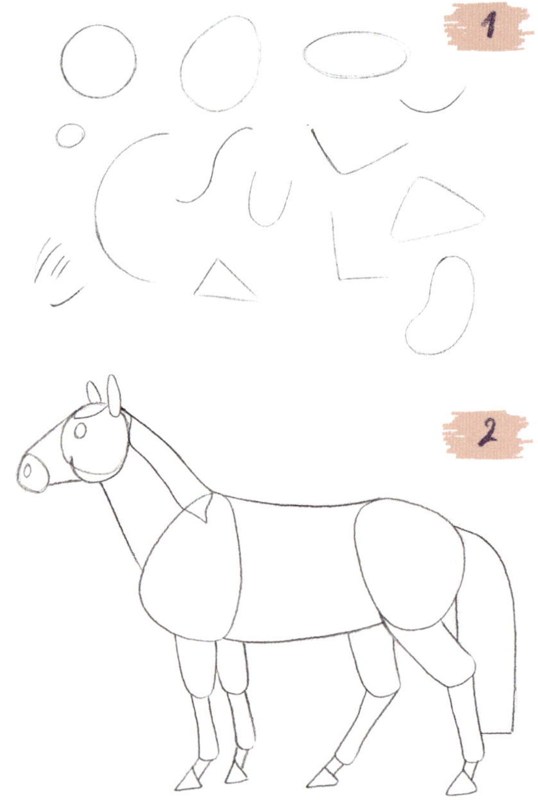

Some examples of shapes you can expect to draw are shown in image 1, and how they all come together to form the shape of an animal can be seen in image 2.

This book is a beautiful beginner's guide for learning how to draw animals. It takes out the confusion of trying to find those shapes that animals are made up of so that you can just get started. In time, seeing these shapes will become easier. Maybe you will start noticing the way animals' rib cages look like ovals, or how their pelvises seem just like cubes. Or perhaps the curve of an animal's leg may appear "S" shaped.

My hope is that you will soon be able to recognize the things you have learned in this book as you go about your day-to-day life.

SKETCH, SKETCH, SKETCH

The famous saying goes "Practice makes perfect." I do think a better alternative to this saying is, "Practice makes improvement." Either way, the emphasis is on practice. The more you attempt something, the better you get. It boils down to muscle memory and wiring your brain to understand the techniques being developed.

When we try something new, we are rarely good at it the first time. Skills take time to develop. This can be frustrating, and many artists spend a lot of time learning to draw something new or develop the skills they're working on.

I want to reinforce that the tutorials found in this book are a great initial step. They will show you how you can easily create the animal you want to draw. The steps are broken down in a way so they should only take one attempt to re-create the animals. But I do encourage practice. Repeat the steps and try the tutorials a few times if you want to. And most importantly, don't worry if your first attempt doesn't look exactly like the images in the book. If this is completely new to you, it's only natural that it may take practice to make the drawings flawless. And that is completely okay.

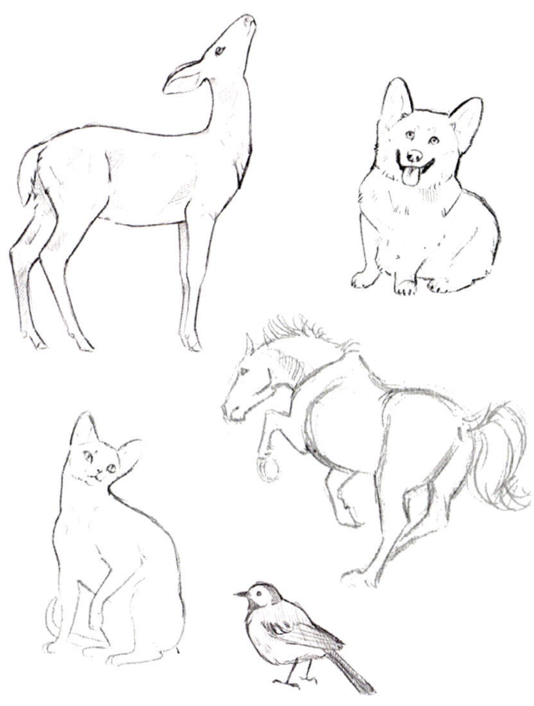

I also encourage you to get familiar with the materials you are using. Explore how they feel. Try different pressures with your pencils or see how much your paper can take before it starts to wear or tear. Play around with what you've got and just scribble away. This play is very helpful in growing your understanding of what your materials are capable of, and that familiarity will make the drawing process easier too.

One thing you may like to do is keep a sketchbook and just draw everything you can. You can use it for these tutorials too. Sketching, playing with your materials and being comfortable with the learning process are all important parts of growing as an artist!

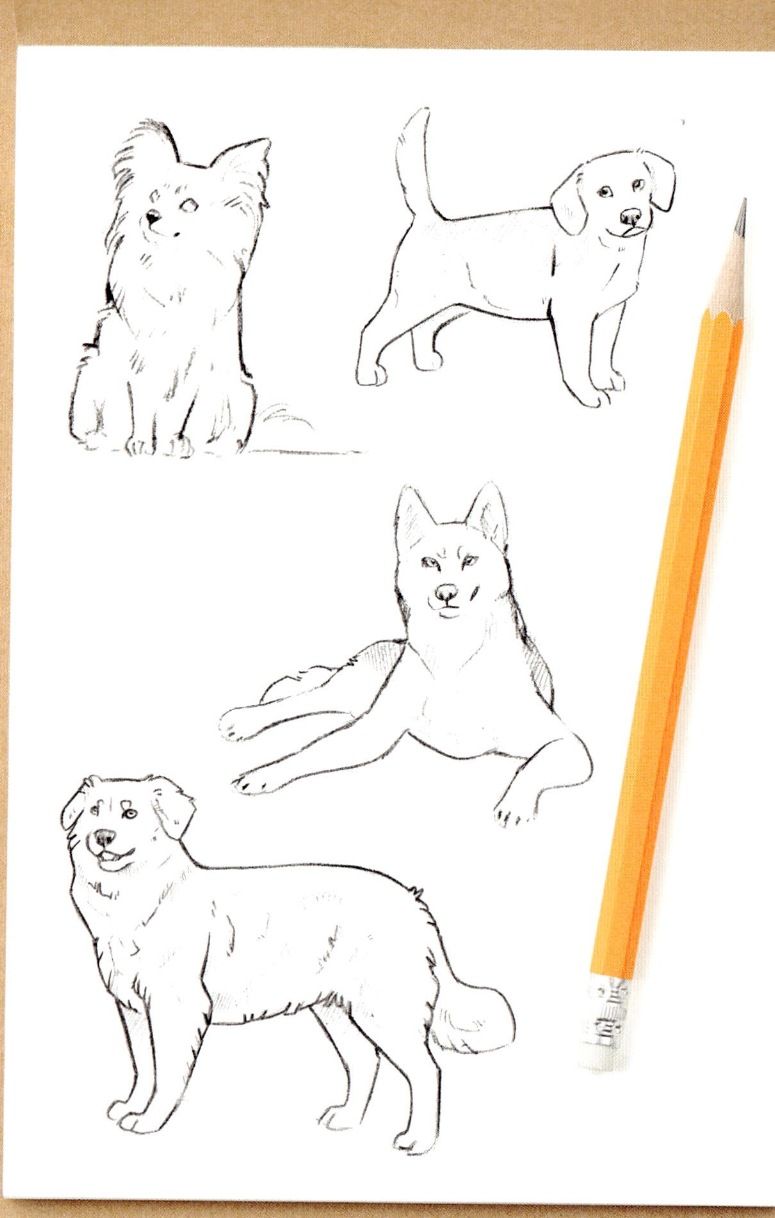

Doodling DOGS

There are few animals as loved and recognized as the dog. Known as man's best friend for a reason, they routinely hit the top of the list for most popular pet. So, to start this book, we are going to look at learning to draw a variety of different dogs.

Now, one thing to bear in mind is that there's no one-size-fits-all set of rules when it comes to drawing this species. Because they have been domesticated for so long and for so many different purposes, they come in an enormous variety of shapes and sizes. The wonderful thing about this is that it means you can't really go wrong.

We will work with a selection of some popular breeds, starting off with nice and simple poses. Then, we will move on to something more dynamic in the form of a pose that shows off the dog's physique. Later, we will use what we've learned when drawing dogs to apply to drawing a wolf. Wolves are the ancestors of our domestic dogs, so they are very similar.

After, we will look at how you can adjust elements to turn the dog into whatever breed you like, and ultimately, how you can use these skills to draw more exotic and wild canines.

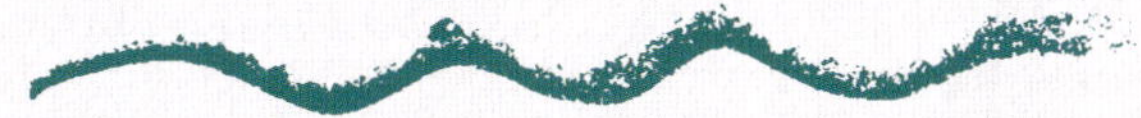

LABRADOR SIDE VIEW

We are going to start with a simple pose for our faithful friend and companion, the domestic dog. Simple poses are great when just starting out as they allow you to get an idea of form and structure before moving on to something more dynamic. To begin with, I have chosen a Labrador. This breed bears all the hallmarks of the creature we imagine when we think "dog," from their friendly floppy ears and smile to their smooth and pettable coat.

We will keep it straightforward so you can get an idea of proportions by drawing a simple standing pose.

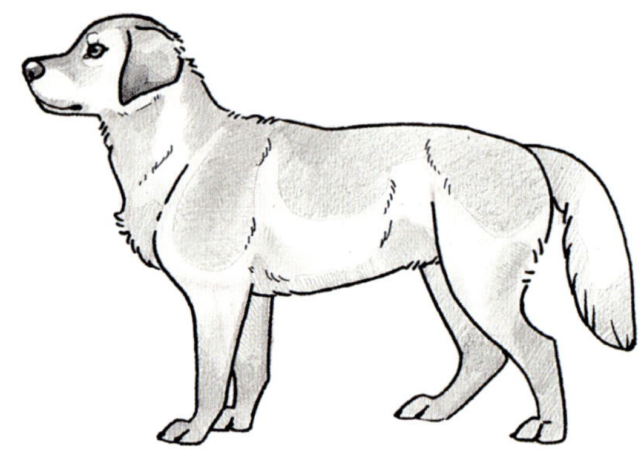

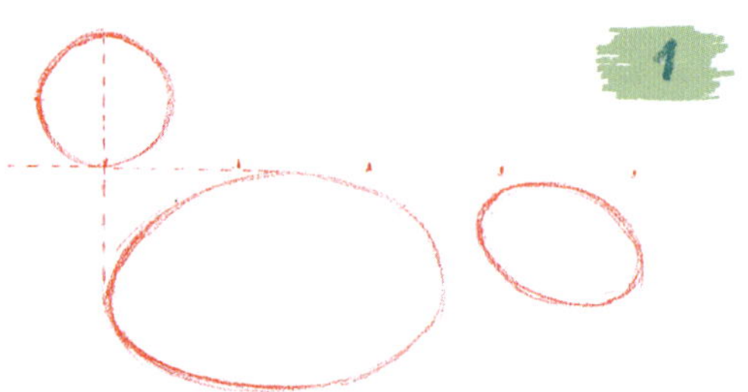

1

Step 1: Draw the ribs, head and hips.

Place the largest, central oval shape in the middle of your page. Give yourself plenty of space around this shape so you have enough room for the rest of the drawing. This oval is for the ribs and chest. The ribs are the largest part, so draw them first to centralize the illustration so you can build up other body parts around it.

Place the circle for the head. Draw your guidelines first. Sketch a horizontal line directly level with the top of the rib's oval and a vertical line up from the front. Start the base of the head circle where these lines intersect, and have the vertical line be its exact center.

Draw the oval for the hips. A good size for the hip oval is if you took the same size circle used for the head and squashed it slightly.

Tip: A useful measure to tell whether the proportions are right while you're drawing these round shapes is that the front of the rib oval to the end of the hip oval is exactly four times the length of the head circle. For example, if the circle for the head is 1 inch (2.5 cm) across, then the body from the front of the ribs to the end of the hips should be 4 inches (10 cm) long. Feel free to include guide marks to help with proportions.

Step 2: **Connect the ovals and add the snout and tail.**

Connect the head circle. From the back of the head circle, extend a straight line that connects to the rib oval. This line should meet roughly two-fifths along the rib oval. At the seven o'clock mark of the head circle, draw a line that connects the head to the chest. This will be the dog's throat.

For the back, connect the rib oval to the hip oval with a lightly curved line. This line starts at the three-quarters point on the rib oval and connects to the highest point on the hip oval. Dogs have a curved spine, and by drawing this curve now, it'll become easier when we finish the illustration later.

Connect the lower part of the rib oval to the lowest point on the hip oval. This becomes the dog's tummy.

Add the snout. At the front of the head circle, place an angular "C" shape. The top of the snout, or angled "C" shape, should fall roughly halfway down on the head circle. The bottom line should run horizontal, level with the top of the rib oval. The snout should be one-third of the Labrador's entire head length.

Draw the tail and attach it to the hip oval. The tail sits just lower than the top of the hips. Tails are extensions of the spine, and the hip bones sit on either side, so bear this in mind. The tail can be almost a sausage shape or like the shape of a peapod. Try to avoid drawing any straight lines for the tail. Dog tails are very flexible, and curvy lines help to show this.

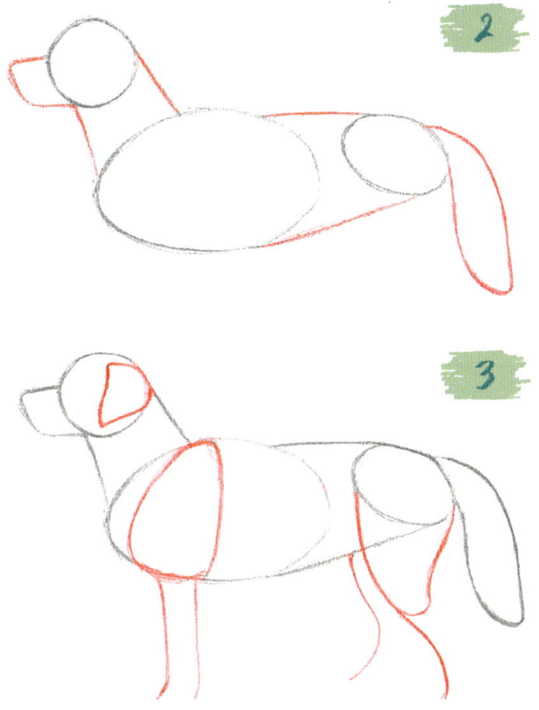

Step 3: **Add the ear and start the legs.**

Add the ear by drawing an inverted tear or triangle. Labrador ears are floppier than other breeds, so the tip of the ear typically points down. The widest point of the ear is where it attaches to the head.

Draw the shoulder. A good shape to use is an oval or egg shape that is more narrow where it sits closer to the back and widens toward the part where it meets the dog's chest. Leave a little crescent of space between the shoulder and front of the ribs where the throat is. When a dog walks or runs, this shoulder shape pivots, so it shouldn't be placed too far forward.

For the near-side back leg, draw a curvy "V" shape that connects the front of the hip oval to the back. The length of the "V" is approximately the same as the longest part of the shoulder oval. This "V" shape is for the Labrador's thigh and knee. The side of the "V" closest to the front legs should curve to form the front of the thigh. The side of the "V" closest to the tail shape should form a gentle wave, creating the dog's buttocks and back of the thigh.

The remainder of the dog's legs will be roughly the same as the height of the rib oval.

Finish off the near-side back leg by extending the front of the thigh down so that the knee or tip of the "V" shape drawn earlier is halfway between the tummy of the animal and the paw.

For the far-side back leg, draw a soft "S" shape.

For the front legs, draw two straight lines vertically, curving a little at the bottom where the paws will go. These lines will become the front parts of each leg. The near-side leg should connect to the middle of the egg used for the shoulder. The far-side leg should be placed slightly to the right. As we won't see the far-side shoulder, this placement can be just a guide, and the far-side leg will mostly disappear behind the near-side leg.

Step 4: Finish the legs.

Place a semicircle to represent the paws at the bottom of each line drawn for the legs. Make sure that the lines of the legs drawn in step 3 meet exactly at the middle of the semicircle. This will help you to draw the toes.

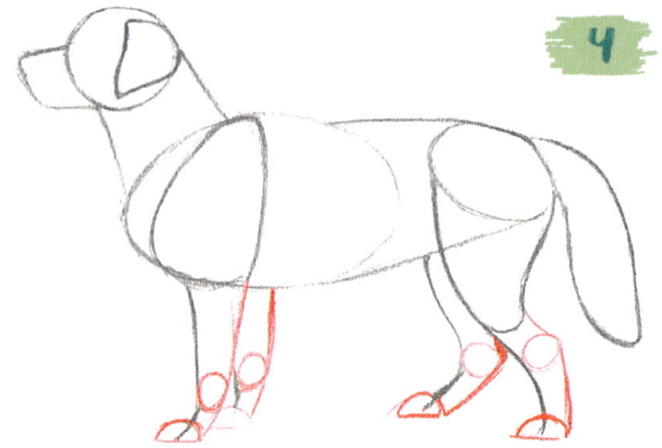

Draw the leg joints. For the front legs, place a circle on the back of the lines that connect to the shoulder, one-third of the way up. This circle is the dog's wrist and should be two-thirds of the width of the paw semicircle. As this is a joint, circles are useful to show volume and help you remember where the wrist joint pivots if the animal is moving.

For the back legs, place a circle directly behind the part of the line that bends backwards. This joint is thicker than the joints for the front legs, so it should be the same width as the hind paw semicircle. This circle becomes the dog's ankle.

Connect these shapes by drawing the backs of the legs. For the front legs, extend a line that joins the base of the shoulder egg shape down past the wrist circle and connects to the back of the paw semicircle shape. For the back legs, connect the near-side leg from the back of the thigh or "V" shape to the top of the ankle circle. Then connect a line from the ankle circle to the back of the paw semicircle on both back legs.

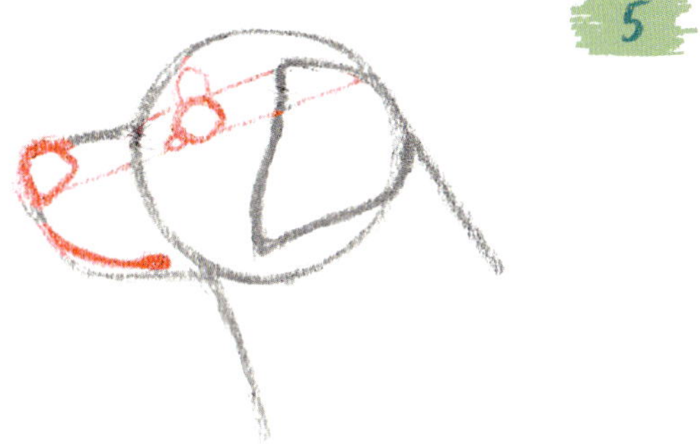

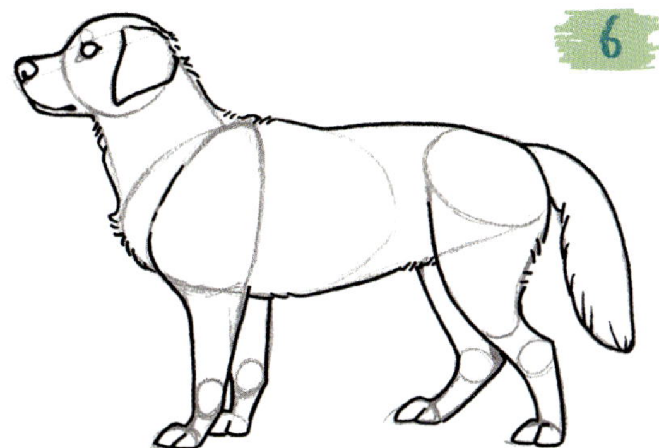

Step 5: Add the facial features.

To draw the nose, sketch in a diamond-like shape at the top corner, farthest from the dog's face on the snout's angular "C" shape.

Add guidelines for placing the eye. You can use the ear triangle and the nose diamond to help with position. You will get two parallel lines by placing a faint line that connects the top corner of the ear triangle to the top of the snout, and then placing a second line between the back of the Labrador's head to the bottom of the nose diamond.

Draw the eye between the previously placed guidelines in the top quarter of the Labrador's head circle. You can finish the eye with a semicircle above for the eyebrow and a smaller one below towards the snout for the tear duct.

Draw the mouth. This will be an upturned curve in the bottom third of the snout. Where the corner of the mouth sits near the head circle, draw a slightly thicker line to represent the edges of the lips, which forms the typical dog "smile."

Step 6: Outline the main features.

Tip: It can be helpful to take your time with these next steps. We will be refining the parts of the dog we want to keep, using some of the lines drawn already to bring out the finished drawing. Other construction lines we will ignore for now.

With a thicker pen, start with the dog's face. Draw over the nose diamond and, towards the middle, add a line to place the nostril. Connect the bottom of the nose diamond to the curve of the mouth, going over the line you drew already in step 5.

Draw the jaw, taking the line from the end of the snout along the guideline towards the throat.

Draw along the top of the snout, towards the head circle and over the top of the edge towards the back of the head. Extend that line down towards the shoulders, leaving gaps and ticks or apostrophe shapes to indicate fur.

Draw over the eye circle and go over the ear triangle, leaving a gap at the top where the ear folds and meets the head.

Go over the throat and extend over the front of the rib circle, again adding ticks to show fur.

For the shoulder, partially draw over the front of the shoulder egg shape, and then extend that line down along the edge of the front near-side leg. Draw the toes by going over the front half of the paw semicircle, along the base of the paw, and add another toe. To finish the front leg, take the line from the back of the paw and extend it up toward the base of the shoulder egg shape. Do the same for the far-side front leg.

Draw the chest and tummy, as well as the back line using the guides drawn in step 2 (page 15). Add some tick marks behind the front leg and before the back leg for fur.

For the back legs, do the same as you did for the front leg. Make sure the thigh line starts near the hip oval, and extend that line down for the rest of the leg. To complete the rump of the Labrador, continue the back line down, adding tick lines for the fluffy rear, and end towards the ankle joint.

Outline the tail. Draw one smooth line over the top of the tail and underneath. Draw fur with more tick lines.

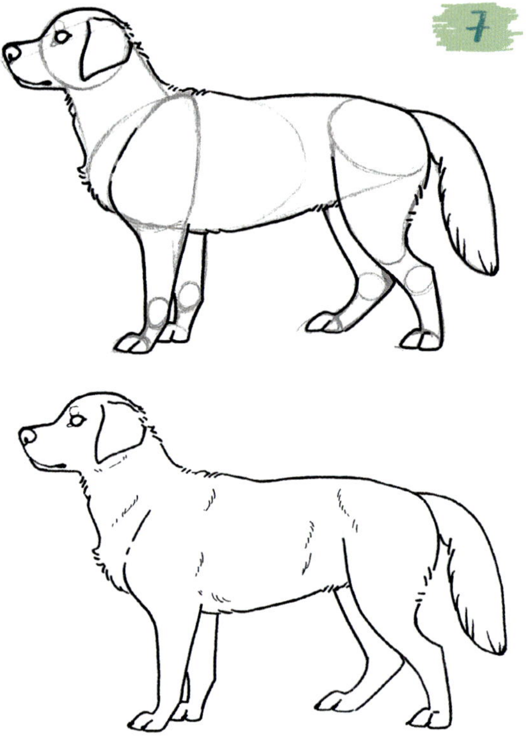

Step 7: Finish the outline.

Draw over the eyebrow and tear duct with a thinner pen.

Add a handful of tick marks and short lines around the round shapes you drew for the head, ribs, shoulder and hips to indicate fur and add texture. These show muscles and edges of the skeleton that lay underneath the skin. You can draw as much or as little as you like, making sure to use the edges of the guide shapes to assist the placement of your tick marks.

Erase all the construction lines.

Step 8: Add shading (optional).

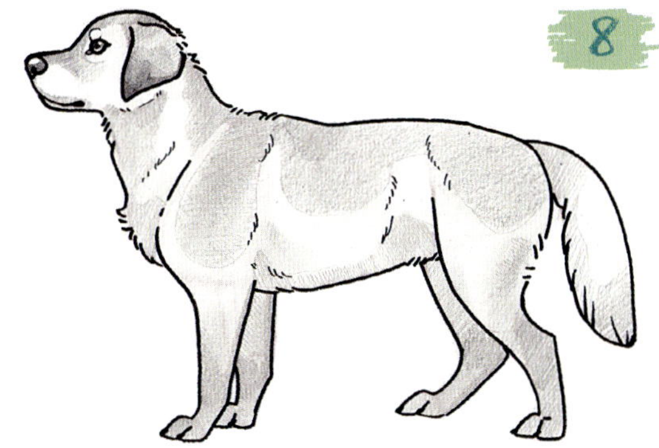

Take this Labrador to the next level by adding some shading. Start off by filling in your dog completely with a layer using your lighter pencil.

Fill in the eye. Leave a small circle at the top of the eye blank for the highlight, and do a very dark circle at the front of the eye for the pupil.

For the nose, leave the top half empty for the shine, and fill in the lower part with a dark layer of shading.

For the ear, shade all of it, but go darker towards the tip and along the lower edge.

Add shading along the top of the head and along the back. This will be the darker fur that some lighter-colored Labradors have. Extend this shading below the eye, around the back of the neck and over a large portion of the shoulders, ribs and hips. Leave a lighter edge to show depth and help define those darker areas.

Shade in the lower part of the animal. Shadow under the jawline, along the throat and below the tummy, works well here.

For the legs, add darker shading at the paws and gradually fade into a lighter shade as you go up the leg. The joints at the wrist and ankle can also be a darker shade.

Add a patch of shading around the rump to emphasize muscles and fur at this part of the dog.

To finish, add a darker patch of shading at the base and tip of the tail, connecting with some shading underneath the tail too.

If you want to smooth this shading, lightly run your finger or a tissue over the pencil to blend these darker areas together.

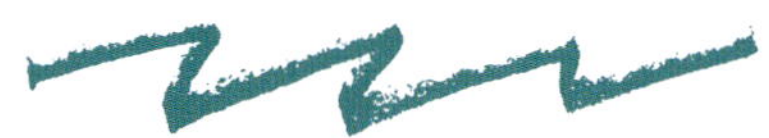

FRENCH BULLDOG "SIT"

The French bulldog, or Frenchie, is a small-but-stocky breed loved by so many. Their large eyes and short snouts make them super adorable. For this tutorial, I've chosen a simplistic yet asymmetrical pose in the form of the classic "sit" from a front view. The asymmetry of this particular drawing adds a bit of flair and character. Drawing a dog from the front, as opposed to the side view of the Labrador tutorial (page 14), helps mix up the angles, which allows you to explore more depth in the drawing.

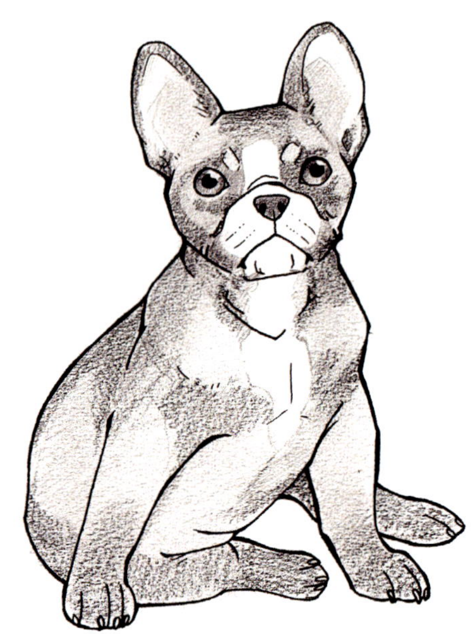

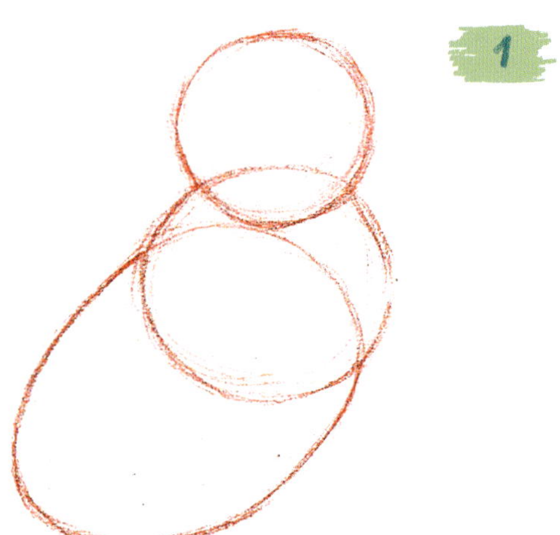

1

Step 1: Draw the head, chest and main body.

Start with a circle for the head. Frenchies are relatively short dogs with large heads. This circle will help you build up the rest of the body placement, so keep the head just above the middle line of your page.

Draw the chest circle. This circle should overlap the head circle, intersecting at the four o'clock and eight o'clock marks of the head. This circle is only marginally bigger than the head circle. For example, if your Frenchie's head circle is 1½ inches (4 cm) in diameter, then the chest oval should be 2 inches (5 cm) at most.

Add a large oval slightly off to the left to act as the dog's main body. This dog is sitting a little off to the side, so the main body will reflect this, and the oval will aim down towards the seven o'clock mark. This oval will overlap the chest circle to the point where the main body oval practically touches the bottom of the head circle. Make the oval as wide as the chest circle (in this example, 2 inches [5 cm] across), and make the length the same as the overlapping head circle and chest circle combined, approximately 3 inches (8 cm).

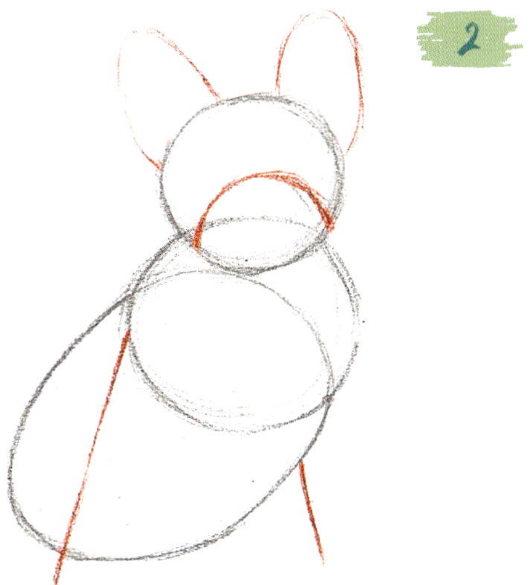

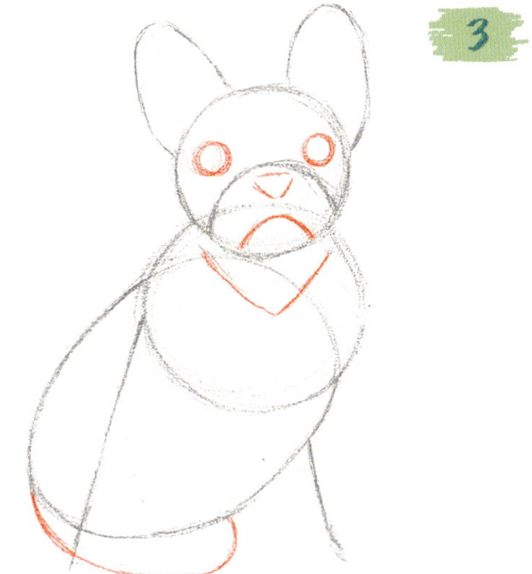

Step 2: **Add the ears, muzzle and the backs of the forelegs.**

Starting with the ears, add two upright ovals with their bottoms cut off at the top of the head circle. French bulldogs have quite large ears, so make these almost as tall as the head circle. You'll want the top parts of the ears meeting at the eleven o'clock and one o'clock marks, and the base of the ears sitting roughly at nine o'clock and three o'clock.

Draw a large curved line for the top of the muzzle. This line should go from the region of eight o'clock to four o'clock, doming up in the middle to the very center of the head circle.

For the backs of the forelegs, you'll need to draw two lines. For the leg on the left of the drawing, have it start at the nine o'clock point of the chest circle. This line then goes down diagonally. So, if nine o'clock to three o'clock is the horizontal axis, with straight down from the nine o'clock mark being 90 degrees, make the left leg aim down to the left at 100 degrees. Extend it slightly past the base of the main body oval.

For the leg on the right side of the drawing, attach it to the side of the main body oval at roughly the middle point of the oval. There should be a 45-degree angle between the leg line at the body oval, so aim the right leg line slightly diagonally to the right. Make sure it ends level with the base of the main body oval.

Step 3: **Time for the eyes, nose, mouth, neck and thigh.**

Start with the eyes. French bulldogs have large eyes, which helps exaggerate their cuteness. Place two small circles in the top half of the head circle, the base of each aligning with what would be the center line across from nine o'clock to three o'clock. They should be one-sixth of the width of the head circle. So, if the head circle is 1½ inches (4 cm) in diameter, then the eyes should be ¼ inch (6 mm).

For the nose, draw an inverted triangle at the top of the muzzle area. Keep this central and as wide as the eye circles.

Add the mouth. This should be a slightly smaller curved line that runs parallel to the muzzle curve, intersecting the head circle at five o'clock and seven o'clock. The peak of the mouth curve should be directly below the point of the nose triangle.

Draw a "V" shape for the dog's neck. This doesn't have to meet the chest oval, but the top of the "V" should be as wide as the head circle, and the point of the "V" should meet the center of the chest circle.

Add the thigh. This dog is sort of sitting at an angle, so the thigh is lying horizontally underneath the main body oval. Once this line is added, the thigh shape should be a flattened tear shape. To add it, extend the top of the main body down in a smooth line that runs horizontally. To finish, round off the line towards a vertical axis to meet the main body. This should attach almost directly below the eye on the left of the drawing.

Step 4: Add the paws, joints and upper parts of the front legs.

Start with the paw for the front leg on the left side. Draw a semicircle flat side down to the right of the back of the leg line. This semicircle should be small, and because French bulldogs have short legs, the base of the paw semicircle should be one quarter as long as the back of the leg line. Do the same for the leg on the right, making sure the paw semicircle is the same size as the left paw and to the right of the line.

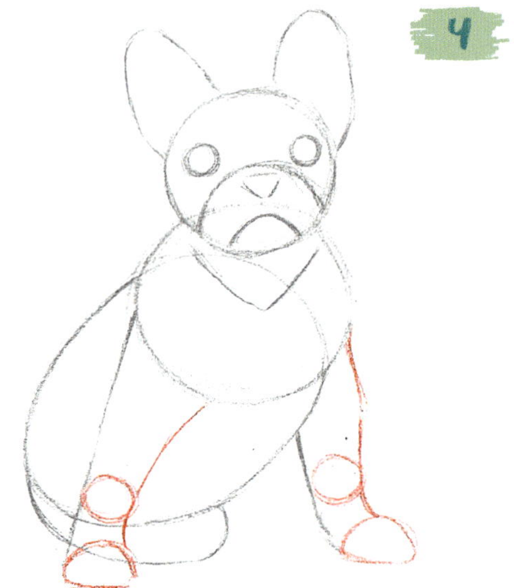

For the joints, draw circles slightly above the paw semicircles. A good placement for the leg on the left side of the drawing is approximately three-quarters of the way down and to the right of the leg line. For the leg on the right of the drawing, make this circle halfway down the leg line. Check that the circles are the same distance away from the paw on both legs to make sure your proportions are good.

Now, finish the leg structure. For the leg on the left, draw one curved line that starts from the paw at the one o'clock mark, goes along the side of the joint circle and then gently curves up to attach to the chest circle at the seven o'clock mark. For the leg on the right, connect the top of the paw semicircle to the edge of the joint circle. For the upper part of the right leg, draw a very slightly waved line from the three o'clock mark of the chest circle down to the right edge of the joint circle. The waved line should make the upper part of the right leg appear slightly wider in the middle to account for the muscles.

Step 5: Add the back legs and feet.

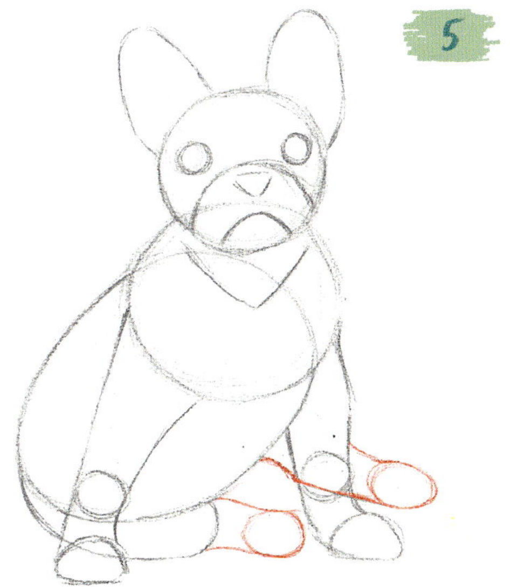

Start with the hind leg on the left. Draw a small oval, roughly the same size as the paw semicircles, level with the front paw on the right of the drawing. This oval should be close to the back of the leg on the right but shouldn't touch it.

Connect the oval to the thigh shape. To do this, draw two lightly curved but parallel lines. The bottom line should curve up ever so slightly and connect the bottom of the paw oval with the lower line of the thigh shape. The top line should connect the top of the paw oval and meet in the corner where the thigh shape connects with the main body oval.

For the hind leg on the right, draw an oval that is roughly the same size as the other hind paw. Place it level with the joint circle on the front leg to the right of the drawing. Add a slightly curved line from the top of this oval and connect it to the leg on the right, just above the joint circle.

Draw the heel for the back leg on the right. Draw a curved line that meets at the nine o'clock point of the joint circle on the right and attaches to the main body oval. This should be almost halfway between where the left edge of the right front leg and the top of the left hind leg meet the body oval. Then, attach the nine o'clock mark of the right front leg joint circle to the base of the hind leg oval. This line will get erased later, so don't worry that it's drawn through the front leg on the right.

Step 6: Draw the outline.

Take your time here. We will be refining the parts of the dog we want to keep, using some of the lines drawn already to bring out the finished drawing. Other construction lines will be ignored.

Start with the dog's face. Using a thicker pen, draw over the eye circles, and draw a little point on the inside corners that are closest to the muzzle. These points are the tear ducts. Draw the nostrils, and then outline the nose triangle. For the mouth, draw an inverted "Y" shape that connects the middle of the nose to the corners of the mouth.

Follow the arched pencil line that implies the muzzle. Instead of making a clean curve, draw some angles and jagged edges. This makes the dog's muzzle seem creased.

For the chin and bottom of the muzzle, add some angled lines. The chin of the dog should follow the base of the head circle, but try to keep it straight with little upturns at the end. This shows off the dog's angular head. The jowls, or base of the muzzle outlining the mouth, look like little "F" shapes, which also add to the wrinkles of the dog's face.

Draw the ears and head circle. For the ears, you can draw directly over the guidelines from the edge of an ear on the top of the head to most of the way around. Then, add a more angular line connecting the middle of the outside of the ear to the head circle, meeting at the two o'clock and ten o'clock marks. For drawing over the head circle, try to draw more angular lines connecting the jowls to the ears. For the top of the head, draw a flat line with two downward angled lines towards the inside of the ears.

Draw the neck over the "V" shape, adding extra lines angled up to indicate the wrinkles.

Draw over the top left and right edge of the chest circle. This circle was a guide, so only draw where the shoulders are. Keep it angular here too.

Round off the back and thigh using the outside of the guidelines left by the main body oval and thigh shape. This can be a more curved line that follows along the pencil guide.

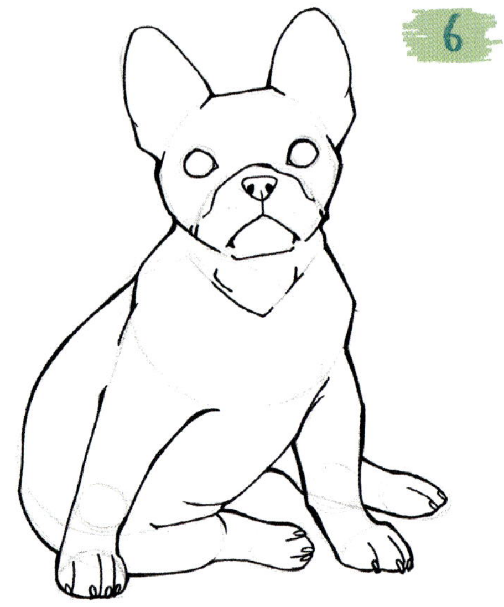

Draw the tummy, connecting roughly the four o'clock mark of the chest circle to the middle top of the thigh shape. Add an extra line that comes off slightly before adding a fold of skin above the thigh.

Add the legs. Start drawing the back of the left-side leg one-quarter of the way down and follow the guideline down. Break up the paw circle on the left into four roughly equal sections, adding a tiny oval at the tip of each section for the claws. Follow the front of the leg guideline until it meets the chest circle. Repeat for the right-side foreleg, breaking the right front paw into three sections, as the leg is angled slightly. Toe one and two should be similar in size, but the third toe should be a sliver.

For the back legs and paws, draw over the outside of the guidelines. The left back leg can be broken into three for the toes, and the right side can be broken into two.

Step 7: Finish the outline.

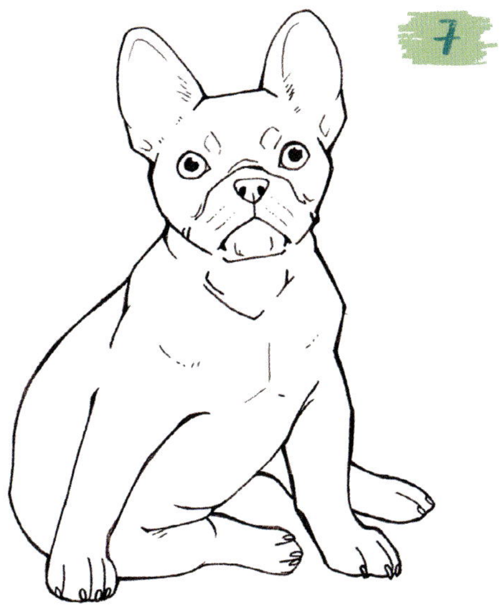

Add more detail with a thinner pen.

Begin with the ears. Just inside the ears, draw a curve that runs parallel with the main outline on the inner left edge of the right ear and an upside-down "L" shape in the tip of the left ear. On the inner parts of the ears that meet the top of the head, add some tick marks to indicate fur. Add more fur in the gap of the main head outline. Then, in the bottom parts of the ears that attach to the side of the head, draw a "C" shape that shows folds of skin.

Draw the pupils. These should be two smaller circles in the center or the eyes with an indent in the top right for the shine.

For the eyebrows, draw two small diamonds just above the eye towards the center of the face. Make sure the shapes are incomplete so it is subtler.

Add some curved lines above the top of the muzzle. Draw one directly at the top and by the muzzle below the eyes. This adds more wrinkles.

Add the dimples along the jowls where the whiskers sit. These can be two parallel and dotted lines. Now add some more lines for the wrinkles on the chin.

On the chest, draw a broken, inverted "Y" shape to define the sternum. Add more dotted lines in the middle of the open shoulder space. This adds more interesting depth and definition.

Erase all of your pencil lines.

Step 8: **Finally, on to the shading (optional).**

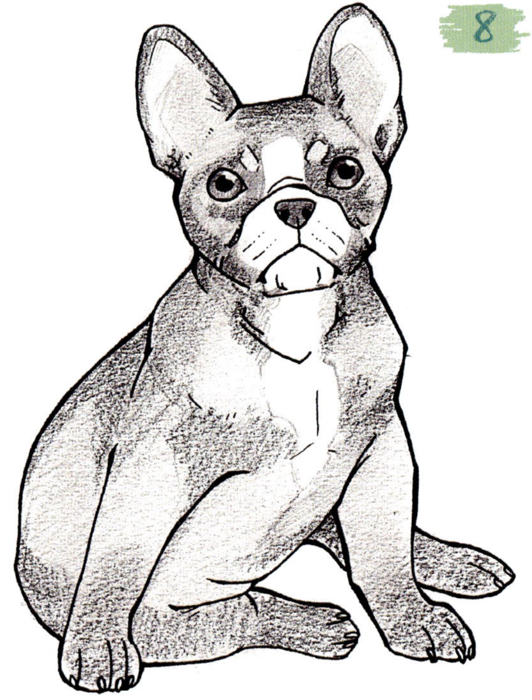

Start with a lighter pencil and fill in the whole dog. If you want to add white markings, now is a good time to define them. I left a dome between the eyes, large areas of the muzzle, the chin and a jagged stripe down the middle of the chest completely blank. Leave the top part of the eye white for the shine.

> **Tip:** Don't worry if you accidently shade these areas in with your pencil. You can always erase it later.

Once the whole dog (minus your white patches) is filled in, you can add some darker areas. I darkened the outside of the ears, the top of the head, around the eyes, along the side of the face, on the tops of the shoulders, down the back, the whole of the back legs, the front paws and the bottom of the chest area.

When you're happy, if you want a smoother finish, you can smudge the shading with your finger or a tissue.

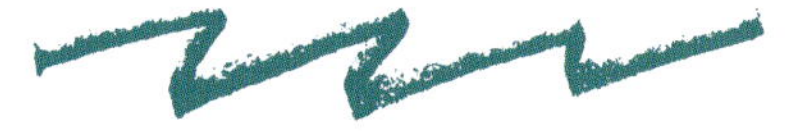

GERMAN SHEPHERD JUMPING

The German shepherd is a classic breed, full of energy and vitality. The mid-leap posture is great for showing off the physique of this breed. Something interesting to take into account when drawing this particular pose is how the body becomes quite elongated, especially when compared to the standing Labrador Side View (page 14). A good comparison is to imagine the dog like a spring at full stretch as it jumps through the air.

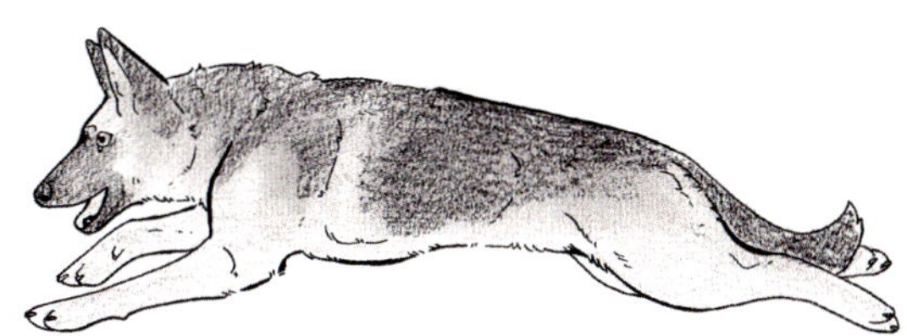

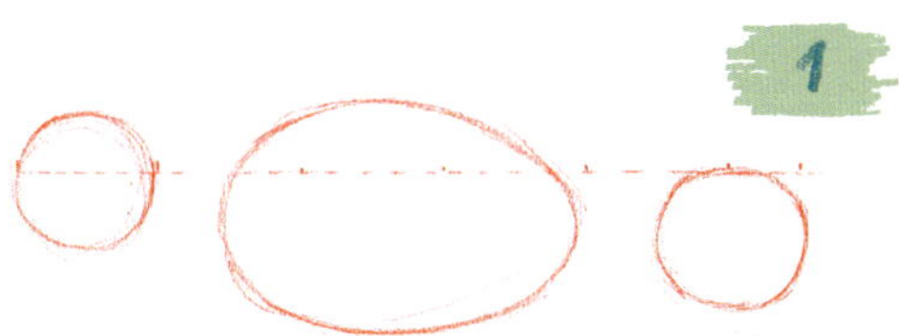

Step 1: Start the base structure for the head, ribs and hips.

To begin, draw a guide to help keep the head, ribs and hips positioned correctly. Draw a dotted line that runs horizontally across the middle of your page. This illustration is going to be much longer than it is tall, so factor that in when you place these objects.

Place a circle for the head at the far left of the horizontal line. The line should intersect through the middle of the head circle, directly through the nine o'clock and three o'clock marks.

Draw an oval for the ribs. The top of the oval should be level with the top of the head circle. The base of the oval should be twice the height of the top section.

Add the hip circle. This circle should meet the dotted line at the very top and fall entirely below the guideline.

Tip: To get the proportions right for this illustration, the head and hip circle should be the same size and be one-fifth the length of the horizontal guideline. The rib oval should be half of the length. For example, make the guideline 5½ inches (14 cm) long. The head and hip circle should be 1 inch (2.5 cm) in diameter and the rib oval should be 2½ inches (6.5 cm). The three shapes should be ½ inch (1.3 cm) apart.

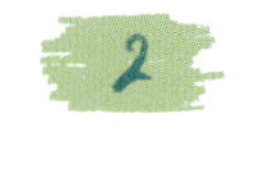
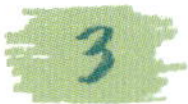

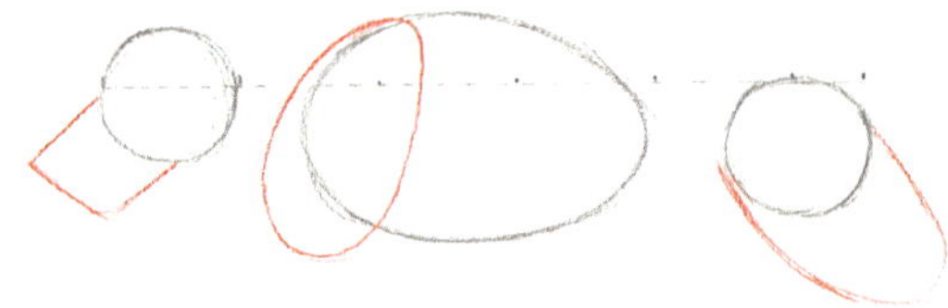
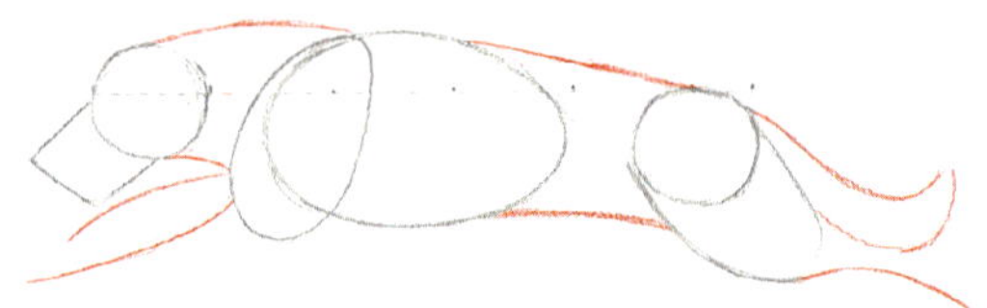

Step 2: Add the muzzle, shoulder and thigh.

Start with the muzzle. The top of the muzzle attaches at the nine o'clock mark, and the base attaches at the six o'clock mark. Draw two parallel lines that point diagonally to the left. These lines should be the same length as the diameter of the head circle. Draw a line connecting the top and base line to create a rectangle.

For the shoulder, draw a narrow egg shape at the front of the chest oval. The bottom of the egg shape should dip below the bottom of the chest oval, and it should be as wide as the diameter of the head circle at the widest point.

To draw the thigh, attach a large "U" shape to the hip circle. The "U" shape should attach at roughly the nine o'clock and two o'clock marks, and the base of the "U" should be angled to the right.

Step 3: Draw the neck, waist, tail and beginning of the legs.

Start with the dog's neck. The top line should be a curve that attaches the twelve o'clock mark of the head circle to the tip of the shoulder egg shape. The lower line of the neck should curve from the six o'clock mark of the head circle to one-third of the way up the shoulder egg.

For the waist, start by drawing the back line. This should connect the top of the rib oval, one-third of the way along to the twelve o'clock mark of the hip circle. For the lower line of the waist, connect the lower part of the rib egg one-quarter of the way along to the thigh "U," connecting it one-third of the way down.

To draw the front legs, you'll need two gently curved lines. The top line, which is the far-side leg, should attach to the point at which the bottom neck line meets the shoulder egg. This line should be a little shorter than the top curve of the neck and should also curve in the same way. For the bottom line, the near-side leg, attach the line to the shoulder egg one-fifth of the way up and have it curve slightly upwards. It should extend a bit farther than the far-side leg.

For the hind leg, draw a curved line that connects to the very bottom of the thigh "U" shape. Make this line dome slightly and be roughly as long as the far-side front leg.

For the tail, start by drawing a reverse, slightly curved check mark from the two o'clock part of the hip circle and extending to the right. This will create the top line of the tail. Then add the bottom line of the tail by drawing a curve from one-third of the way up on the right of the thigh "U" to the tip of the reverse check mark.

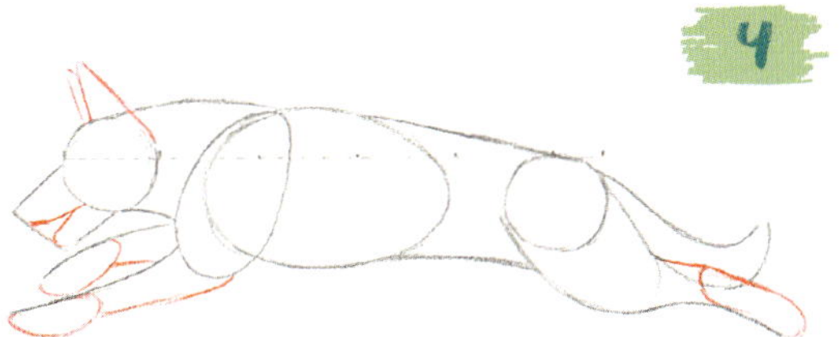

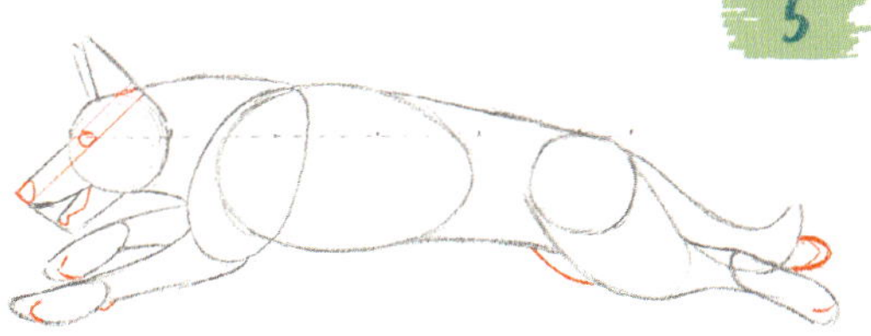

Step 4: Draw the ears and mouth and finish the leg structures.

For the ears, start with one erect triangle that points diagonally to the left. The back of the ear should connect to the two o'clock mark of the head circle and be roughly the same length as the muzzle. The front of the ear should connect between the eleven o'clock and twelve o'clock mark. To add the far-side ear, draw an upside-down tick that runs parallel to the near-side ear. Make sure the tips of the ears are level.

For the mouth, it'll mimic a "Y" shape, with the bottom of the "Y" attaching at the seven o'clock mark of the head circle. The split of the "Y" should occur one-quarter of the way toward the end of the muzzle. The top split line of the "Y" should curve up and meet the end of the muzzle rectangle one-third of the way down. The bottom of the "Y" split should curve down and meet three-quarters of the way down the end of the muzzle rectangle. Round off the bottom shape slightly to represent the chin.

Finish off the legs. Start with the front paws by drawing two flattened ovals below the front leg lines. The ovals should be as long as the muzzle and one-third its height. Then connect the bottom of the near-side oval to the base of the shoulder egg. Draw a line that connects the far-side front paw oval to one-fifth of the way along the near-side top leg line.

For the hind leg, draw a sausage shape to represent the paw and ankle of the dog. This shape should be a little longer than the other paw oval, but the same height. Then connect the top of the sausage shape to the "U" shape to make the back of the leg.

Step 5: Add the nose, eye, tongue, far-side hind leg and toes.

For the nose and the eye, start with a guideline that runs parallel to the top muzzle line and intersects the head circle at the eight o'clock and one o'clock marks. Extend the top muzzle line toward the ear so you have two parallel lines. Then place the eye, which will be a small circle that sits between these two lines right on that horizontal line that you started the illustration off with. For the nose, draw a triangle at the end of the muzzle between the two parallel lines.

The tongue is a bit of a complicated shape, so start with a little "U" shape right at the front of the mouth. Then draw a flatter "U" shape that connects the tip of the first "U" to the point where the "Y" for the mouth meets the head circle.

For the far-side leg, add a curved line that connects at one-fifth of the lower waistline to halfway down the thigh "U" shape. Then add a flattened and backward "C" shape tucked between the tail tip and near-side hind paw sausage shape.

For the toes, draw sideways "V" shapes at the end of each front paw oval. They should be sort of parallel to the tips of the paw shapes, with the point of the "U" shapes aimed at the end of the paws. Also, add a little "V" shape at the base of the near-side front paw to represent a small pad on the back of the dog's leg.

Step 6: Draw the outline of the main features with a thick pen.

Starting off with the dog's face, outline along the guidelines of the muzzle, mouth, jaw and tongue.

Draw the nose triangle, adding a small dot toward the bottom for the nostril.

For the eye, draw around the main circle and add a little notch at the seven o'clock mark for the tear duct.

Draw the ear shapes. Add some small broken lines to indicate fur where the ears attach to the back of the head circle.

Draw the neck lines. Using the top and base guidelines that connect the head circle to the shoulder, add fur by drawing broken tick lines and zigzags. German shepherds typically have lots of fur around their necks, so feel free to make the drawing very fluffy.

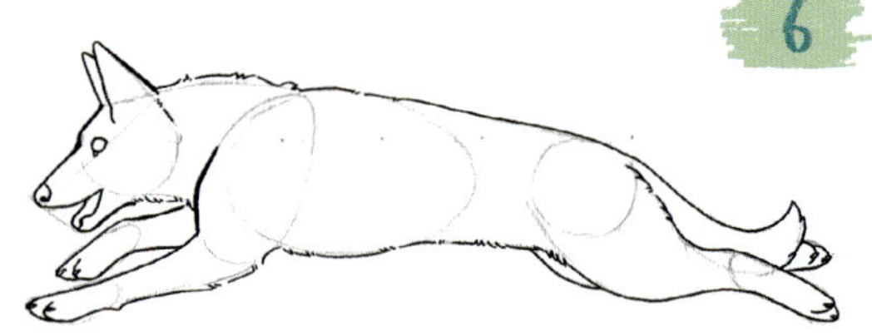

Extend along the back line, starting with some broken lines over the rib oval for fur, but draw one continuous line along towards the hip oval. Keep this line going until you reach the tip of the tail.

Draw the front legs. Start a line halfway down the shoulder egg shape and extend until you meet the top of the near-side leg guideline. Draw along the top line, add the toes and continue around the bottom of the leg line. Add some more ticks and broken lines around the elbow to show the fur. For the far-side front leg, draw the outside of the guidelines. For each toe, add a tiny oval for the claws.

Draw the chest and tummy. German shepherds have a lot of fur along their tummy, so draw a broken line and extra tick marks to make it look fluffy.

Add the outline for the back legs and paws. Start with the curve from the thigh and along towards the toes. Draw the toes and around the back of the foot and leg towards the rump. Draw some zigzags and tick marks for the rump to indicate fur. Follow the guidelines for the far-side rear legs and paws. Add the tiny ovals for claws at the tip of each toe.

Draw the underside of the tail. This is a series of little curved ticks to show the fur.

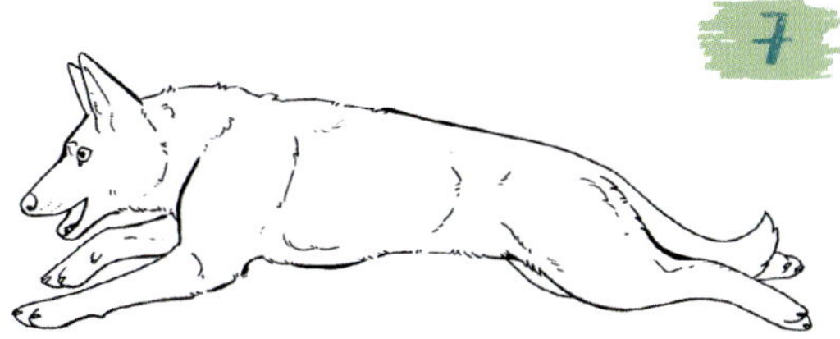

Step 7: Add the finishing details of the outline with a thinner pen.

Starting with the German shepherd's head, draw the whisker dimples, a lower canine tooth, a pupil, an eyebrow and an inner ear. The whisker dimples should sit between the nose and mouth opening—two parallel rows of dots will do it. Draw a small oval in the nook of the tongue for the canine tooth. Draw a small black dot in the center of the eye, with an indent at the top for the shine. Just above the eye, draw a broken rectangle for the eyebrow. Add the inside of the near-side ear with a central vertical line and a few broken lines to indicate the fur.

On the far-side front paw, right where the foreleg bends, add a small "U" shape and a notch for the dewclaw.

Draw along the remaining guidelines of the head circle, shoulder egg, rib oval and hip circle, and add lines to accentuate fluff and fur.

Erase all your pencil guidelines.

Step 8: Add shading to finish your German shepherd drawing (optional).

Start with a lighter pencil and shade in the entirety of your dog drawing. Make sure the top of the eye stays white for the shine.

Once the dog has been filled in, take a darker pencil and fill in dark areas of the German shepherd. These dogs typically have a dark muzzle, ears and nearly black fur that runs along the back of the animal. Fill in the back of the neck, tops of the shoulders and along the ribs. Fill in the tail too.

When you're finished shading, use your finger or a tissue to blend the pencil if you want a smoother finish.

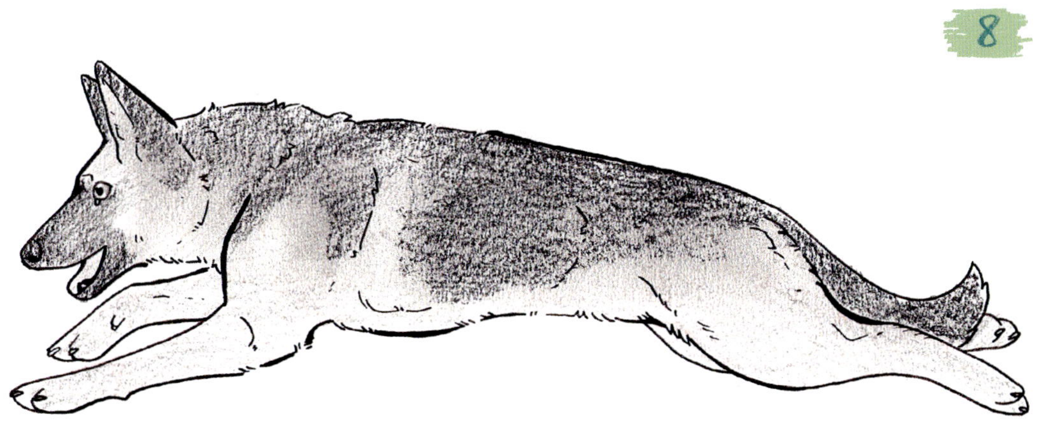

WOLF ON A WALK

For this tutorial, we are going to draw a walking wolf. These animals are ancestors to the domestic dog, so many of the proportions are very similar. And although these exact animals may not be something you see very often, there may be some familiarity with them when it comes to re-creating them for the page. This pose, while not quite as dynamic as the German Shepherd (page 27), still has a lovely movement to it, which will give life to the drawing.

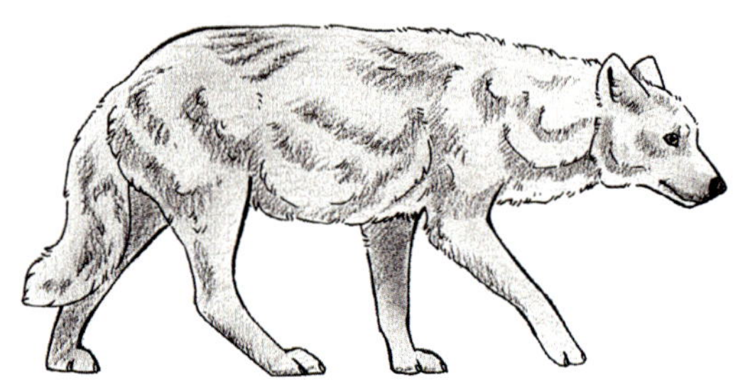

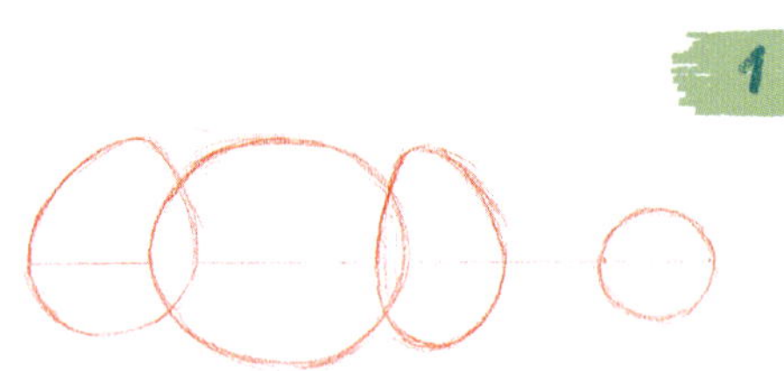

Step 1: Start with the head, shoulders, middle and hip shapes.

Begin by drawing a horizontal line as your guide. Wolves tend to carry their head lower than dogs when walking, so this horizontal guideline will help place the remaining shapes. For this exact illustration, I made the guideline 6½ inches (16.5 cm) long and placed it three-fifths of the way up from the bottom of the page.

For the head, draw a circle at the far right of the line. The head should make up one-sixth of the guideline, and the guideline should cut through the middle of the circle. In this drawing, the head circle is 1¼ inches (3 cm) in diameter.

Draw the shoulder. This should be an egg shape, roughly 1 inch (2.5 cm) wide and 2 inches (5 cm) tall. Set it to the left of the head by 1 inch (2.5 cm). The horizontal line should fall directly through the middle of the shoulder egg.

For the middle circle, overlap the shoulder egg by ¼ inch (6 mm). Wolves typically have a larger, more barrel-like middle, hence the more central chest/tummy shape. This circle should be 2½ inches (6.5 cm) long and 2¼ inches (5.5 cm) tall, so it's ever so slightly squashed. Again, make sure the horizontal guideline runs right through the center.

Draw the hips, which is an egg shape like the shoulder, only a little wider. It should be almost the same height as the shoulder egg and 1½ inches (4 cm) wide. Overlap it with the middle circle.

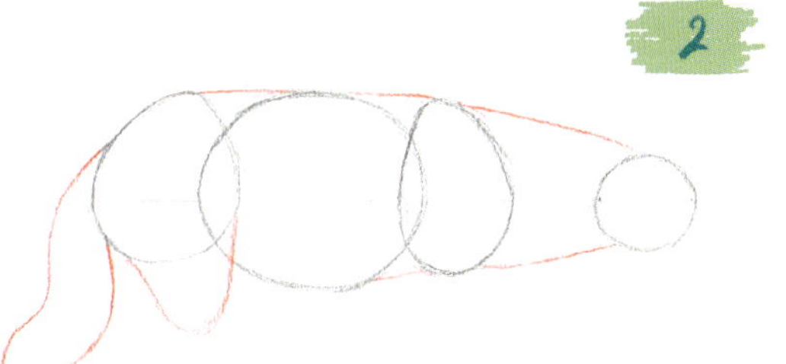

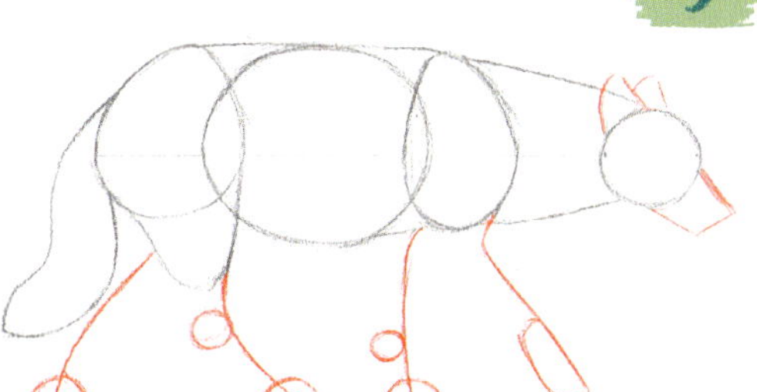

Step 2: Draw the neck, back, chest, tail and upper thigh on the near-side leg.

For the neck, draw a line that connects the twelve o'clock point of the head circle to the top of the shoulder egg. Draw another line from the seven o'clock mark of the head circle to the base of the shoulder egg.

For the back, connect the top of the shoulder egg to the top of the middle circle and the top of the middle circle to the tip of the hip egg.

Draw a short line for the chest by connecting the bottom of the shoulder egg to the right side of the middle circle.

Add a "U" shape for the upper thigh. Attach the top of the "U" to the seven o'clock and three o'clock marks of the hip egg shape. The tip of the "U" shape should be ¾ inch (2 cm) below the hip egg.

For the tail, start a line from the ten o'clock mark of the hip egg. Draw a gentle "S" shape until you're level with the tip of the thigh "U." Then draw another line that connects to the eight o'clock mark of the hip egg. Do a curved line that runs parallel with the "S" you've drawn and finally curve up and back to attach to the "S."

Step 3: Add the ears, muzzle, and begin the legs.

To draw the ears, attached two triangular shapes to the head circle. Start with the near-side ear, attaching it to the ten o'clock and twelve o'clock points. For the far-side ear, attach it to the one o'clock mark. The tips of the ears should be level with the wolf's back.

For the muzzle, draw two lines, one from the four o'clock mark and one from the six o'clock mark. Angle them diagonally down slightly. They should narrow slightly as they leave the head circle and be half the length of the diameter of the head circle. In this instance, ½ inch (1.3 cm). Draw a line across that connects the two lines to finish the muzzle shape.

For the legs, begin with the near-side foreleg. Start with a short line that connects to the bottom right of the shoulder egg and points diagonally to the left. Draw until it is level with the bottom of the middle circle. Then draw a second line from the end of the first, pointing down to the right and creating a 100 degree angle. This second line should be about the same length as the top neck line. Add an oval for the paw that's roughly one-half of the second line and about three times as long as it is wide.

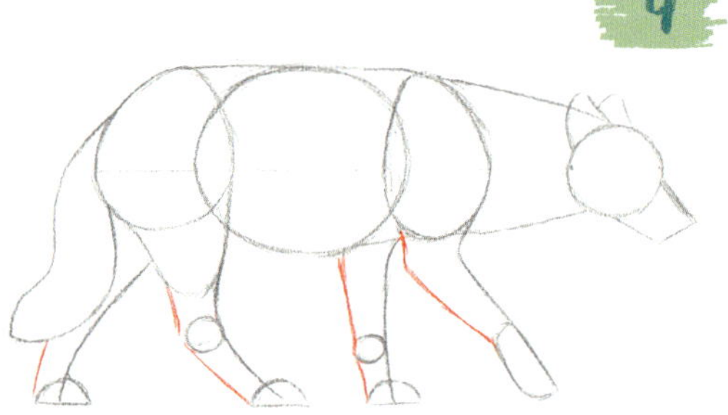

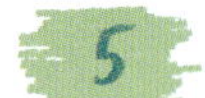

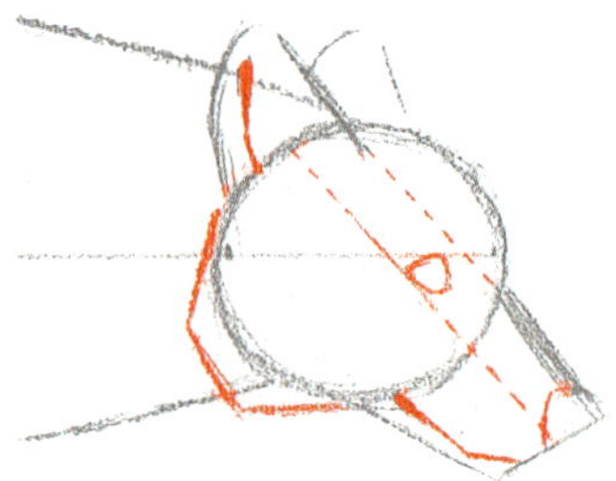

For the second leg from the right, the far-side foreleg, draw a lightly curved line vertically down from where the shoulder egg meets the small chest line. This line should extend very minimally past the near-side front paw. Place a small semicircle, flat-side down with the leg line directly in the middle to form the paw. One-third of the way up, place a small circle for the wrist.

For the third leg from the right, the near-side hind leg, draw a lightly curved line starting at the front of the thigh "U" shape. Extend this line as far down as the far-side front leg. Again, draw a central semicircle for the paw, same side as before, and add a small circle two-thirds the way up from the bottom for the ankle.

For the last leg, draw a curved line that extends from the middle of the left side of the "U" shape and extend it to be level with the previous two legs. Add the semicircle again. Don't worry about the ankle circle for this leg as it's hidden behind the tail.

Step 4: Finish the legs.

For the leg farthest to the right, draw vertically down from the back of the shoulder egg. Then, extend it almost parallel with the front of the foreleg until it meets the paw oval.

For the second leg from the right, draw a vertical line down from the five o'clock mark of the middle circle. Connect it to the wrist circle and the back of the paw semicircle.

For the third leg from the right, draw a line down that connects the back of the thigh "U" shape to the ankle circle. Connect the ankle circle to the back of the paw semicircle with a parallel line to the front of the hind leg.

For the last leg, draw a parallel line up from the back of the paw semicircle until it meets the underside of the tail.

Step 5: Add the facial features including the nose, eye, mouth, inner ear and cheek fluff.

Extend the top of the muzzle back until you have a line that connects to the back of the near-side ear. This is just a guide. Then draw a parallel guideline that connects halfway down the front of the muzzle to the eleven o'clock mark on the head circle.

Draw the nose, which is a triangle at the front of the muzzle. It should fit between the guideline and the top of the muzzle, one-quarter of the way along.

Add the eye just below the horizontal line drawn in the first step. This can be a rounded triangle shape that sits on the second parallel guideline.

For the mouth, draw a very flat "V" shape that connects just below the nose shape to the five o'clock mark of the head circle.

For the inner ear, draw up from the ten o'clock mark and run parallel along the back of the near-side ear. Don't connect it to the ear tip.

To add the cheek fluff, draw three lines that are the same length. A good length is as long as the wolf's near-side ear. First draw one that's horizontal, meeting the head circle at the six o'clock mark. Then draw one that attaches to the base of the near-side ear and runs slightly diagonally to the left. Then draw a line that connects the two at the ends.

Step 6: Draw the main outline.

With a thicker pen, draw over the muzzle, nose and along the mouth. For the nose shape, draw a small semicircle for the nostril. Draw along the mouth line, making it thicker as you reach the head circle for the corner of the lips.

Draw over the eye, along the top of the head circle and over the cheek fluff. Make sure the cheek line is broken with ticks and apostrophes to indicate fur.

Draw the ears with a broken line around the base of the near-side ear close to the cheek fluff.

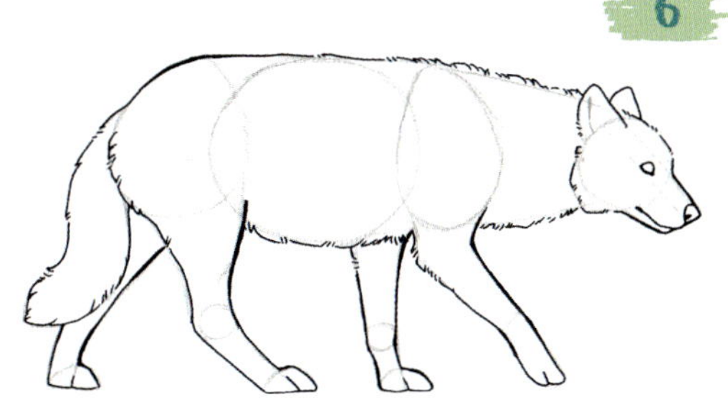

Draw along the neck lines. Wolves are typically very fluffy, so add lots of ticks and apostrophes just outside the guidelines to indicate thicker fur.

Extend the line along the back, going from the occasional tick mark for the fur to one smooth line that meets the base of the tail. For the tail, continue those curves, ticks and apostrophes to make the tail nice and fluffy.

Draw the legs. For the front of the legs, draw along the guidelines, and for the backs of the legs, add ticks and apostrophes around the elbows and along the rump for the fur. Start the front of the near-side foreleg where the guideline meets the shoulder egg. For the near-side hind leg, start the line partway between the tummy and where the leg guideline meets the hip egg shape. For the two hind legs and the far-side front leg, draw over the front of the paw semicircle for the toes, and then two-thirds of the line along the center line for the back toes. For the near-side front leg, add a toe halfway down the front of the paw oval.

Draw the tummy. Along the curve of the base of the middle circle, draw ticks and apostrophes all the way between the back of the near-side foreleg and front of the near-side hind leg.

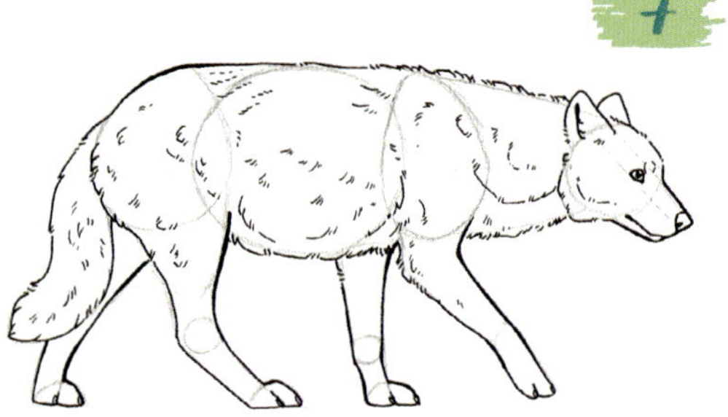

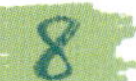

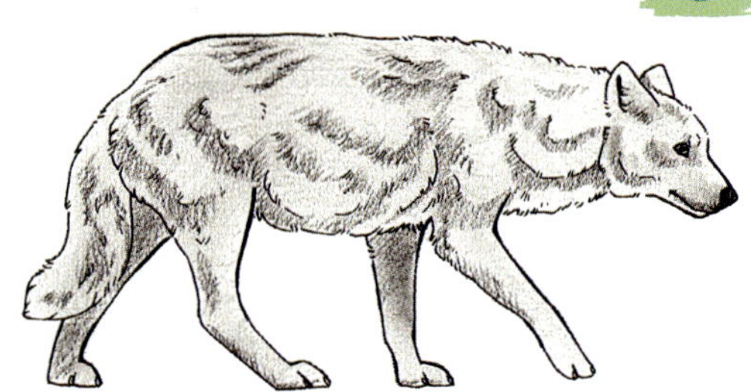

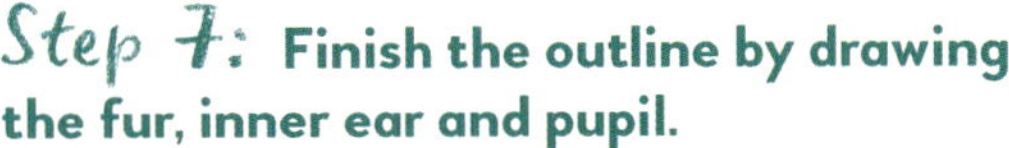

Step 7: Finish the outline by drawing the fur, inner ear and pupil.

Add an extra line parallel to the cheek fluff, keeping it broken and made of ticks and apostrophes for the fur.

Do an extra layer of fur along the neck, starting at the cheek fluff and run parallel to the bottom of the neck. Curve to the middle of the front of the shoulder egg. Again, keep it broken for the fur. Add patches of ticks and marks in the upper part of the neck.

Use the middle circle as a guide to add more fur marks along the curves. Fill in the shapes of the guidelines with sporadically placed groups of marks. Less is more here. You just want to indicate the fur.

Fill in a row of the back of the near-side hind leg, running parallel to the rump. Also fill in the tail with randomly placed groups of ticks and apostrophes.

Add the central line for the inner ear with a few short lines to indicate ear fur.

Draw the pupil, which is a small black circle with a clear indent for the shine.

Add the eyebrow slightly above and to the right of the eye as two "C" shapes opposite each other.

Erase your guidelines.

Step 8: Add the shading (optional).

Using a lighter pencil, fill in the entirety of your wolf.

Then, with a darker pencil, add some shadow. For starters, you can make the far-side legs darker to show some depth. Then, apply darker pencil beneath all of the fur lines you made in step 7. This helps to add volume. A good technique is drawing similar ticks and apostrophes for the darker shading too, which helps emphasize the fur.

Then, for a smoother finish, feel free to blend the pencil together with your finger or a tissue.

A Few Puppy Portraits

Dogs can have pointy ears or floppy ears. Long muzzles or short ones. They can have curly tails, straight tails, deep chests or barrel-like bellies. Fluffy coats, smooth coats or shaggy coats.

For this section, I have created some alternative dog breeds you can draw. Each starts with the head and chest oval, plus the top of the muzzle curved line as per the French Bulldog "Sit" tutorial (page 20). With some variations of proportions and shapes, you can easily create a wide range of dog illustrations.

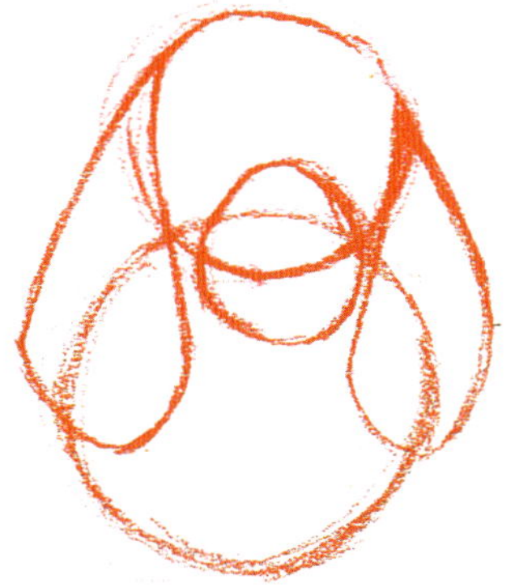

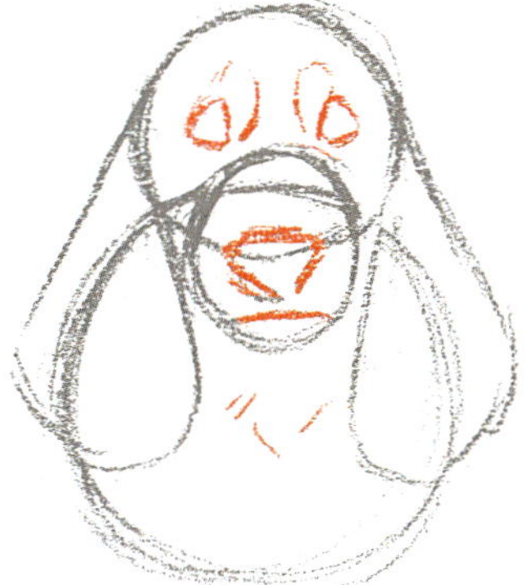

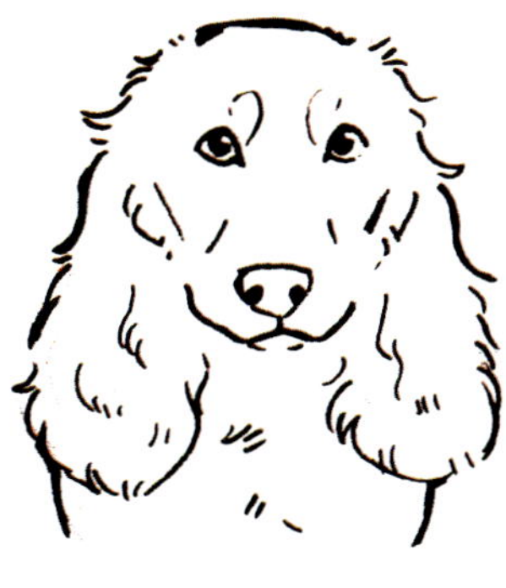

COCKER SPANIEL

For this portrait, keep the proportions of the head circle and the chest circle like that of the French Bulldog "Sit" (page 20). But then, make these changes.

For the muzzle, start with the arched line that connects the four o'clock and seven o'clock marks. But instead of leaving it there like the French Bulldog tutorial, turn that shape into an egg.

Place the ears, which are two elongated water droplet shapes. They should connect to the head circle at the ten o'clock and two o'clock marks and extend all the way to just past the horizontal halfway mark of the chest oval.

Add the eyes, nose, mouth and a few lines to indicate the base of the neck. The nose should be an inverted triangle taking up 50 percent of the end of the muzzle egg shape. The top line should rest just above the bottom of the head circle. Draw a straight line across the bottom of the muzzle egg for the mouth. Then, draw two small and rounded triangles for the eyes. The base of the triangles should be level with the top of the muzzle egg and sit on either side of it. Add two "C" shapes, with the left one being backwards, on the inside of the eyes for the eyebrows.

When outlining, make sure to add lots of wavy lines along the ear shapes to show long fur. Cocker Spaniels have very hairy ears, and the wavy lines help emphasize this. Outline the rest of the shapes as normal.

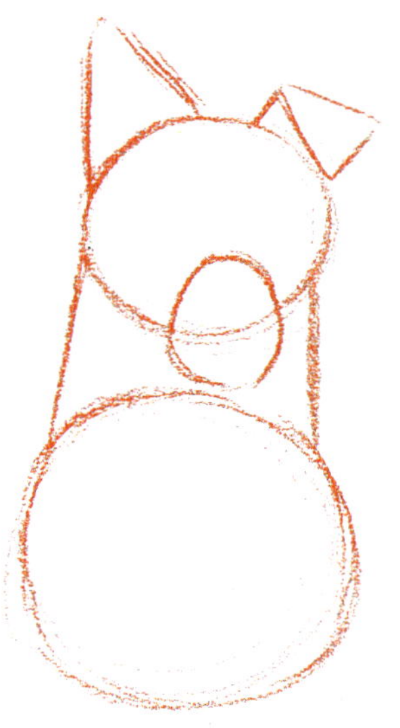
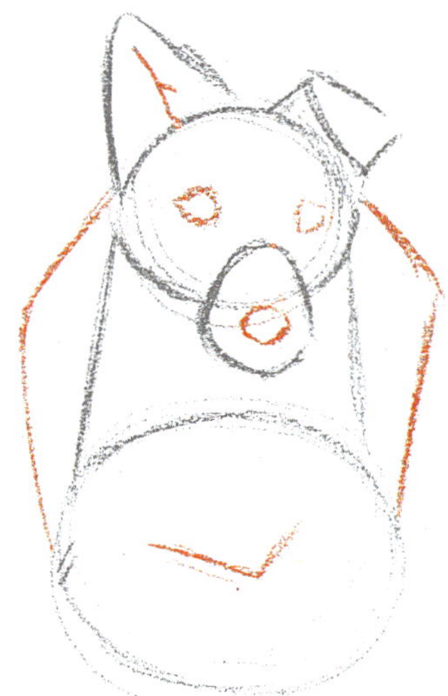
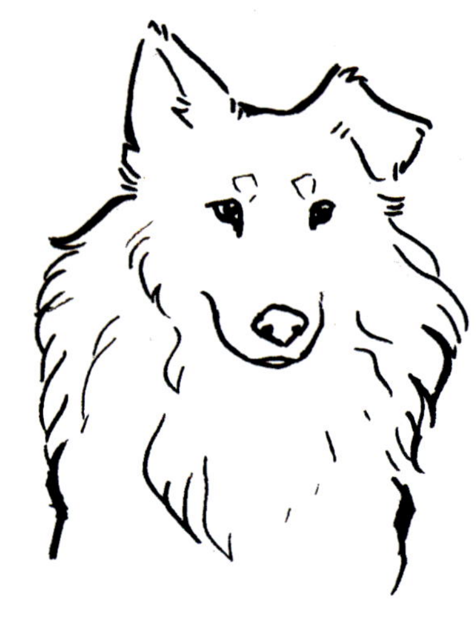

ROUGH COLLIE

This breed has a longer neck than the French Bulldog "Sit" (page 20), so while the proportions of the head circle and chest circle are the same as in that tutorial, make sure the two circles are separated and have a gap in the middle.

Connect the two circles with a pair of vertical lines from the eight o'clock and four o'clock points on the head circle meeting at the ten o'clock and two o'clock marks of the chest circle.

Add the muzzle egg like the Cocker Spaniel (page 37), but make it half the size proportionally.

For the ears, do one triangle from the nine o'clock and twelve o'clock marks of the head circle. Add an inverted triangle with the tip sitting just above the three o'clock mark. Make the triangle as wide at the base as the other erect ear triangle. Then have a small line connecting the one o'clock mark to the left point of the triangle.

Add a line for the inner ear, place the eyes on either side of the top of the muzzle and the nose centrally on the lower part of the egg muzzle.

Add a "V" in the middle of the chest circle to show the base of the neck.

Add guidelines for the thick neck fur. This should be two diagonal lines that extend from the nine o'clock and three o'clock marks of the head circle. Then, when level with the base of the head circle, bend those lines and carry them down until they meet the three o'clock and nine o'clock points of the chest circle.

Time to outline. The Rough Collie has a lot of long fur, so draw wavy lines all the way along the guidelines drawn in the previous steps. Add a little bit of fur at the base and tips of the ears too. For the right ear, make sure you don't fully draw the left line of the triangle. This is where the ear folds.

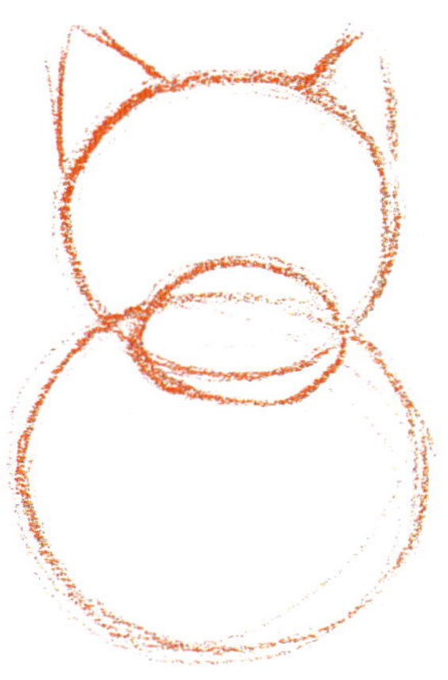
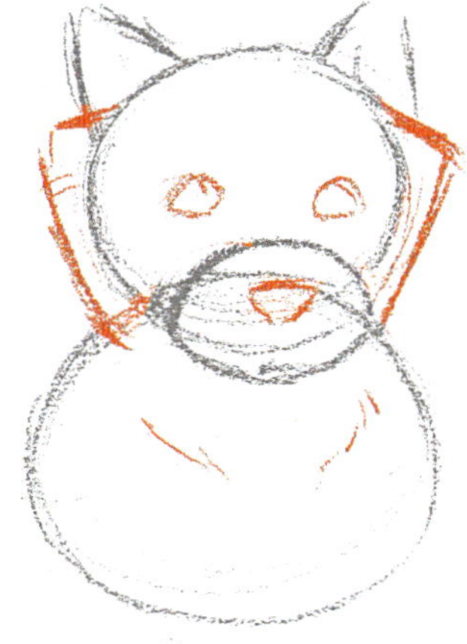
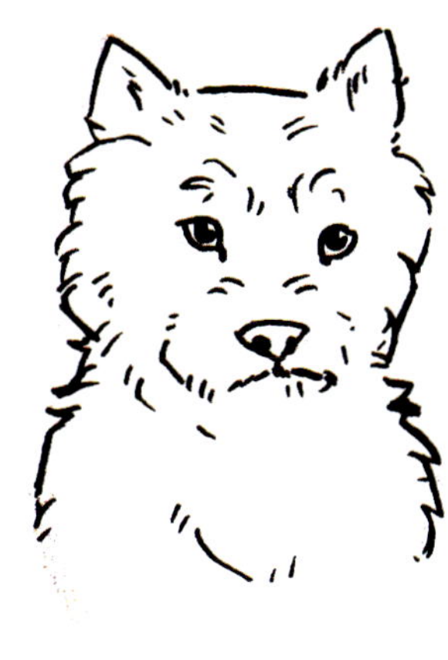

WEST HIGHLAND TERRIER

Also known as a Westie, these little dogs have similar proportions to the French Bulldog "Sit" (page 20). So start there with the two overlapping head and chest circles.

The muzzle curved line should be similar in size to the French Bulldog "Sit" but extend down into a squashed oval shape.

For the ears, add two very small triangles. The left ear should sit at the nine o'clock and eleven o'clock marks. The right ear should sit at one o'clock and three o'clock.

Add some cheek fluff. Draw short diagonal lines from the eleven o'clock and three o'clock marks, and then draw them downwards until they meet the tops of the shoulder circle.

Add the eyes and nose. The nose should be a centered inverted triangle that sits in the muzzle oval. The eyes should be on the central horizontal line of the head circle, on either side of the muzzle.

For the outline, draw along the guidelines in broken ticks and apostrophe marks. Westies, when unclipped, have wiry white fur that can look disheveled. Don't be afraid to make it look messy.

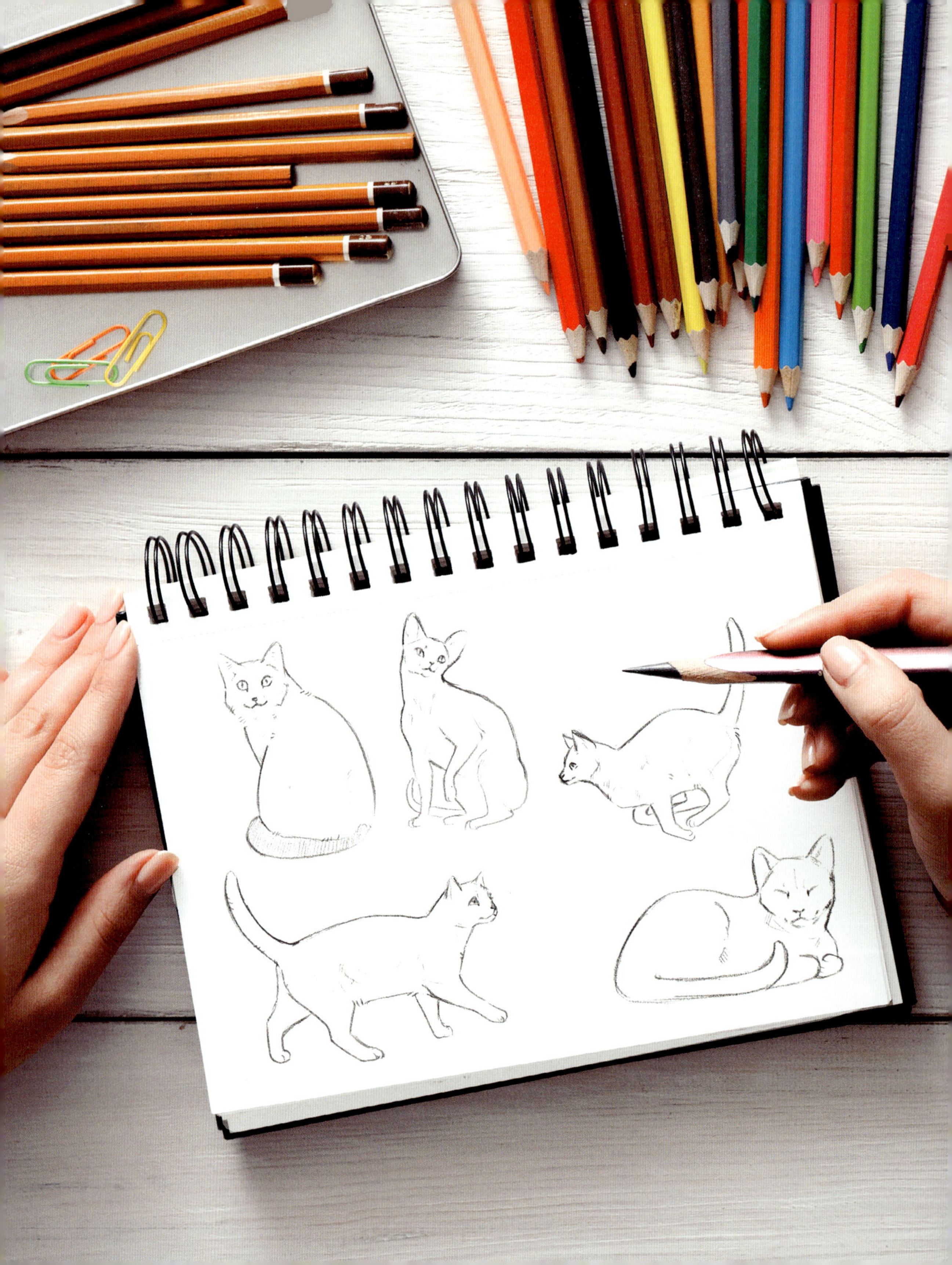

Constructing CATS

Cats are endearing creatures famed for their cuteness, charisma and confident independence. They often leave us wondering whether we own them or they own us. And are we in fact their butlers as they stroll through life with us at their beck and call?

There are many different breeds, but I've narrowed them down to longhair and shorthair for these tutorials. As well as some adult cats, you'll learn how to draw a sweet and playful kitten too. One thing that can be tricky for artists that are new to drawing cats is getting their proportions right, especially their facial features. For example, muzzles can be hard to get just right. The tutorials will delve into this, so take your time when placing the shapes to get the proportions nice and realistic.

Later in this chapter, we will look at how you can draw a variety of cat portraits with a few adjustments to sizes and shapes. One of these tutorials will be drawing a tiger's portrait. Their proportions, while not exactly the same as a house cat's, are remarkably similar. It may be enjoyable to reflect on these similarities as you draw.

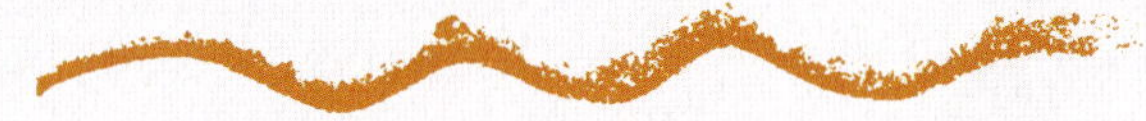

LONGHAIR LYING

There are so many varieties of long-haired cats. This tutorial is perfect for drawing nearly all of them. You've got Birmans, Maine coons, Norwegian Forest cats, Persians and so many more. Their faces and colors tend to be the main things that set them apart from each other. For this tutorial, we will draw a generic long-haired cat.

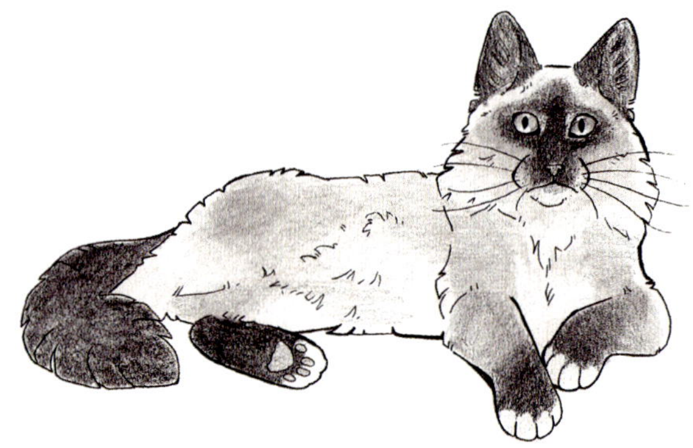

Tip: Long hair can pose a bit of a challenge to draw. When adding the hair in the later stages of the illustration, you may find that the original guidelines get obscured or lose definition. That's okay! The focus of this project will become showing off the longer fur anyway. But to help you when you do place the fur lines and shapes, focus on adding the lines carefully along the original guidelines. This will help create the long fur without losing too much definition.

Step 1: Start with the head, shoulders and hips.

Draw a rectangle shape. If the page was dissected into a three-by-three grid, place the rectangle within the middle box of the column on the right. This will represent the shoulders. For a good guide, make this shoulder rectangle 2 inches (5 cm) wide and 2¼ inches (5.5 cm) tall. This shape should be ever so slightly wider at the base than at the top.

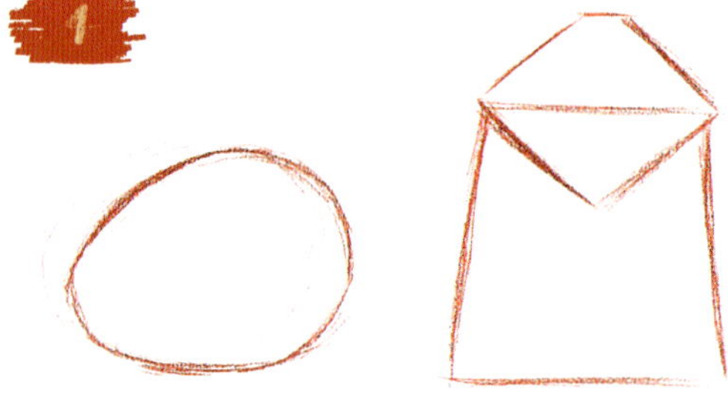

Draw the head as a pentagon shape using the rectangle as a guide. The two bottom lines should extend downward from the top corners of the shoulder rectangle and meet in the vertical center of that same shape, one-third of the way down. Then, from the same corners of the shoulder rectangles, draw upward as if you were drawing the head as a diamond. Before those two lines meet, however, leave a gap and draw a short line for the top of the head, parallel to the top of the shoulder rectangle.

Draw an egg shape lying on its side for the hips. Leave a gap between the shoulder rectangle and the hip egg shape that is half as wide as the shoulder rectangle. The tallest part of the egg should be level with the halfway point between the top of the shoulder rectangle and the bottom of the head pentagon. The egg shape should be as wide as the shoulder rectangle.

Step 2: Add the ears, muzzle, thighs, shoulder shapes and ribs.

For the ears, using the head pentagon as a guide, draw two triangle shapes connecting the side corners to the upper two corners. The outside lines of the ear shapes that connect to the sides of the head should be as long as the head is tall. The inner lines should be half the length of the outsides of the ears. The tops of the ear triangle shapes should be rounded slightly.

For the muzzle, start with a horizontal line that goes through the middle of the head pentagon connecting the side corners. Then, you'll want to create a shape that looks like a miniature version of the head pentagon. To do this, draw two lines that connect the horizontal guide to the two bottom edges of the pentagon. The lines should start two-fifths away from each side corner and go diagonally down until they meet halfway along the bottom lines of the head pentagon.

To add the thighs, draw a sideways "Y" shape inside the hip egg. If the egg was a clock shape, draw the bottom tip of the Y at the eight o'clock mark. Then the fork of

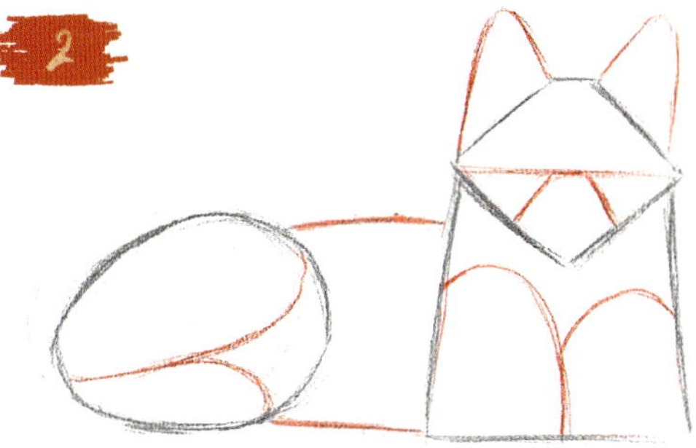

the "Y" should split one-third of the way up from the central vertical line of the egg. The fork that aims towards the top of the hip shape should curve up until it meets the two o'clock point, and the fork that aims to the bottom of the hip shape should curve down and meet the five o'clock point. When you're done, the upper thigh shape should be twice the size of the lower hip shape.

For the shoulders, let's draw another "Y" shape. Start the bottom tip of the "Y" at the center of the shoulder rectangle. Draw the left side of the "Y" first, forking up and over to the left until you create a gentle dome or upside-down "U" shape. Do the same for the right-hand fork of the "Y," only make sure that the right shape is slightly shorter than the left.

Connect the shoulder rectangle to the hip egg. For the bottom of the ribs that are flush with the ground, draw a line that is almost level with the bottom of the shoulder rectangle until it meets the bottom of the sideways egg shape. For the top of the ribs, connect the hip egg at roughly one o'clock until you meet the shoulder rectangle one-sixth of the way down on the left.

Step 3: Add the forelegs, hind paws and facial features.

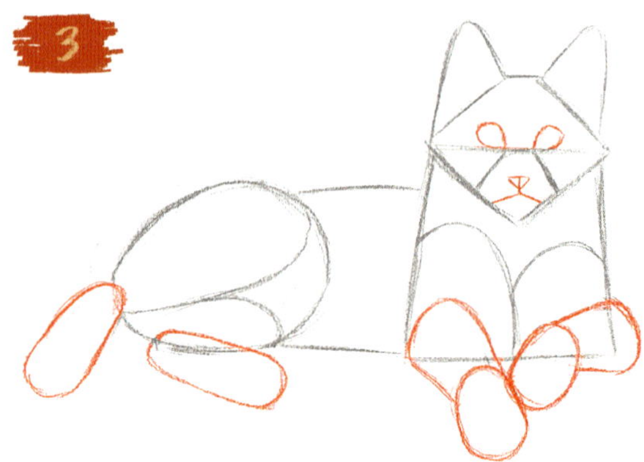

Start with the right-side foreleg by drawing an oval overlapping the bottom of the shoulder rectangle within the right shape drawn by the "Y" from step 2 (page 43). The oval should be tilted slightly and should hang two-thirds of the way below the rectangle shape. Then, draw a sideways "U" shape that connects to the top of the oval and halfway down the oval on the right side of the shape. This "U" should be narrower where it meets the paw oval, and one-third of it should extend past the shoulder rectangle.

For the left-side foreleg, start with an oval that tilts in the opposite direction of the right-side paw oval. This oval should sit with a tiny gap between it and the base of the shoulder rectangle and be resting against the end of the right-side paw oval. Both paw ovals should be the same size. Then draw another "U" shape, this time almost upside-down. The left side of the "U" should sit flush with the left of the shoulder rectangle, and the top should be level with the right-side foreleg "U" shape.

For the back paws, you're going to draw two elongated oval shapes. They should be roughly twice the length of the front paw ovals, but the same width. Place one overlapping the bottom thigh shape with a good four-fifths of the shape just below it to represent the paw. For the other paw, connect a narrow edge to the very left end of the top thigh shape with the paw angled down until the opposite end is almost level with the first hind paw shape.

For the face, start with the eyes. Draw two egg-like shapes on both sides of the top edge of the muzzle pentagon. The bottoms of these shapes should be resting on the horizontal line drawn in step 2 (page 43). Cats have comparatively large eyes, so they should each be as wide as one-fifth of the horizontal line.

Draw the nose and mouth. Draw an upside-down "Y" shape in the middle of the muzzle pentagon, with the tail part of the "Y" half the length of the two forks. Connect the forks of the "Y" exactly halfway along each of the bottom two lines of the muzzle pentagon. For the nose, draw an inverted triangle that's twice as wide as it is tall with the tail of the "Y" shape right down the middle.

Step 4: Draw the tail, hind paw pads, cheek fluff and inner ears.

To draw the tail, draw a curved line at the nine o'clock mark of the hip egg and extend it out and around the hind paw oval on the left. Proportionally, you should be able to fit another hind paw oval in the space between the tail line and the left hind paw. Extend the tail's curve until it's level vertically with where the left hind paw meets the upper thigh shape. Then, one-third of the way down the left hind paw, draw a curve that attaches to the first tail line, forming the tip of the tail.

For the paw pads on the second hind paw, in the third of the paw oval that is farthest from the body, draw a rounded triangle and four tiny oval shapes. To help with sizing, all four of the toe pads should fit within the larger paw pad.

For the cheek fluff, draw two diagonal lines that extend from the side corners of the face pentagon. They should aim away slightly from the shoulder rectangle. Then, draw two diagonal lines up from where the forks of the "Y" drawn in step 2 (page 43) meet the edges of the shoulder rectangle, until they meet the first two diagonal lines.

Draw the inner ears by drawing two "C"-like shapes, with the "C" in the left-side ear mirrored. They should connect the tip of the ear triangles to the head pentagon one-third of the way between the top and bottom edges of the ear shapes.

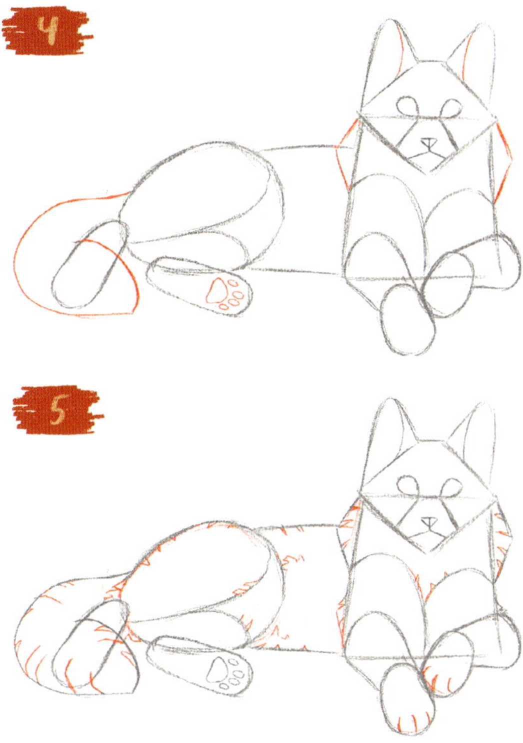

Step 5: Draw the front paw toes, and add some guidelines for the fur.

For the toes, draw three lightly curved lines separating the end of the paw oval on the forelegs into four almost equal sections. The center two toes may be slightly larger than the outer two toes on each paw.

Start adding the fur guidelines. Feel free to refer back to the tip at the introduction of this tutorial (page 42) for this step.

Start along the inner edges of the cheek shapes, add a few little "V" shapes with the fork attaching to the outside line and the point of the "V" aiming inwards towards the shoulder rectangle. Add some more "V" shapes upside down in the crease left by the "Y" shape drawn within the shoulder rectangle in step 2 (page 43).

Repeat the "V" shape along the inside edges of the rib lines, both top and bottom. Also draw the "V" shapes along the top edge of the hip egg.

For the tail, add an occasional "V" shape as well as longer tick shapes to indicate the thicker fur that the tail has.

Add a few zigzag lines for extra fur connecting the top of the hip egg to the upper edge of the left-side paw oval. Also add a zigzag connecting the tail to the bottom of the lower thigh shape, bringing more fur to the hind end of the animal.

Throw in a couple of small zigzags inside the rib area towards the thigh shapes for tummy fluff. Then add a zigzag and a couple of "V" shapes that attach to the shoulder rectangle at the bottom left edge for the elbow fluff.

Step 6: Draw the main outline.

Grab your thicker pen and begin with the outside edge of all of the pencil guidelines laid out so far.

For the head, you're only going to draw the very top edge of the head pentagon shape. The rest of the shape is just going to be a guide for extra fur later.

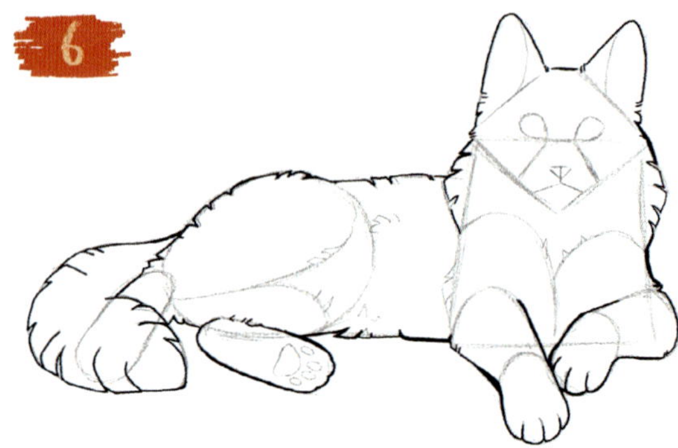

Draw the ears, keeping the line intact except for where the ears meet the side corners of the head pentagon. For the lower part of the line, draw some apostrophes to indicate fur.

Extend the base of the ears along the cheek fluff, this time drawing over the "V" shapes placed in step 5. This shows off the shaggy and thick neck fur.

Draw over the right-side of the shoulder rectangle and the right-side foreleg. Draw the toes and up around the top of the leg, ending the outline halfway along the sideways "U" guideline.

For the left front paw, draw the upside-down "U" guideline at the point that's level with the right foreleg. Draw down and around the toes, and then over the bottom part of the left foreleg. Add some apostrophes for fluff where the elbow meets the lower line of the ribs.

Draw along the back and over the top of the hip egg, again following the "V" shape guidelines from step 5. Do the same for the tummy and over the top of the visible hind paw to enhance the tummy fur. Then draw the bottom section of the hind paw oval.

Draw over the tail, making sure to include the "V" shapes and tick marks drawn in step 5.

Step 7: Finish the outline using a thinner pen.

Add all of the extra fur lines over the guides drawn in step 5. This includes fur around the tummy, and along the "Y" shape, draw inside the hip egg. Use ticks, zigzags and little apostrophes for these lines.

Draw over the hind paw pads.

Add a few more ticks and apostrophes along the "Y" guideline of the shoulder rectangle. Also add a few lines along the guidelines where the head pentagon meets the shoulder rectangle. Add some ticks and lines that cross the space of the inner ear area. Make this nice and fluffy.

Add the eyes and pupils. Start by drawing the eye oval guidelines. Then add the pupils. These are two almost diamond shapes that sit centrally in the eye circles. Then draw over the nose triangle, adding two small dots on the bottom two edges for nostrils. Extend down from the point of the nose triangle over the inverted "Y" to form the mouth. Draw a broken line along the bottom point of the muzzle pentagon to form the fluffy chin.

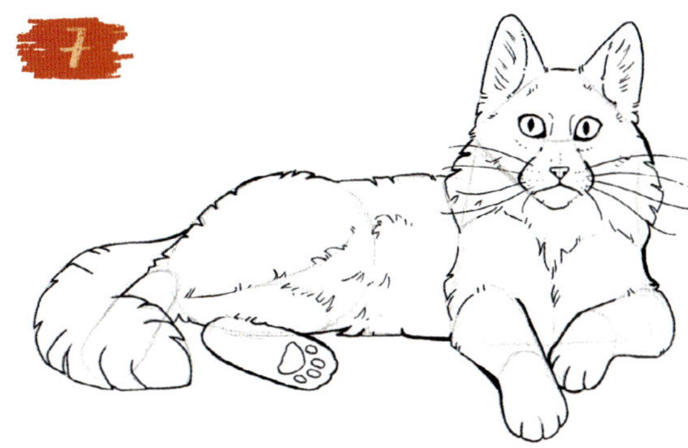

Finish the muzzle shape by drawing from the bottom tips of the "Y" mouth fork up in a curve until halfway along the top edges of the muzzle pentagon. Add the whisker dimples, which can be two or three rows of dots that run parallel within the muzzle above the mouth.

Draw the cat's whiskers. Less is more here. Start with five curvy lines on each side coming out of the muzzle and extending past the cheek fluff.

Erase your guidelines.

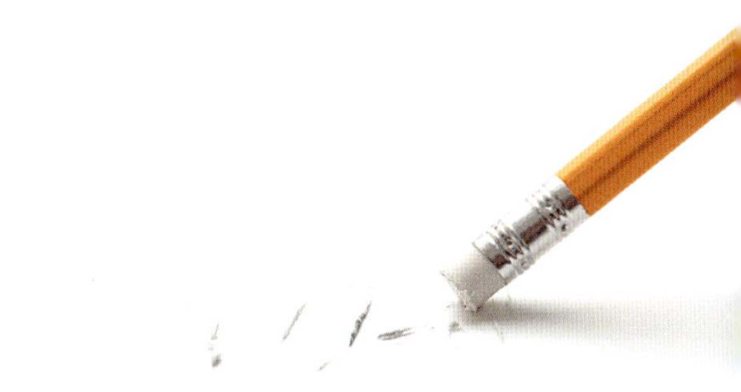

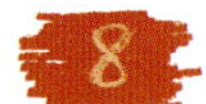

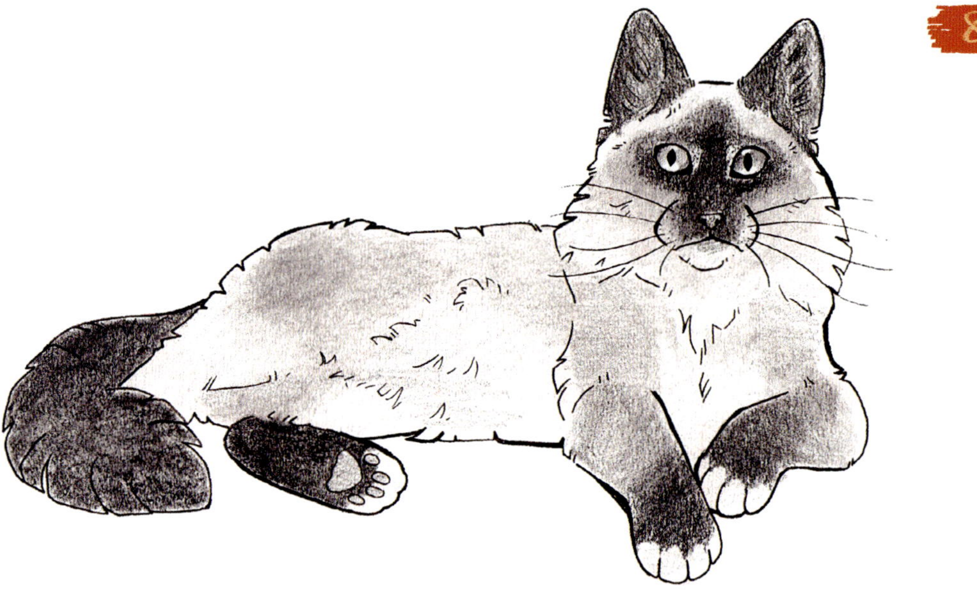

Step 8: Add some shading (optional).

For this cat, I've gone with the markings of a Birman. This breed typically has dark faces, legs and tails, while the rest of their fur is pale.

Fill in the entire space with a lighter pencil. Even though Birmans appear white, it's good to shade them to help them stand out on the page.

For the eyes, add a little more shading to the top of the eyes with a clear spot for the sheen. Use less shading on the lower portion of each eye. This gives the eyes depth.

For the markings, take a darker pencil and fill in the patches of dark fur. Some Birmans are darker than others, so I've made this one almost black. I added darker ears and filled in the tail entirely. I also added darker fur around the eyes like a bandit mask and filled in the center of the muzzle, leaving the edges lighter in a crescent shape.

For the paws, I left the toes pale. Birmans often have little socks, which is characteristic of the breed. For the hind paw, fill in the whole foot minus the tips of the toes. For the forelegs, start with darker shading just behind the pale toes, and then fade to lighter shading as you approach the shoulders.

Go back with your lighter pencil to add some gentle shading along the back and in the shoulder region.

Finally, blend everything together with your finger or a tissue.

SHORTHAIR STRETCHING

For this tutorial, you're going to draw one of the most famous of cat poses: the arched back. This particular drawing is one of a shorthair stretching, but the advantage of this pose and tutorial is that you can do the same shapes for a cat or kitten that is playing or one that is spooked. Cats in play mode sometimes do the arched back accompanied by sideways bounces or hops. Then, cats who have been spooked do the same pose with their back up high and fur standing on end. They usually hiss or try to make themselves look big.

The proportions for this tutorial are fairly exclusive to the three situations just described. When cats arch their back, their body compresses somewhat in the middle as it arches up. It extends the appearance of the legs at the same time. So this should make the illustration seem like it would fit within a square.

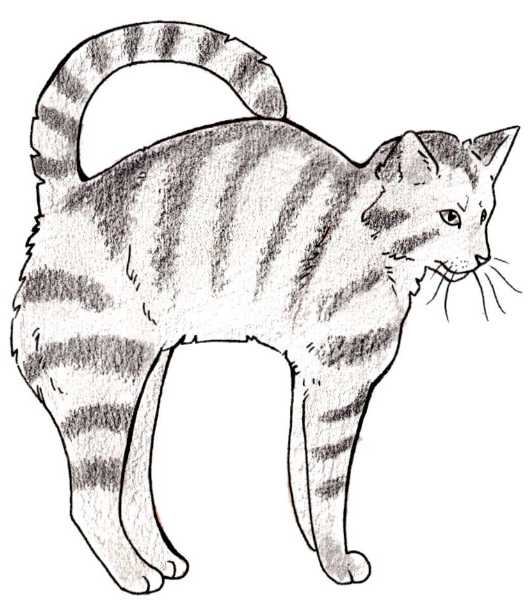

1

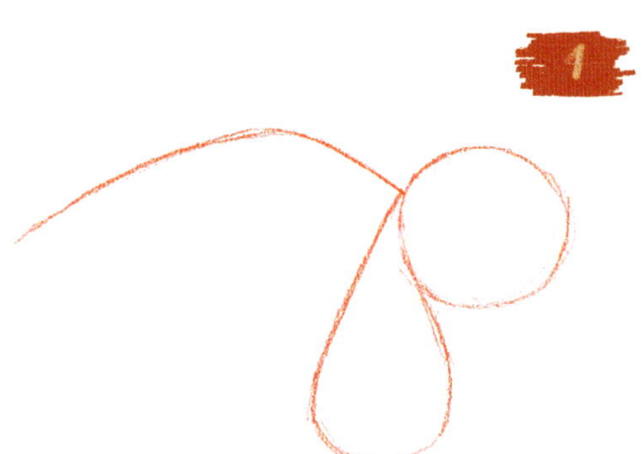

Step 1: **Begin with the head, shoulders and the line for the back.**

Draw a circle for the head of this cat. Place the circle to the right of your page, two-thirds of the way up from the bottom. The rest of the illustration will be on the left.

Add a water droplet shape to the left of the head circle. This is the shoulder shape. The tip of the water droplet should sit at the ten o'clock mark of the head circle. Extend the water droplet down until the distance from the bottom of the droplet shape to the bottom of the head circle is the same height as the diameter of the head circle.

Place the arched back line. Start the line at the ten o'clock mark of the head circle, just where the shoulder shape meets the head circle. Draw this line up to the left at a roughly 90-degree angle away from the side of the shoulder shape. Then, once the line is level with the top of the head circle, create a curved line. That line should be three times as long as the head circle diameter.

Step 2: Draw the neck, hip, thigh shape and tummy.

Connect the base of the head circle to the front of the shoulder water droplet shape to create the neck. Add a straight line from the six o'clock mark to the front of the shoulder shape approximately one-third of the way up.

For the hips, you'll need to draw a shape that is similar to a water droplet with the tip cut off. Draw down from the end of the back, parallel to the left line of the shoulder water droplet shape. Draw the line in a curve, level to the base of the shoulder water droplet, and then, once the hip and thigh shape is slightly wider than the shoulder shape, draw upwards until you meet the spine line.

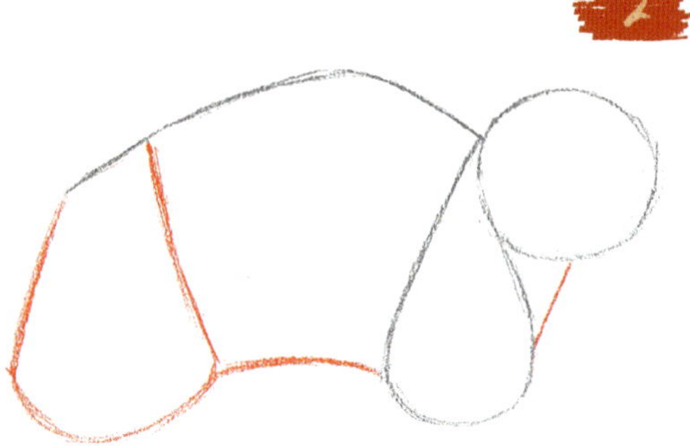

Draw the tummy, which is a domed line connecting the left side of the shoulder droplet, one-eighth of the way up. Make the curve slight and connect it to the right side of the hip and thigh shape at a point level to where you started the line.

Step 3: Add the ears and snout, begin the legs, draw the tail and add a guideline for the eyes.

Draw the ears. For the ear on the right side of the head circle, draw a triangle that connects the one o'clock and two o'clock marks. The length of this triangle should be one-third of the diameter of the head circle. Draw an upside-down "V" on the inside left of the head circle, the same size as the first ear. The point of the "V" should sit between the eleven o'clock and twelve o'clock marks on the head circle.

For the snout, draw two lines diagonally to the right from the four o'clock and six o'clock marks on the head circle. These lines should be half the length of the ears. Then draw a line between the two to form the end of the snout.

Draw the front lines for the near-side foreleg and the two hind legs. Start the foreleg at the base of the shoulder water droplet shape. If the bottom of this shape was the lower half of the clock, this line should start at the five o'clock mark. For the two hind legs, start the leg on the left at the point where the hip and thigh shape meets the tummy line. Then, slightly to the right of this line, draw a parallel line for the other hind leg. The length of the legs should be the same as the distance between the peak of the arched back line to the tummy.

To add the tail, draw two arched lines from the left end of the back line to the peak of the arch of the back line. The top line of the tail should start at the tip of the back line and dome up and to the right to connect to the back line. It should meet roughly one-quarter of the way along from the head circle. Draw a parallel line just inside the semicircle created with the first line.

Add a horizontal line across the head circle connecting the nine o'clock and three o'clock marks as a guide for where to place the eyes.

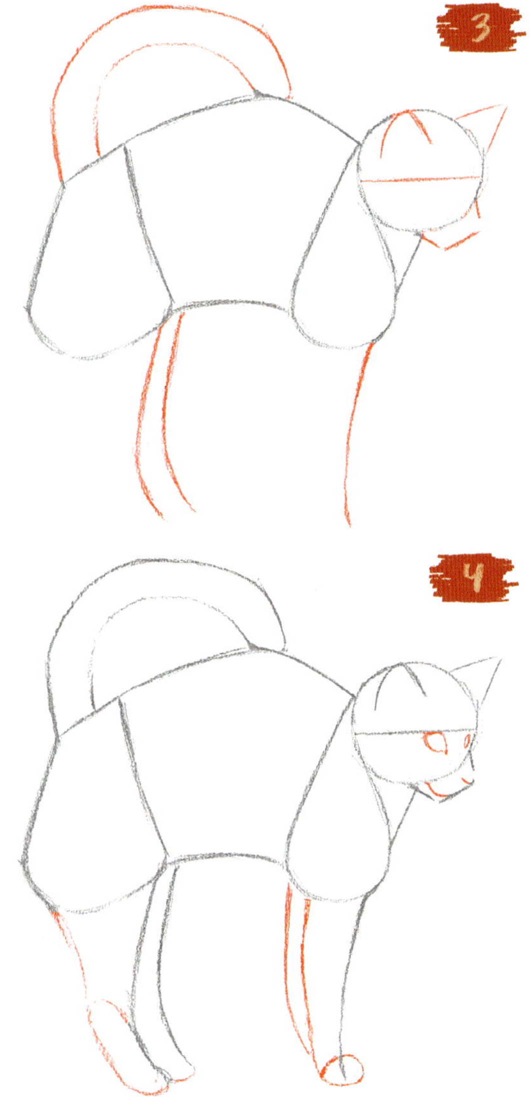

Step 4: Draw the eyes, nose and mouth and finish the legs.

Draw the eyes using the guideline drawn across the head circle. The right eye is barely visible from this angle, so draw a tiny oval just below the guideline, leaving a sliver of a gap to the right between the eye and the head circle. For the left eye, draw an oval with the top flush with the bottom of the guideline. The eye should start one-quarter of the way from the right of the line and end just short of the center.

For the nose, draw a little line from the right corner of the snout shape to create a little "V" shape.

For the mouth, draw a flattened "U" shape connecting roughly the five o'clock mark of the head circle to one-quarter along the line of the front of the snout.

To finish the legs, start with the near-side front paw by adding a small egg at the bottom of the line drawn for the front leg. Make sure the front leg line intersects the middle of the paw egg shape. Next, draw a line connecting the left edge of the paw egg up to the shoulder water droplet shape at roughly the seven o'clock mark. Then draw a line for the far-side front leg, starting where the tummy line meets the shoulder shape, and then running parallel with the back of the near-side front leg until it meets roughly level with the top of the paw oval.

For the near-side hind leg, start with an elongated oval for the foot. This should be half the length of the leg line and four times as long as it is wide. With a curved line, attach the back of the hip and thigh shape to the foot oval. This should create one smooth line between the shapes. Draw the base of the far-side hind leg paw with a short, curved line between the two front lines drawn in step 3 (page 51).

Step 5: Add guidelines for fur, and draw the back toes, eyebrows and inner ears.

Add a handful of "V" shapes along the neck line, back of the shoulder shape and both sides of the hip and thigh shape. These "V" shapes should be small and subtle. Draw a few upside-down "V" shapes just above the belly line, to the left of the shoulder shape. Also add some that run along the top line of the tail, a few near the base of the tail and a few closer to the tip to indicate fur that's parted as the tail bends. Add a little zigzag behind the near-side ear, and a line that connects the left base of the ear to the nine o'clock mark on the head circle.

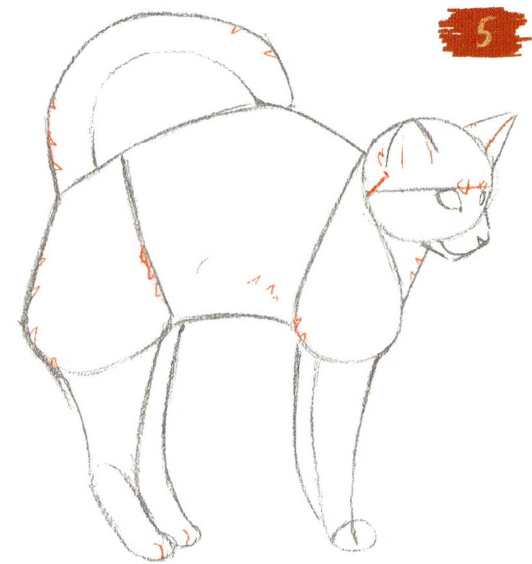

For the back toes, in the middle of the very tip of the paw, draw two backwards "C" shapes—one for each paw.

Add the eyebrows. Add two upside-down triangle shapes between the eyes. Half of the triangles should fall on either side of the face guideline.

Add lines for the inner ears. For the far-side ear, draw a line that connects the head circle to the tip of the ear triangle. The line should start one-third of the way up between where the ear lines connect to the head circle. For the near-side ear, draw two lines down from the tip of the ear creating three sections, about as long as the lines drawn for the outside of the ears. The central section should be the widest, then the left section, and the farthest right should be the narrowest.

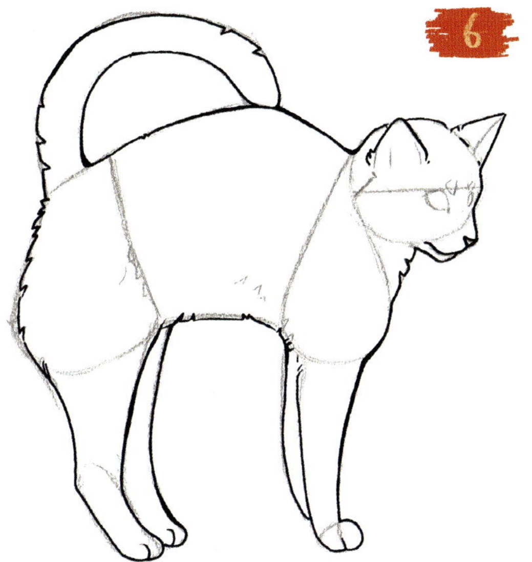

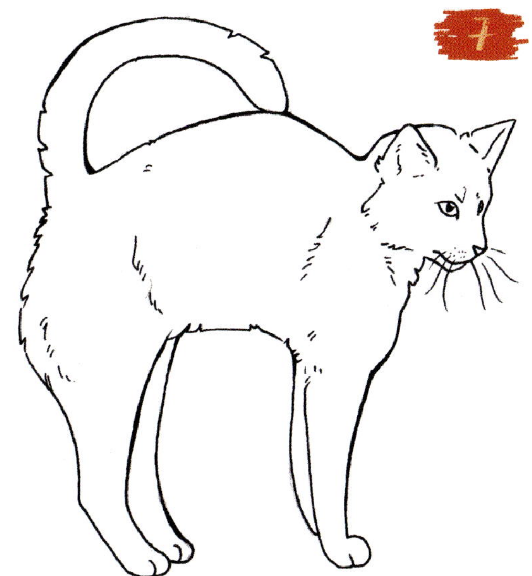

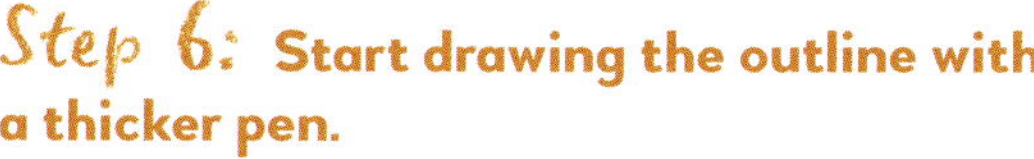

Step 6: Start drawing the outline with a thicker pen.

Starting with the far-side ear, draw the peaks of the ear triangle, and add a dash where the ear meets the head circle. Draw down around the edge of the head circle to where it meets the top of the muzzle. Draw the muzzle shape, nose shape and along the mouth line. Draw over the top of the head circle and over the upside-down "V" for the near-side ear, with a little zigzag on the left to indicate fur.

Draw down the neck line and over the "V" shapes for the fur. Continue down over the shoulder shape, along the front of the near-side foreleg and over the top of the paw egg shape. Add a dash for the toe, and then draw up around the back of the foreleg until you meet the elbow. Add a few ticks and apostrophes for the elbow fluff.

Draw over the far-side foreleg, along the tummy. Add some fur on the tummy by drawing some zigzags.

Follow the guidelines for the back legs with your pen, making sure to add a line for the toes and zigzags over the "V" shapes drawn in step 5 for the fur along the rump.

Draw over the tail, adding the fur where you placed the "V" shapes. Then draw over the back line.

Step 7: Finish the outline using a thinner pen.

Go over the inner ear lines and add some ticks and apostrophes along the bottom of the head circle for the fur of the cheek. Add some additional ticks, apostrophes and zigzags along the left of the shoulder shape, the right of the thigh shape and around the base of the rump.

Draw the eye ovals, adding an oval on the near-side eye with the top missing for the pupil and its shine. For the other eye, just draw a dot for the pupil as perspective makes it hard to see the eye anyway.

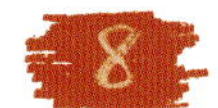

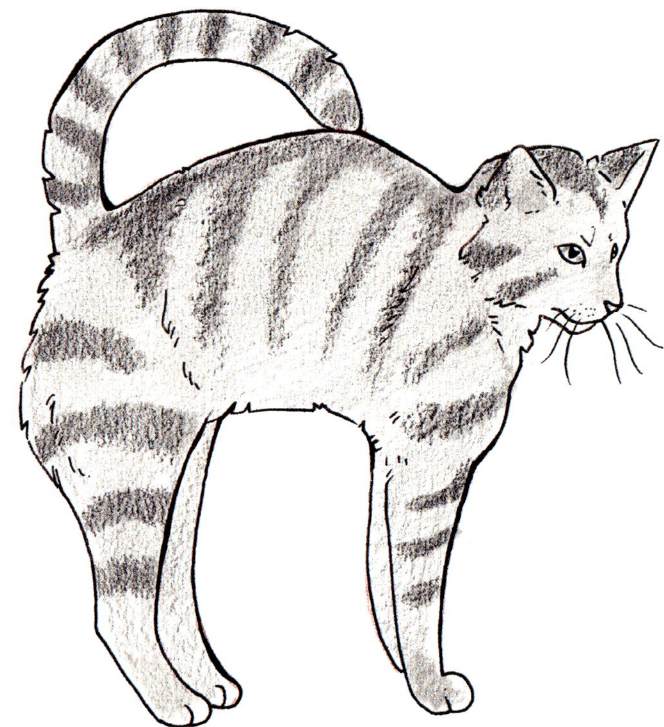

Draw a series of dots in the muzzle space between the mouth and the nose for the whisker dimples. Then draw the whiskers. Gentle wavy lines are perfect for these. Add them on both the left and the right side of the nose.

Erase your pencil lines.

Step 8: Add some shading (optional).

Using your lighter pencil, fill in the entire cat.

Add markings with your darker pencil. For this cat, I've shaded her like a classic tabby. Add bands of darker lines, evenly spaced with and as wide as the lighter fur. The tail should be stripy with bands running all the way along it. Shade some darker fur that runs all the way along the back, with stripes that come off towards the tummy but finish before they meet the tummy space.

For the back legs, add bands of fur like the tail. For the foreleg, add stripes that start at the front of the leg but don't quite meet the back of the leg.

For the head, shade in the top and along the back of the far-side ear. Then add some triangle shapes that go from the cheek towards the eye.

Finally, for a smoother finish, blend the pencil with your finger or a tissue. If you want to keep the stripes more defined, be careful not to overblend.

Playful Kitten

Who doesn't love a feisty kitten, learning to explore and become a grown-up cat through playing with toys and balls of yarn? For this tutorial, we will draw a kitten playing with a ball. The thing to bear in mind about drawing this kitten compared to the adult cats from the Longhair Lying (page 42) and the Shorthair Stretching (page 49) tutorials is that the proportions will be very different. The choices of shapes will be the same, but the size of the shapes in proportion to certain areas of the body will vary. For example, the kitten's head will be much larger compared to its body. The same goes for the paws, but the opposite is true for the tail.

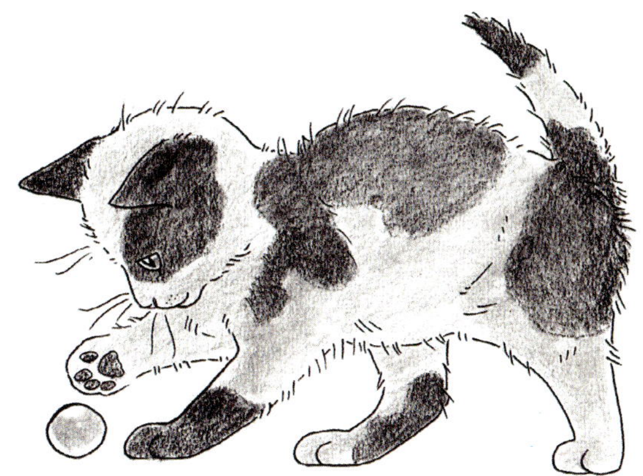

Tip: To ensure you get that characteristic cuteness of the kitten, the facial feature proportions will be important to consider. While the kitten's head is large, the eyes, ears and muzzle will appear quite small in comparison.

Step 1: Draw the head, shoulders and main body of the kitten.

On the left side of your page, draw a circle for the head. Place it just above the horizontal middle of the page. Bear in mind that the head of the kitten will be quite large, so if you find a guide helpful, aim for a diameter of 1½ inches (4 cm).

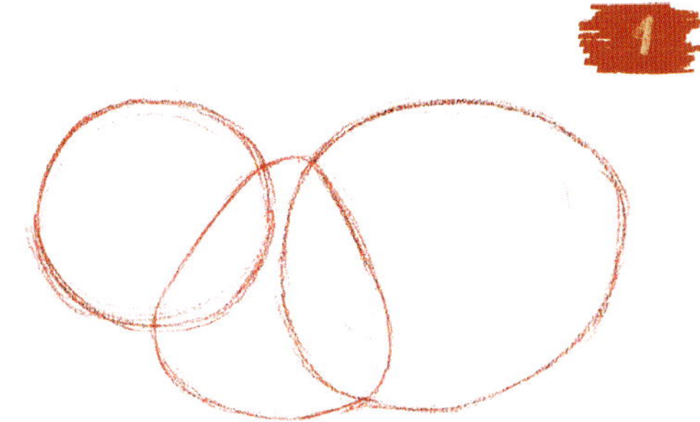

Add the shoulder shape. This will be a rounded triangle. The peak of the triangle should sit to the right of the head circle, one-quarter of the way down from the top of the head circle. The left side of the triangle should overlap the head circle, intersecting at the two o'clock and six o'clock marks. The shoulder triangle's widest point should be the same width as the head circle.

Add the oval shape for the main body of the kitten. This should be a bit larger than the head circle, so 2 inches (5 cm) at the widest point. Overlap the shoulder triangle, just to the right of the peak and slightly below the bottom right corner. The oval should nearly but not quite meet the edge of the head circle.

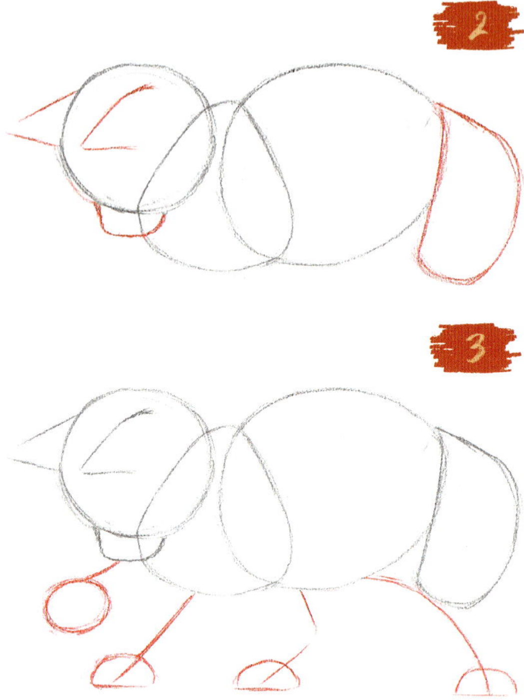

Step 2: Add the ears, snout and thigh shape.

For the ears, draw two sideways "V" shapes on the head circle. The far-side ear should connect at the nine o'clock and halfway between the ten o'clock and eleven o'clock marks on the head circle. The bottom line, which indicates the front of the ear, should slant slightly upward. The top line or back of the ear should angle down. Where the two lines meet, the tip of the ear should be at an almost 45-degree angle. For the ear on the near side, draw a "V" of the same size within the head circle. The bottom line should originate in the exact center of the head circle. Then with the same 45-degree angle at the tip of the ear, draw towards the top of the head circle, curving the back of the ear slightly and finishing with a gap below the one o'clock mark.

Draw the muzzle. This shape is like a squashed "U," and twice as wide as it is tall. Attach the left of the "U" shape to the seven o'clock mark and the right to the five o'clock mark.

Draw the thigh shape. Think of this shape as a rounded rectangle. Draw a line that starts at the two o'clock mark of the main body shape. Draw the line down and to the left, ever so slightly off-vertical until you are level with the base of the shoulder triangle. Draw to the right in a light curve that bends upwards into a light "U" shape. Follow with the right-hand line in another light curve, similar to a reverse "C" shape until you meet back at the starting point. This shape should be roughly twice as tall as it is wide.

Step 3: Draw the first stages of the kitten's legs.

For the far-side front leg, start with a short line that meets one-third of the way along the snout "U" shape. This line should be a little shorter than the width of the snout shape. Draw an oval shape that is as wide as the snout shape and twice the height, with the short line attached to the one o'clock mark of the oval shape.

For the near-side front leg, draw a diagonal line from the center of the shoulder triangle. This line should be at the same angle as the short line drawn for the far-side front leg and three times as long. For the paw, draw a semicircle flat side down that is half the size of the oval drawn for the far-side leg. Make sure the diagonal line finishes just to the left of the center of the semicircle, creating a pizza slice–like shape on the right.

For the far-side back leg, start with a mirrored capital "L" shape that connects just to the left of the six o'clock mark on the main body shape. The line connected to the bottom of the main body shape should aim down diagonally to the right, and then bend at approximately 90 degrees. Continue this line down until it's level with the near-side front paw. Draw a semicircle for the paw just like the one drawn for the near-side front paw.

For the near-side back leg, draw one curved line that connects the main body to the base of the thigh shape and down to the paw. Start the curve between the five o'clock and six o'clock marks and draw towards the thigh shape. As you meet the edge of the thigh shape, continue that curve until the line is level with the two paws on the left. Add another semicircle for the paw, this time with the curved line splitting the shape directly down the middle.

Step 4: Add the eye, nostril, the finishing lines for the legs and the tail.

Add a guide to help you with drawing the eye and the nostril. Use a dotted line to connect the tip of the near-side ear to the snout, approximately one-third of the way from the left on the snout "U" shape.

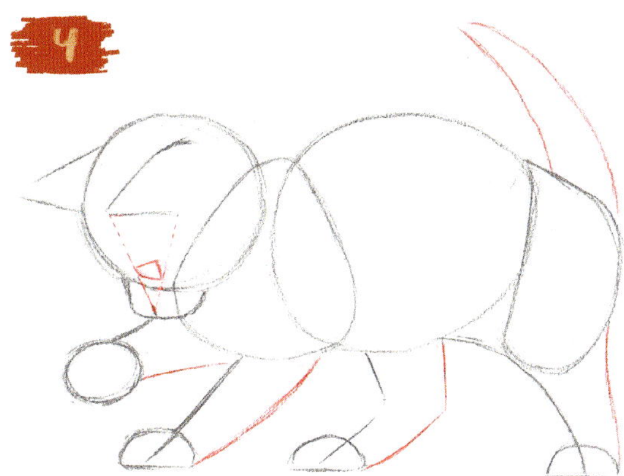

Draw a second dotted guideline that connects the center point of the head circle, where the ear "V" also meets, and draw to the point where the first line meets the snout shape. You will then have a dotted "V" shape to help place the eye and nostril.

For the nostril, draw a little notch right at the point where the two dotted lines meet.

For the eye, draw a triangle shape between the two dotted lines. The bottom of the triangle should be curved, and sit with a small gap between it at the edge of the bottom of the head circle. The triangle shape should then meet at the peak with the left line being a little longer than the right line.

Finish off the legs by drawing lines that run almost parallel to the first leg lines you've already drawn. For the far-side front leg, connect a line at the four o'clock mark of the paw oval to the front of the near-side front leg, just below where that line meets the middle of the shoulder triangle.

For the near-side front leg, connect the right of the paw semicircle to the shoulder triangle, slightly to the right of the point of where it meets the main body shape.

Draw another "L" shape for the far-side back leg, starting at the point where the near-side back leg meets the body shape. Draw almost vertically down until you're level with the bend in the front of the far-side leg, and then connect to the back of the paw semicircle.

For the near-side hind leg, draw the faintest of "S" shapes that connects to the middle point of the right of the thigh shape down to the back of the paw semicircle.

To draw the tail, do an elongated upside-down "V" shape. This shape should be as long as the main body shape is tall. Start at the point where the right of the thigh shape curves to the left and draw the right edge of the tail up in a curve. Once the line is long enough to be as tall as the main body shape, draw down and meet one-quarter of the way along the thigh shape to the right of where it meets the main body shape.

Step 5: Add the pupil, top of the nose, mouth, paw pads, toes, ball and fur.

Start by drawing the pupil. Within the eye triangle, add a shaded oval shape with the portion nearest the top left of the eye empty for the shine. This should make the pupil look almost like a "V" shape with a thicker bottom.

For the top of the nose, draw a line from the edge of the snout "U" to the tip of the nostril line.

Draw the mouth by adding a curved line to the very right of the snout "U" shape.

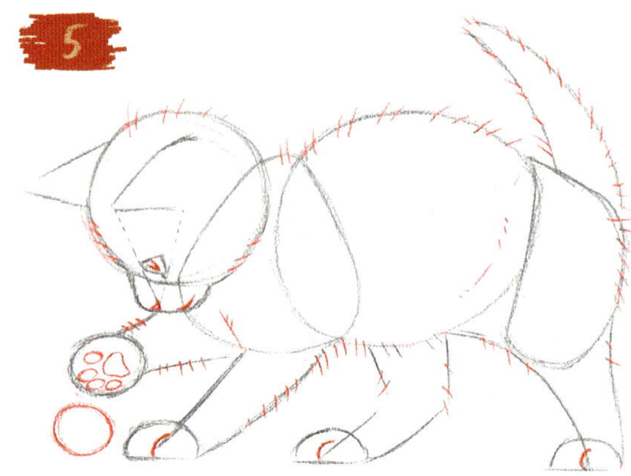

Draw the paw pads by drawing four small oval shapes for the toes and a rounded triangle shape inside the far-side paw oval. The ovals should all be the same size and in the left half of the paw oval. The bottom three should sit on the lower left edge of the paw oval. The top one should sit directly above the second one from the bottom, with a gap left between the top pad oval and the top edge of the paw oval. The large paw pad triangle shape should be three times the size of one of the toe pad ovals and sit to the right of the four toe pads.

Draw the toes for the remaining three paws within the semicircles drawn. For each one, draw a "C" shape starting centrally on the flat line and finishing two-thirds of the way up from the bottom.

Add a circle for the ball. This circle should be placed just below the far-side paw oval with the bottom of the circle level with the flat edges of the paw semicircles.

Add guidelines for the fur. Kittens often have scruffy fur with long hairs that stick out more than the rest. Draw ticks that indicate the fur all along the outside of the kitten. Concentrate them on the top edge of the head circle, between the far-side ear and snout shape and on the lower right of the head circle between the snout "U" and the three o'clock mark. Have the ticks run along the top of the shoulder triangle, over the top of the main body shape, on both edges of the tail and down the right of the near-side hind leg. Do the same for the bottom of the main body shape, along the edges of the far-side back leg and along the backs of the front legs. Add a few on the top line of the far-side back leg. Make sure the lower half of the back legs and the paws are free from these hairs.

Add a line with two tick marks on it that runs between where the front of the near-side front leg meets the shoulder triangle to two-thirds of the way towards the right edge of the snout "U."

Step 6: Begin drawing the outline.

This stage helps build up the fluffiness with lots of short tick marks. This process can be very fun, so feel free to be loose and random with these lines.

Begin drawing the face of the kitten with a thicker pen. Follow the edge of the far-side ear shape and along the forehead, drawing the ticks for the fur instead of doing one long shape. Draw over the snout "U" shape, the nose and the mouth.

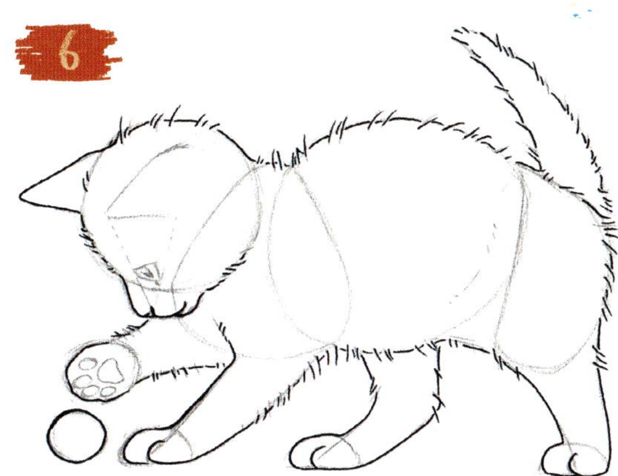

For the majority of the kitten, draw broken lines using the tick marks drawn in step 5 as a guide. That's along the top of the head, back, tail, tummy and areas of the legs. For sections where there are no tick marks, draw lines that follow the original edges of the guide shapes. Where there are tick marks for the fur, leave gaps and draw over the tick guide. This broken line indicates how fluffy the kitten is.

Draw over the paws and toe lines drawn for the near-side front paw and the two back paws.

Draw the ball circle.

Step 7: Finish the outline by adding the ear, eye, paw pads and whiskers.

Add a few extra ticks and apostrophe marks within the main body shape for additional fur markings. Keep the fur lines short, and where they are grouped together, make sure they flow in the same direction. Add a few extra ticks at the base of the ears and within the shoulder triangle.

Draw over the near-side ear "V" shape with a few tick marks where the ear meets the head.

Draw over the eye shape, filling in the pupil shape and adding a tear duct. The tear duct is a short line in the bottom right corner of the eye triangle that points towards the nostril.

Draw over the paw pad ovals and triangle shape.

Add a cluster of dots between the mouth shape and nose for the whisker dimples. Finish the outline by drawing some whiskers. These can be gentle curves that stick out from the left of the snout shape and also vertically down from the nose shape. Add a couple of whisker lines for the eyebrows in the vicinity of the eight o'clock mark.

Erase the pencil lines.

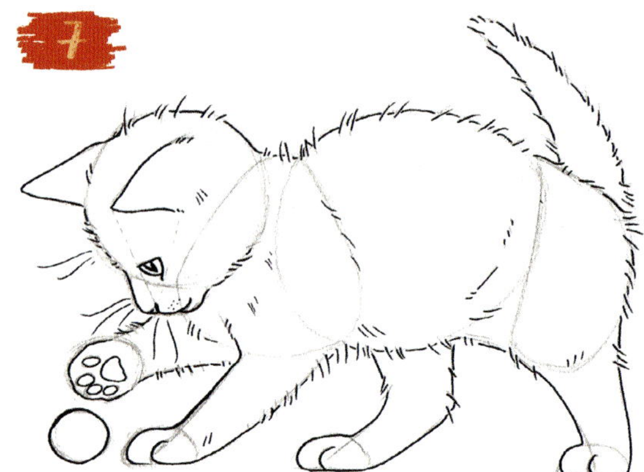

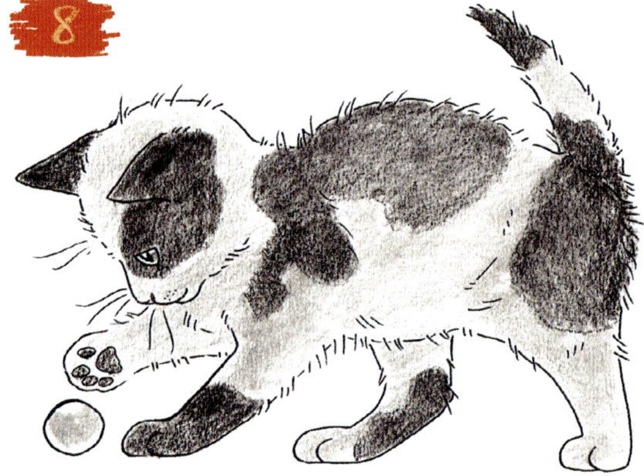

Step 8: Add some shading (optional).

I went with black and white for this kitten. The joy of these markings is that they can be completely random and drawn exactly how you want.

Start with a light pencil and shade in the entire kitten. Don't forget the ball shape.

With a darker pencil, draw some random splotches to fill in. For this kitten, I shaded the ears dark and extended the near-side ear splotch to include the eye.

Add a completely dark front paw, and shade in the paw pads too. For the far-side back paw, I added a random splotch from the paw to the middle of the leg.

For the body, draw a splotch that covers a portion of the shoulder and over the top half of the main body shape.

Add a splotch that covers most of the thigh shape. Add a black tip of the tail.

For a smoother finish, blend all of your shadings with your finger or a tissue. Take care with blending around the markings you've drawn for the splotches if you want those edges to be sharper.

Fabulous Feline Faces

Felines come in all shapes, sizes, colors and fur patterns. For this group of mini-tutorials, you'll learn how you can vary the shapes and proportions of facial features to draw a couple of different breed portraits plus one famous large cat: the tiger.

These mini-tutorials are based off the tutorial for the Longhair Lying (page 42). Refer to that tutorial so you can adjust the shapes and proportions to create these new breeds.

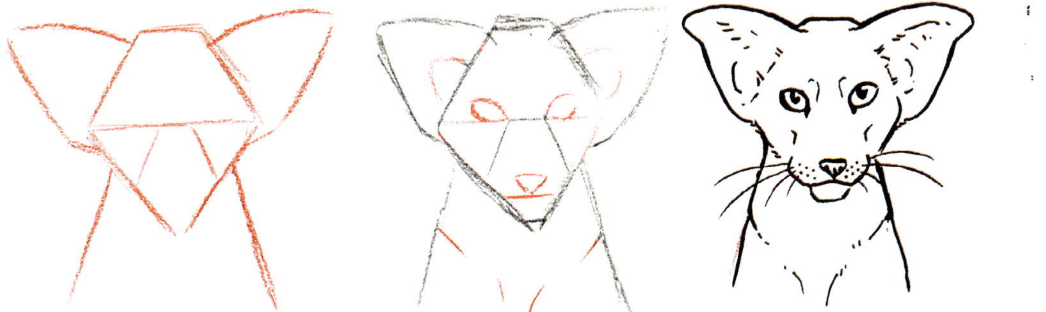

THE ORIENTAL SHORTHAIR

This spectacular breed is famous for its extraordinarily large ears. Their faces are angular and narrow with ears that protrude like satellite dishes. So let's look at the key differences that create this intriguing cat.

Narrow the head pentagon. When drawing the head, pay attention to the height and width of the shape. It's ever so slightly taller than it is wide. The bottom half of the pentagon is slightly taller than the top half.

This means that the muzzle pentagon is also narrower. So, to add the muzzle, draw one line down approximately two-fifths from the left along the horizontal line down to the center of the bottom left line of the head pentagon. Draw the opposite line two-fifths from the right down to the center of the bottom right of the head pentagon.

The ears point out more to the sides instead of sitting erect. Start with opposing curved lines that start just below the very top of the head pentagon. Extend them out, curving until they're level with top of the head pentagon. Then, from just below the horizontal line that goes across the head pentagon, draw two short lines. Connect the long, curved line to the short line. Each ear should be roughly as long as the head is wide.

The neck lines should taper so they're narrower at the top than the bottom. The base of the shoulder shape should be as wide as the head, and the lines should connect almost halfway between the lines of the muzzle and the corner where the horizontal guide connects.

For the eyes, draw almond shapes on either side of the top of the muzzle. Instead of wide, round eyes, Oriental Shorthair eyes are narrower.

The nose and mouth are much closer to the bottom of the muzzle oval. For the inverted nose triangle, draw the top level with where the muzzle lines meet the head. For the mouth, draw a horizontal line rather than the "Y" drawn in Longhair Lying (page 42).

When outlining the Oriental Shorthair, make sure to use continuous lines. This is because they're smooth-haired without any really long fur.

The whiskers are short too, compared to the longhair, so stick to a couple of short, curved lines.

THE SCOTTISH FOLD

Scottish Fold cats have very short muzzles and folded ears, like their name suggests. Here are the variations you can make to draw yourself one of these charismatic kitties.

A broad head pentagon will do well for this cat. Make it wider than it is long. This makes the muzzle pentagon broad, which will help emphasize the short muzzle that this breed has.

For the ears, add two very small triangles that slope down from the top of the head pentagon. Although these triangles are technically pointing up, when drawing the outline, you will add a little nook at the base next to the left and right corners to emphasize the folded ears.

The neck lines also taper out here like the lines drawn for The Oriental Shorthair (page 61). Because the head is broader, the neck naturally appears thicker in comparison.

The Scottish Fold's eyes are quite small in comparison, so draw them as two nearly circular shapes on either side of the top of the muzzle.

Add some cheek fluff that connects the right and left corners of the head pentagon to the very bottom point.

Add the nose and mouth. The top of the nose should be one-sixth of the way up from the bottom corner of the head pentagon. Then draw the inverted "Y" shape for the mouth. The angles between each of the three lines of the "Y" shape should be an equal 120 degrees.

When outlining, make sure the lines are rounded and solid. The Scottish Fold has thick fur, but it's dense enough that it makes it look fairly smooth and shorthaired.

The whiskers are fairly long and droopy, so add curved lines from the muzzle that all angle downwards.

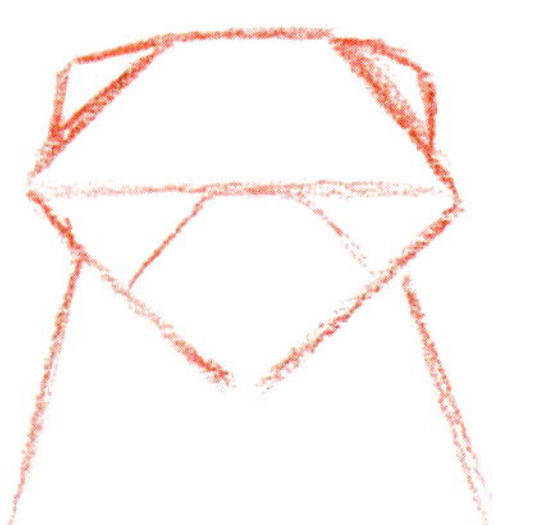

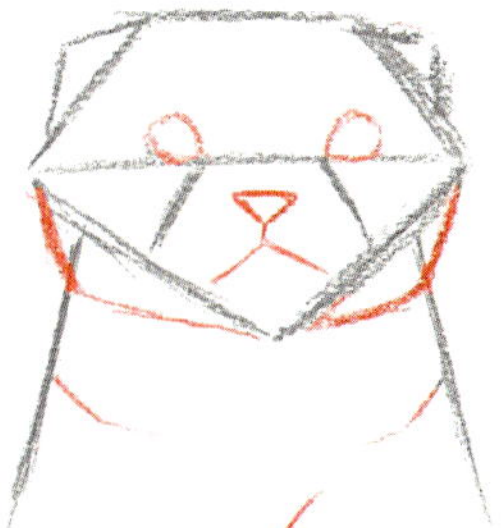

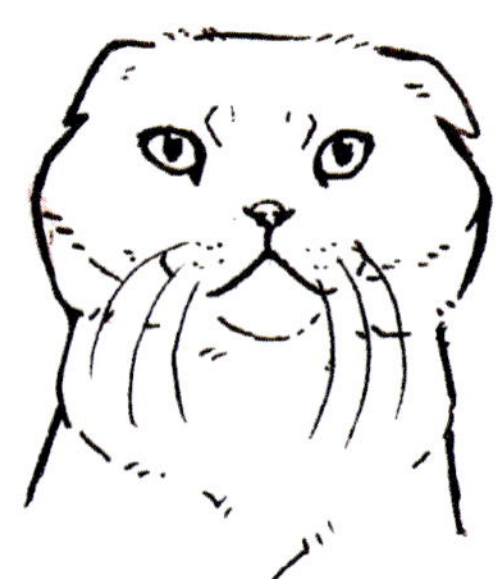

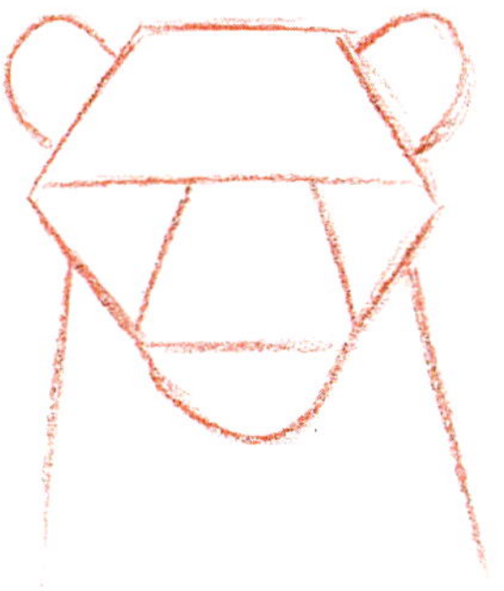

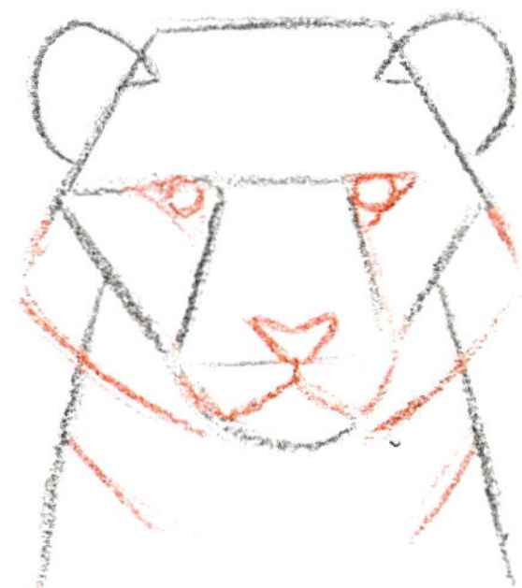

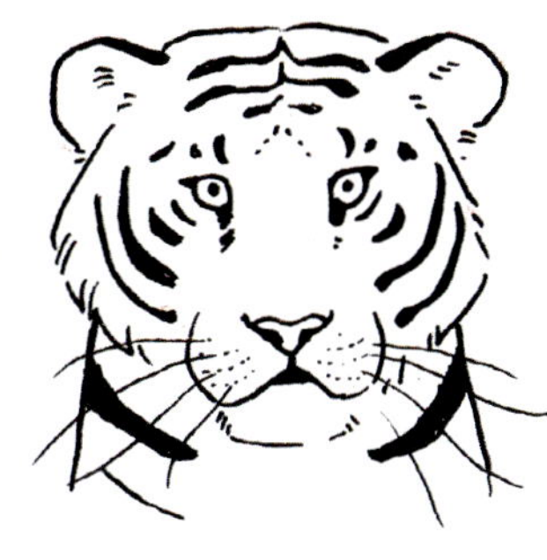

TIGER

Tigers have fairly long faces with broad muzzles and chins. So with just a couple of adjustments you can easily learn to make this fierce feline.

Start with a head hexagon instead of a pentagon. The sides should all be the same length.

Place a horizontal line that connects the leftmost corner to the rightmost corner.

Draw the nose and muzzle. Draw a line connecting one-third from the left of the horizontal line to the bottom left corner. Draw another line connecting one-third from the right of the horizontal line to the bottom right corner.

Add the chin, which is a "U" shape connecting the two bottom corners of the head hexagon. The tallest part of the "U" should be half the distance between the bottom of the head hexagon to the horizontal guideline.

For the ears, add two "U" shapes to the top right and top left sides of the head hexagon. The shapes should be the same height as the "U" shape used for the chin.

Add cheek fluff. Draw two "L" shapes that curve down diagonally away from the head hexagon and then bend down towards the base of the chin "U" shape.

For the eyes, draw two straight lines that connect the horizontal guideline to the sides of the muzzle lines. Create two triangles, and then draw circles to create the eyes.

For the nose, draw a heart-like shape just above the bottom line of the head hexagon. The width of the heart should be one-third of the bottom line of the head hexagon.

For the mouth, draw an an upside-down "Y" shape from the bottom tip of the nose heart shape. The two prongs of the "Y" should meet the chin "U" shape at the seven and five o'clock points.

Time for the outline. Now is the time to add the tiger's markings. On the cheeks, you can add some curved lines that vary from thick to thin. Draw an exact mirror of the shapes on the opposite side of the head. Add some ticks along the cheek fluff guidelines to indicate the longer fur along a tiger's jaw. On the top of the tiger's head, draw a few stripes that look like upside-down "V"s. Don't make these perfect and have them thicker in some places.

Tiger whiskers are very long. Draw out from the muzzle in long curves that extend past the neck.

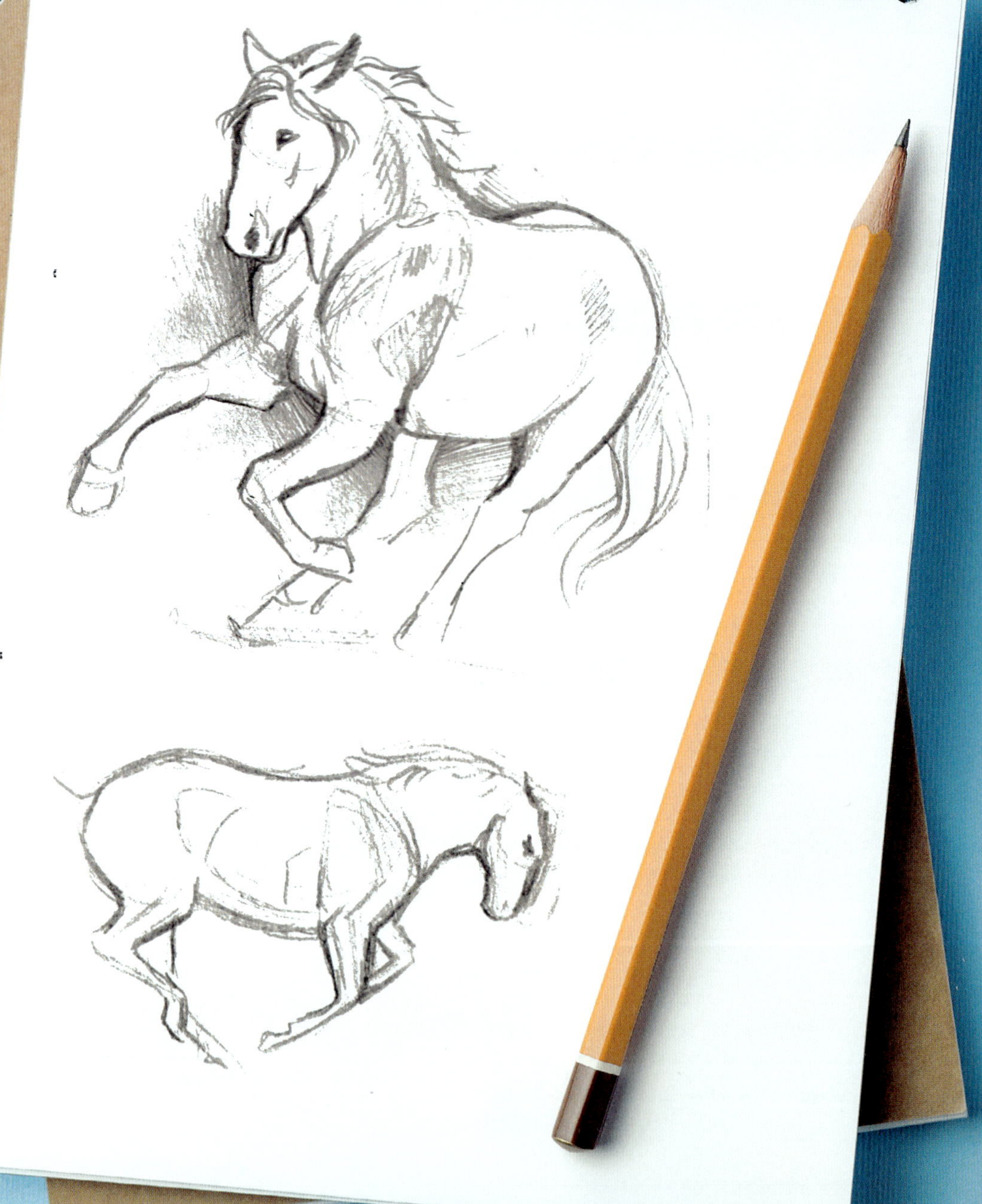

Portraying PONIES

Horses are large animals that can often cause challenges for artists. Because of their size and anatomy, they can be quite intimidating. Their movement is quite distinctive. For example, their spines aren't particularly flexible. Because of this rigidity, the majority of their movement comes from the shoulders and legs as they walk or buck. You'll find through the full-body tutorials that the main body of the animals don't flex very much and that a lot of the dynamism comes from the placements of the heads, necks and limbs.

Horses' appearances vary wildly across the breeds, depending on what purpose they initially had. For this chapter, we will look at drawing a portrait of a generic horse before moving on to dynamic full-body poses for two breeds: the Clydesdale and a famous symbol of the Wild West, the paint horse. While many iterations of the horse family are domesticated, we will take a look at one of their wild cousins too—the zebra.

Finally, we will look at the changes and adjustments you can make to the Pony Portrait tutorial to create a different breed.

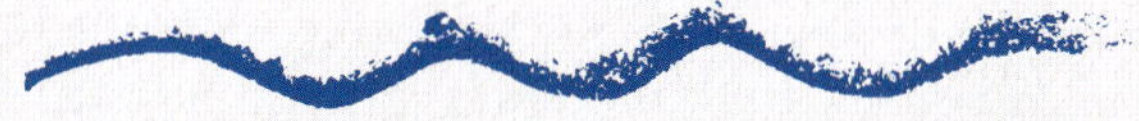

PONY PORTRAIT

With their long and intriguing faces, horses can be very appealing to draw. They can also be a challenge because their facial structure can be more complicated than other animals. That's why for this tutorial we are going to focus on just the horse's portrait, breaking down the face into easier and more manageable shapes.

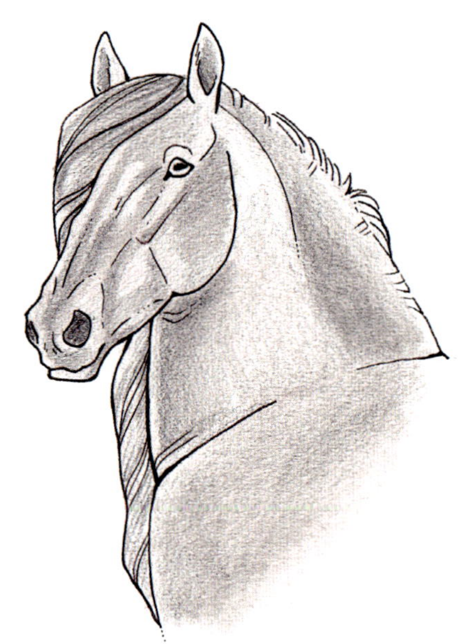

Tip: I really recommend taking your time with this one, and having patience as you go. Horse faces can be tricky, but the result will be worth it if you allow yourself the time to get the placement of all of the features just right.

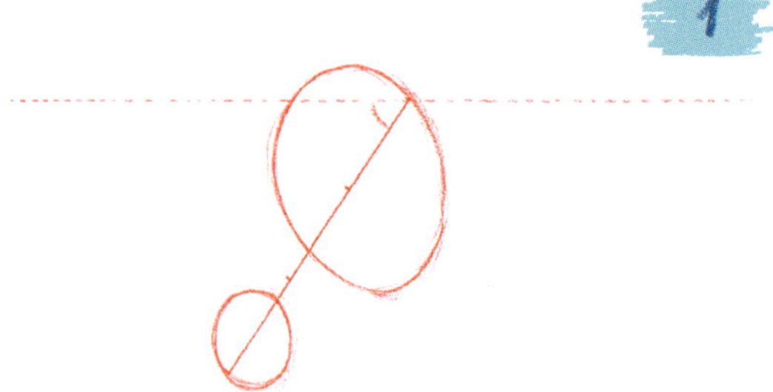

Step 1: Start with bases of the head and mouth.

Add a horizontal dotted line across the page, one-quarter of the way down from the top of your page. This is to help with the angle of the face.

In the approximate center of your page, draw a diagonal line that points down and to the left at a 45 degree angle. Make the diagonal line 3 inches (7.5 cm) long.

Draw an oval for the mouth that takes up approximately ¾ inch (2 cm) at the bottom of the diagonal line. The line should split this oval into two equal halves.

Draw a larger oval for the main head section. This shape will be four to five times larger than the mouth oval, again with half of the shape falling on either side of the diagonal line. It should also sit with a segment of one-sixth of the top of the shape over the top of the dotted horizontal line.

Step 2: Add the ears, eyes, nostrils, lower lip and neck line.

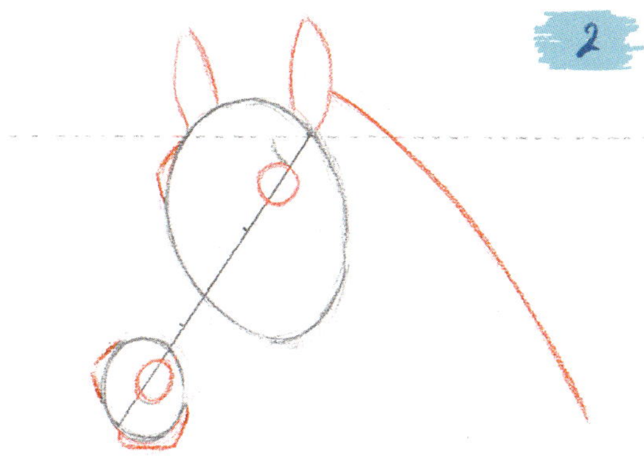

For the ears, draw two narrow ovals that have had the bottoms cut off on either side of the main head oval. Start with the ear on the left, drawing where the horizontal dotted line intersects the head oval. The height of the ear should be one-third of the height of the main head oval. Once the line is long enough, bring the right line of the left ear down until you meet the top of the head oval. The ear should be three times as tall as it is wide. Draw the opposite shape for the right ear.

For the eyes, draw a "C" shape for the eye on the left. This should start at the base of the left ear and meet again at almost nine o'clock on the main head oval. For the right eye, draw a circle along the diagonal line drawn in step 1. The circle should take up the exact middle ⅓ inch (8 mm) of the diagonal guideline.

Add the nostrils. For the left nostril, repeat that "C" shape you drew for the left eye on the left edge of the mouth oval. Make it the same size and shape as the eye "C" shape. For the right nostril, draw an oval that is similar in size to the right eye circle. This shape should sit on the diagonal guideline with one-third to the left of the line and two-thirds to the right.

For the lower lip, draw a sideways "V"-like shape with the two prongs of the "V" curving inwards and attaching to the mouth oval. Start by drawing down just below the end of the diagonal line, around the bottom of the mouth oval, and then when you're level with the right of the nose oval, form the point of the "V" before drawing up and connecting to just below the three o'clock mark of the mouth oval.

For the neck line, draw a curve from the right side of the right ear shape. This line starts one-third of the way up and then curves out and down until the line is level with the lower lip line.

Step 3: Draw the bridge of the nose, the jawline, the cheek, the eyeball, the throat and the shoulder.

Start with the bridge of the nose. Draw a line that connects the bottom of the "C" drawn for the left eye to the top of the "C" drawn for the left nostril.

For the jaw, draw a straight line that connects the lip line to the six o'clock mark of the main head oval.

To draw the cheek, add an "L" shape that connects to the point where the jaw meets the head circle. Draw up at a 90-degree angle from the jawline until you're two-thirds of the way to the diagonal line drawn in step 1. Then draw parallel to the diagonal line until you meet the top right of the head oval.

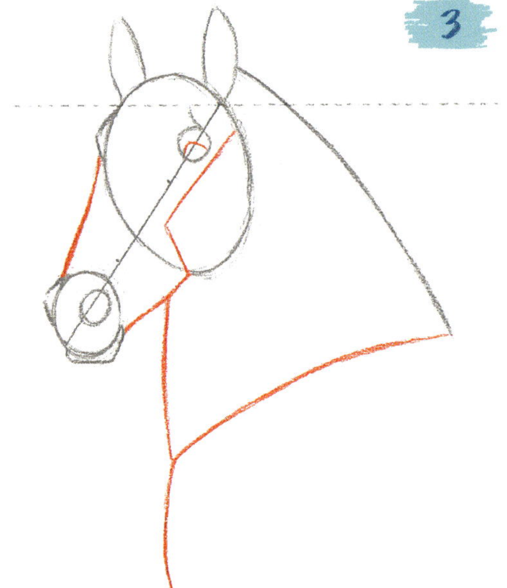

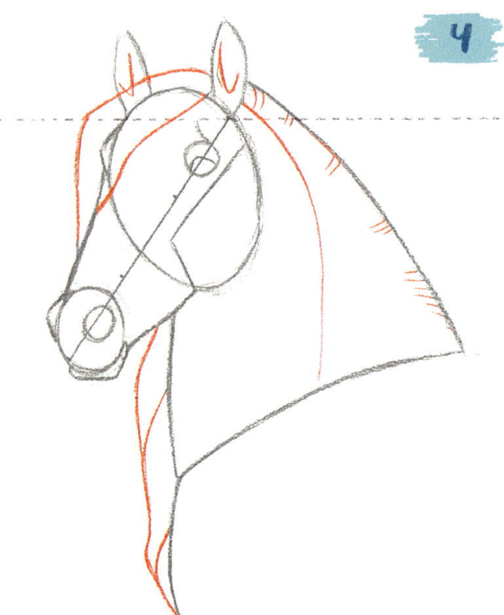

Refine the eyeball shape. Inside the right eye circle draw an upside-down "U" shape that connects the seven o'clock and four o'clock points of the eye circle.

To draw the throat, add a lightly curved line starting at one-third of the way from the right of the jawline. This line should be half of the length of the neck line drawn in step 2 (page 67).

Add a sideways "L" shape for the shoulder. Start from the point where the neck line finishes and connect it to the end of the throat line. Then draw vertically down in a light curve for the front of the shoulder shape. This line should be almost as long as the throat line.

Step 4: Draw the mane, inner ears, forelock and neck muscle.

Add a series of tick marks along the neck line to indicate where the mane attaches to the neck. These can be in pairs, threes or larger clusters of ticks as you prefer.

On the left of the throat and shoulder shapes, below the jaw, add a series of curved lines stacked next to each other for the longer flowing hair.

Draw two "V" shapes for the inner ears inside the ear oval shapes. These "V" shapes will have a longer edge and a shorter edge. Draw the longer edge two to three times as long as the shorter edge on the side of the ear that is closer to the opposite ear.

For the forelock, or the part of the horse's mane that flows over the face, start with a curved line that starts on the left side of the right ear. This line should start level with the back of the neck line. Maintain the distance over the top of the main head oval, over the left eye "C" shape and down until you connect it just past the middle of the line for the bridge of the nose. For the bottom line of the forelock, draw a light "S" shape that connects from the bottom line of the left side of the right ear down to just past the one-quarter mark of the bridge of the nose line.

Add a curved line within the neck shape for some muscle. Start the curved line at the bottom right of the right ear oval, exactly equal between the head oval and the neck line. Extend that curve down until you meet the shoulder "L" shape, just right of the middle of the line between the throat and the right neck line.

Step 5: Add some additional detail and structure for the horse's face.

Draw a line for the center of the horse's face. This line starts at the forelock, almost level with the top of the left eye "C" shape and runs parallel to the bridge of the nose line. Connect it just to the left of the twelve o'clock mark of the mouth oval.

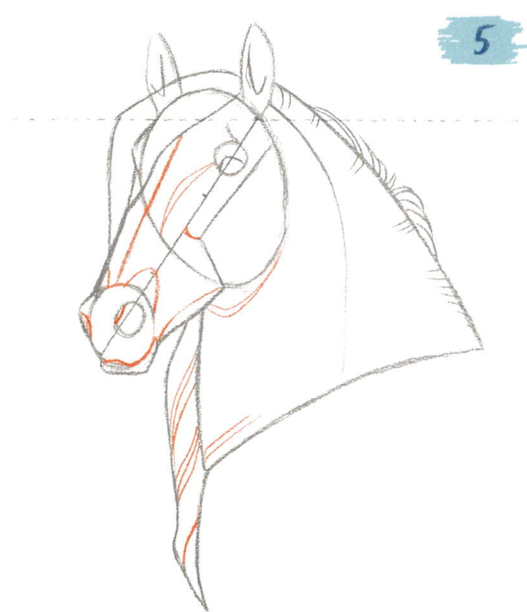

Add some extra volume to the nostrils. Do this by first drawing an upside-down "U" shape on the top right of the mouth oval, connecting the twelve o'clock mark to the three o'clock mark. The peak of the "U" should be on the diagonal guideline and should be as tall as the widest part of the right nostril oval. Then draw a short line from the eleven o'clock mark of the mouth oval to the bridge of the nose line, connecting level with the peak of the upside-down "U" shape you just drew.

Add some definition to the nostril holes. For the left nostril "C" shape, draw another backwards "C" that connects the middle of the first "C" to just where it meets the mouth oval at the bottom. For the right nostril, do a backwards "C" that connects the nine o'clock and eleven o'clock marks of the nostril oval.

Draw the mouth. For this, draw a "W" shape along the bottom of the mouth oval where the lip line sits that connects the two points where the lip line meets the mouth oval.

Add some definition to the jaw with a curved line just above the jawline. Start the curved line at the points where the jawline meets the mouth oval and the main head oval, and dome this curved line up until you create a shape similar to a willow leaf.

Draw some definition for the cheek with a short curved line connecting the bend in the cheek "L" shape to the diagonal guideline.

Add more definition above the cheek to the left of the right eye. For this, you're going to create a curved willow leaf shape by drawing two curved lines that connect the nine o'clock mark of the right eye to the eight o'clock point on the main head oval. Both lines should start and finish at the same point, curve in the same direction with the peak away from the first diagonal line and have a slight gap between them.

Add some wrinkles for the folds of skin on the throat. Draw two lines below the cheek and two above the shoulder line. For the top two lines, start them at the four o'clock mark of the main head oval. Have them both curve upwards to meet the jawline, one finishing just right of the point where the throat begins and the other right where the throat meets the jawline. For the bottom two lines above the shoulder, draw two lines with a slight gap between them arching away from the throat line towards the back of the neck. These lines can be as long as you like, but for this guide, make them one-fifth of the top shoulder line.

Add a few extra wavy lines in the flowy mane section to add some extra hair.

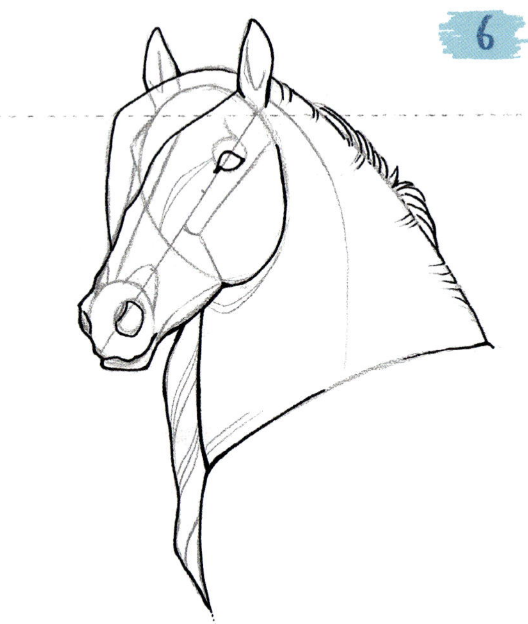

Step 6: Start drawing the outline.

Draw over the outside of the guideline shapes with a thicker pen.

Draw over the forelock shape, over the bridge of the nose and around the nostrils, mouth shape and lower lip. Then draw along the jawline and over the bottom of the head oval until the point where the cheek "L" shape meets the back of the oval.

Draw over the eyeball shape, adding a notch along the diagonal line for the tear duct. Draw the nostrils, making sure to go over the lines added in step 5 (page 69).

Draw over the top part of the left ear oval, which is visible above the forelock, then over the outside of the right ear oval.

Draw over the throat line and outside of the flowy main section. Partially draw over the shoulder "L" shape, leaving a gap in the middle of the top of the shoulder to soften the look of the muscles in this area.

Along the neck line, draw along the ticks and break the main neck line slightly to indicate the longer hair here. Draw a series of "C" shapes stacked to the right of the neck line to show the mane growing out and folding away from the neck.

Step 7: Finish the outline.

Add the finer details with a thinner pen. Draw some additional lines within the forelock to make the hair appear to flow. These lines can be as you like, but make sure to stick to waves, "S" shapes and "C" shapes for that elegant look.

Draw over the mane guidelines.

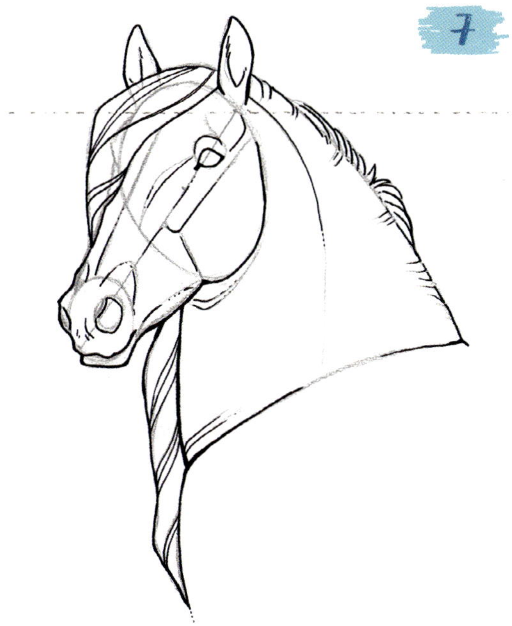

Draw over the additional definition added in step 5 (page 69). For the facial features, don't draw over the guides completely. Break those lines up using shorter lines or dots, which soften the appearance of the structures. Draw over the added nostril volume, jaw definition, central face line, cheek "L," neck wrinkles and along the neck muscle.

Also add some extra wrinkles in the form of ticks and apostrophes above the mouth line and between the two nostrils.

Draw over the very top of the eye circle. As another aspect of definition, draw a sideways "L" between the top right of right eye shape and the point where the diagonal line meets the head oval.

Erase your pencil lines when you're done.

Step 8: **Shade in your horse (optional).**

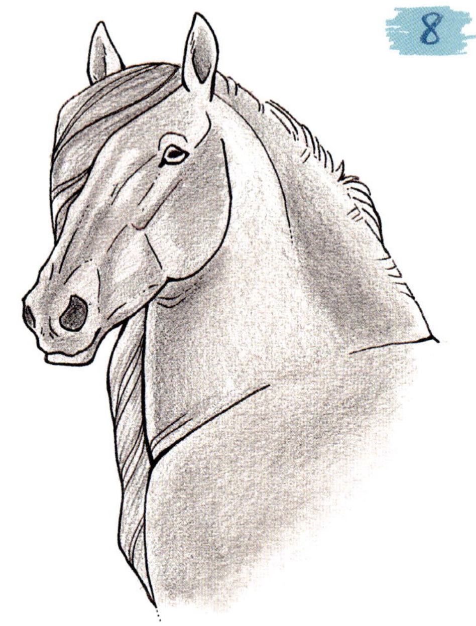

You'll just need a lighter pencil, which you will layer to create softer areas of darker shading.

Fill in the entirety of your horse portrait with one light layer of pencil. Then, go back with the same pencil and add areas of shading. To do this, go over areas you want to darken with the same light pressure from before. You'll blend this all together later.

Darken along all of the additional definition lines that were structured in step 5. This will create bands of darker areas along the muscles and facial bones to create depth. Add a band of shadow along the throat section, leaving a light strip to the left of the shadow immediately along the throat line. This will create some reflective light that adds extra volume. Add shadow just to the right of the muscle in the neck. Again, this adds depth and volume.

Darken the nostrils completely, and add a rounded rectangular shape for the pupil with a "C" shape of lighter shading to the left of the pupil for the iris. Also shade within the inner ear "V"s.

When shading the mane and forelock, draw along the flow of the hair to add more detail.

When you're finished, for a smoother look, blend together the pencil with your finger or a tissue. As the shoulder isn't connected to a body, blend out the shading into a nice faded gradient.

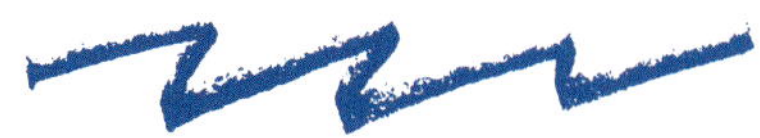

CANTERING CLYDESDALE

For this tutorial, we are going to look at one of the larger breeds of horses, the Clydesdale. One interesting feature of these horses is the long hair that grows around their hooves. These are quite complicated shapes to draw, so it's worth being patient and drawing them slowly. The same goes for the Clydesdale in general. There will be quite a few smaller stages to take within each of the steps to this tutorial, so going steadily will make it much easier and less overwhelming.

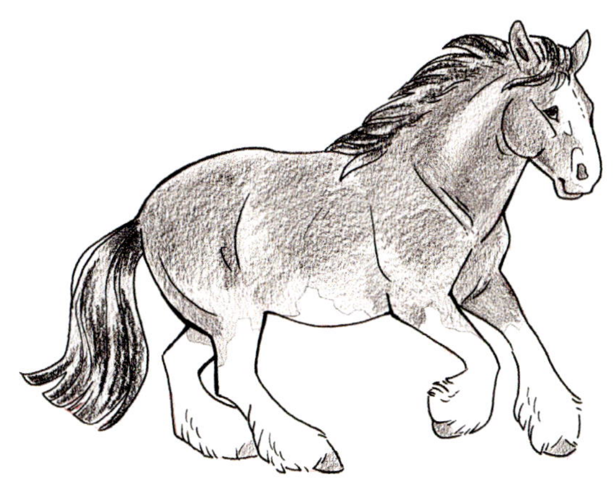

1

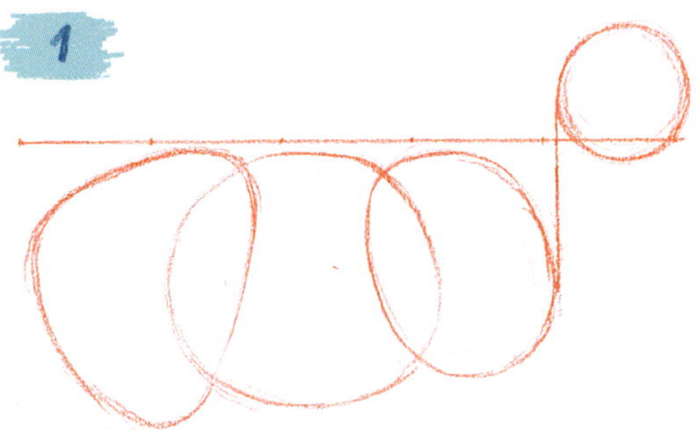

Step 1: Draw the main body and begin the head shape.

To help you get the proportions right, draw a horizontal line two-thirds of the way up your page. A good length of this line is 5 inches (12.5 cm). This will aid in creating the right size shapes.

Place the hip shape. This is almost triangular, as if the corners were cut off and rounded. Drawing beneath the horizontal guideline, place the top right rounded corner just below the 1⅔-inch (4.2-cm) mark from the left of the horizontal line. Draw the line to the right, and then down, slightly slanted to the left. Add the bottom rounded corner of the triangle. Then draw up to the left to the next corner, which falls flush with the start of the horizontal guideline. The shape should be ½ inch (1.3 cm) taller than it is at the widest point, and the left corner should be almost 1 inch (2.5 cm) below the horizontal guide.

Add the middle circle. This circle should be to the right of the hip triangle, with almost one-quarter of the middle circle overlapping it. The middle circle should be 2 inches (5 cm) in diameter, sitting to the right of the 1-inch (2.5-cm) and 3-inch (7.5-cm) marks on the horizontal line.

Draw the shoulder oval to the right of the middle circle with one-third of the shape overlapping it. The right edge of the shoulder oval should sit slightly right of the 4-inch (10-cm) mark and be 1⅓ inches (3.5 cm) wide and just shy of 2 inches (5 cm) tall.

Add the head circle. Using the right edge of the shoulder oval as reference, draw a line directly vertical upwards to intersect with the horizontal line just past the 4-inch (10-cm) mark. Draw the head circle with the left edge sitting on that vertical line. The head should be almost 1 inch (2.5 cm) in diameter, and the bottom of the head circle should sit below the horizontal line, intersecting it between the eight o'clock and four o'clock points.

Step 2: Add the snout and neck, and begin drawing the legs.

Place a circle for the end of the snout. If the head circle is almost 1 inch (2.5 cm) in diameter, the snout circle should be ⅓ inch (8 mm) in diameter. Place this shape at roughly the five o'clock mark of the head circle, leaving a small gap between the two shapes. This placement should leave the right edge and one-third of the snout circle to the right edge of the head circle.

Draw the top and bottom lines for the snout. The right line will form the bridge of the nose, connecting the two o'clock mark of the snout circle to the three o'clock mark of the head circle. The left line will be the jaw and connect between the eight o'clock and nine o'clock marks of the snout circle to the seven o'clock mark of the head circle.

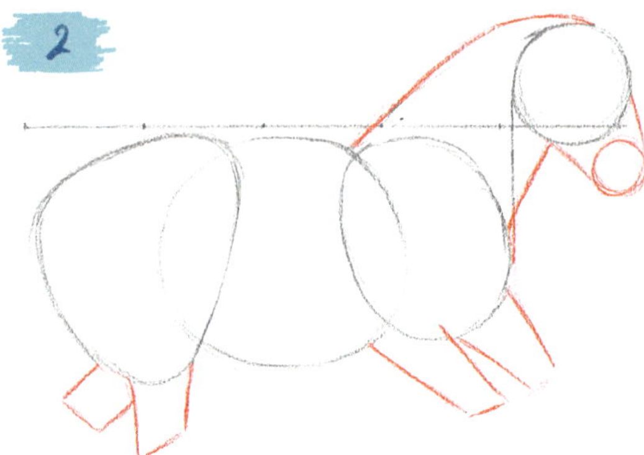

Draw the lines for the neck. For the top of the neck, start a curved line at the one o'clock mark of the head circle. Leaving a slight space, draw over the head circle and straighten out the line until you finish at the middle circle, just to the left of the shoulder oval. For the bottom line of the neck, start where the jaw meets the head circle and draw straight towards the shoulder oval, meeting just above the vertical guideline.

Add the upper portions of the legs. Start with the far-side foreleg. Draw two lines that leave the shoulder egg at roughly the four o'clock and six o'clock marks. These lines should be half as long as the shoulder egg is tall, so in this case, 1 inch (2.5 cm), and aim diagonally down and to the right.

For the near-side foreleg, draw a "U" shape that is flat and angular instead of rounded. Have the top right of the "U" start just above the bottom line drawn for the right leg. Extend the line 1 inch (2.5 cm) to the right in the same direction as the first two lines. Then draw the left part of the "U" shape from the five o'clock mark of the middle circle, again pointing in the same direction and 1 inch (2.5 cm) long. Draw a shorter line across connecting the two and forming the bottom of the "U" shape.

Draw the near-side hind leg. Draw an angular "U" shape. Both the right and the left lines should be directly vertical and approximately ½ inch (1.3 cm) long. Connect the right line to the right of the bottom corner of the hip triangle and the left line just to the left. This should create an almost seamless straight line down from the right edge of the hip triangle, and a slight bend or 120-degree angle where the left of the "U" meets at the hip triangle. Draw a line that connects the left and the right of the "U" shape.

Add the far-side hind leg. The three lines of this "U" shape are the same length. Think of it as square with one edge removed. Place the left line one-fifth of the way up from the bottom corner of the hip triangle, aiming down and away to the left. Draw the right line one-third of the way down of the left side of the near-side hind leg "U" shape. Then connect the two lines to finish the far-side leg "U" shape.

Step 3: Add the eyes, nostril, ears and lower legs.

> **Tip:** The shapes for the lower legs are a little more complex than your average shape. Take your time with these.

Draw the eyes. Draw a cross that cuts the head circle into equal quarters. For the near-side eye, place a circle with its left side flush with the vertical guideline, and the top quarter of the circle overlapping the horizontal line. For the far-side eye, draw a backwards "C" shape attached to the right of the head circle, meeting at either side of the face's horizontal guideline.

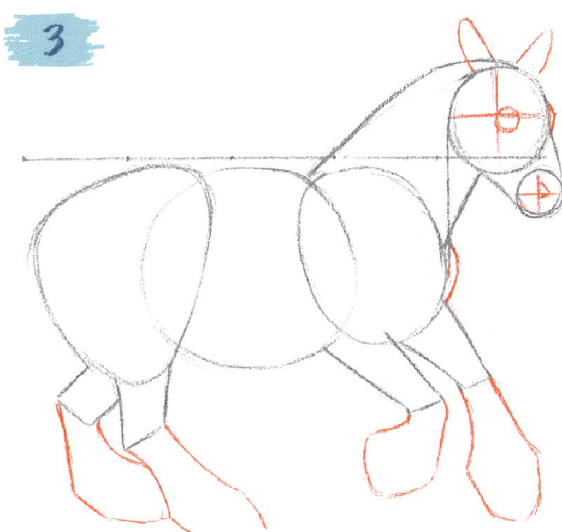

For the nostril, draw the same vertical and horizontal lines within the snout circle to cut it into four equal quarters. Draw a triangle shape in the top right quarter by drawing a line from the middle of the top half of the vertical line to the middle of the right half of the vertical line.

Draw the ears. These are two inverted "U" shapes at the top of the head circle. Have the near-side ear meet the head circle at the eleven o'clock and twelve o'clock marks and the far-side ear meet the head circle at the one o'clock and two o'clock marks. The "U" shapes should be half the height of the head circle.

Add the far-side shoulder to the right of the shoulder oval. This is a lightly curved line that connects where the lower neck line meets the shoulder oval to where the top line of the far-side foreleg meets the shoulder oval.

Draw the lower legs. All of these shapes are narrower at the top and wider at the bottom, with the width at the widest points being almost twice as wide as the narrowest parts.

Start with the far-side foreleg. Continue the right line of the leg down straight for the same length, in this case 1 inch (2.5 cm). Then draw the left line, which is again 1 inch (2.5 cm)—but this time in a light curve so that the distance is double at the opening compared to where the lines meet the upper portion. Connect the two lines with a "U" shape to form the hoof. The "U" should be as wide as it is tall, approximately ¾ inch (2 cm).

For the near-side foreleg, each line is going to be the same length—approximately ¾ inch (2 cm). For the right line, extend the top line of the near-side foreleg to create a 120-degree angle. Then draw the left line down from the bottom line of the upper leg, creating a 45-degree angle. The distance between the ends of these two lines should again be twice as wide as where they meet the upper leg. Again, draw a "U" shape to connect the two lines.

Draw the near-side hind leg by first drawing two lines leaving the left and the right side of the angled "U" shape drawn in step 2. This should create two 120-degree angles as the lines slope diagonally down to the right. Make these lines 1 inch (2.5 cm) long, getting slowly wider as they curve apart. Then, at the end of these two lines, draw two shorter, diagonal and parallel lines that extend until they are both level with what would be the ground. Connect those two lines with a horizontal line.

For the far-side hind leg, start with the right line for the front of the leg by drawing a curve from the bottom corner of the "U" shape. Have this curve meet one-quarter of the way down the back of the near-side hind leg. For the left line forming the back of the far-side hind leg, draw down almost vertically by 1 inch (2.5 cm). Then draw a diagonal line that's parallel with the shorter diagonal lines drawn for the bottom of the near-side hind leg. This line should be almost half of the previous line, so ½ inch (1.3 cm) long. Then draw a horizontal line that connects to the back of the near-side hind leg.

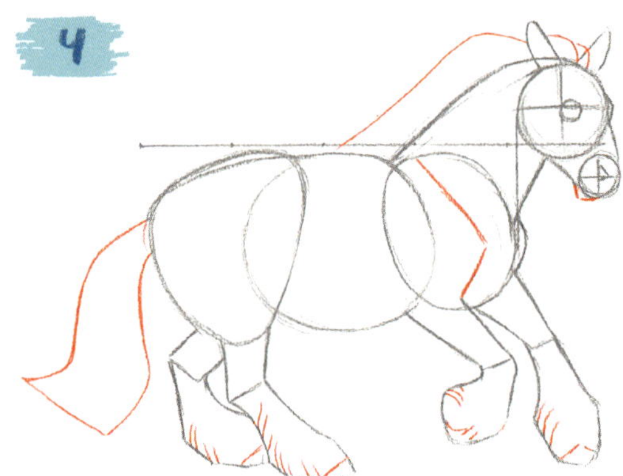

Step 4: Draw the mane, tail, shoulder, chin and hair around the hooves.

Draw the mane. Draw two backwards "C" shapes between the ears. Draw one up from the one o'clock mark of the head circle and arch it back to meet the near-side ear, one-third of the way down from the tip. Then draw a smaller "C" closer to the two o'clock mark and curve it back to meet the middle of the previous "C" shape. Then from the left side of the near-side ear, draw a curve from one-third of the way down from the tip. Arch the curve up until its peak is almost level with the tip of the near-side ear. Then straighten the line down and connect to the twelve o'clock point of the middle circle.

For the tail, draw two "S" shapes that leave just below the left corner of the hip triangle. The two lines should be three times as wide at the end of the "S" compared to where they meet the hip triangle. Connect the two "S" shapes with a straight line.

To draw the shoulder, add a backwards "L" shape within the shoulder oval. Start the top of the "L" at roughly the eleven o'clock mark of the shoulder oval and draw towards the four o'clock mark. Before you reach the four o'clock mark, draw a new line towards the front of the near-side front leg. The bend in the "L" should be 90 degrees.

Draw the horse's chin by adding a "V" shape at the end of the snout. Connect it to the six o'clock mark of the snout circle and then back to the jawline just below the nine o'clock mark of the snout circle.

Add the hair around the hooves. Draw the hoof shapes to the lower part of the legs. For the hind legs, this will be a diagonal line that goes up and to the right from the bottom horizontal line of the lower leg shapes. Connect it one-third from the right and up towards the front of the lower leg shape. For the far-side foreleg, draw an upside-down "V" shape at the end of the lower leg shape. Then for the near-side foreleg, draw some ticks around the end of the lower leg shape to indicate the hair hanging over the hoof. Along the backs of all of the legs, add a series of stacked "C"s and ticks to show the hair.

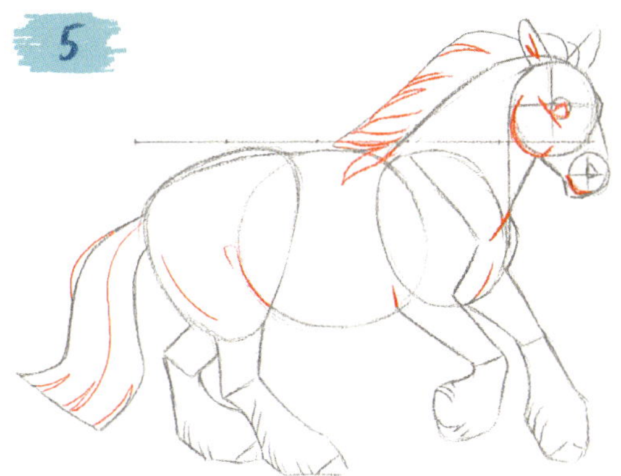

Step 5: Refine the facial features, add some muscle and define the hair of the mane and tail.

For the face, add a "V" shape within the left ear. The "V" should be twice as long on the right as on the left. Add an upside-down "U" shape within the near-side eye circle to create the actual eye shape. Add the mouth by drawing a flattened "U" shape over the bottom of the snout circle between the six o'clock and nine o'clock mark to emphasize the mouth placement.

Add the cheek. To do this, start with a "U" shape that goes over the bottom left quarter of the head circle. The "U" should start just above and to the right of the nine o'clock mark of the head circle, curve around the bottom left of the head circle, and then finish right where the vertical guideline drawn in step 3 (page 75) meets the initial horizontal guide from step 1 (page 73). To finish the cheek shape, add a short diagonal line that runs flush with the near-side eye circle, between the two tips of the cheek "U." Leave a gap between the ends of the "U" and the diagonal line.

Draw muscle definition for the remainder of the body. Extend the bottom neck line into the shoulder oval, leaving a gap as the line nears the bend in the "L" shape drawn in step 4 (page 77). Draw a short, curved line where the back of the far-side foreleg meets the shoulder egg and finish it level with the far-side shoulder "C" drawn in step 3 (page 75). Where the back of the near-side leg meets the middle circle, draw a little line vertically to form the elbow. Add a curve that follows the middle circle from the point where the thigh triangle meets the belly up to the nine o'clock mark of the middle circle. Then create a line that curves back to the left creating a shepherd staff shape. Last, along the left of the thigh triangle, draw a curved line that runs parallel to the left line. Leave a space and make this line roughly 1 inch (2.5 cm) long.

Add the hair detail for the mane and tail. For the mane, draw a series of "V" shapes and tick marks that run the length of the mane curve drawn in step 4. At the bottom where the curve meets the main body circle, draw an elongated "V" to add a lock of hair that's flowing to the side of the horse's body.

For the tail, draw one long "S" shape that divides the tail shape in two. Then along the diagonal line at the end of the tail shape, add three upside-down "V" shapes to show where the tail hair has parted. Add a light curve over the top "S" shape to create more volume for the tail.

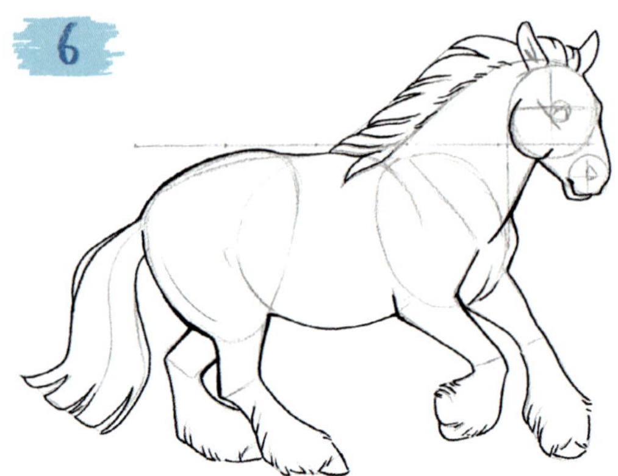

Step 6: Draw the main outline for the horse using a thicker pen.

Starting with the face, draw over the top right of the head circle, over the far-side eye "C" shape, down over the bridge of the nose and over the mouth and chin. Continue that line along the jaw and over the cheek "U" shape.

Draw over the ear shapes. For the mane, draw over the portion that sits between the ears, adding a notch in each shape to show more hair definition. Then run along the mane drawing and over the tick shapes drawn in step 5. Where the mane meets the top neck line, add a few ticks and apostrophes so the line is softer and broken.

Draw over the top of the main body circle, over the top of the thigh triangle, leaving a little gap where the tail meets the thigh triangle, and then down the back of the leg. For the hind legs, draw unbroken lines over the upper portion of the legs and along the front of the lower parts of the legs, and then add broken lines along the back of the lower parts of the legs. Add the ticks over the hair guidelines to show off the hair. Draw over the hoof shapes.

Draw over the bottom of the middle circle for the tummy, along the upper portions for the forelegs and then up along the bottom neck line for the throat. Draw over the lower part of the shoulder "L" shape to define the muscles, and draw over the curve for the chest muscle. Finish the hooves and draw broken lines with ticks and apostrophe marks for the long hair on the lower parts of the forelegs.

Draw over the outside of the tail, including the curve for extra volume drawn in step 5. Draw over the "V"s at the end of the tail to show the hair parting.

Step 7: Finish the outline with a thinner pen.

Draw over the smaller eye shape. Then draw over the diagonal cheek line, over the nostril and add two "U" shapes for facial definition. Have one with the two tips of the "U" pointing to the eye and another with the two tips of the "U" pointing to the nostril. Add a few dashed lines as an extension of the bridge of the nose running up parallel to the eye "C" shape to define the center of the horse's head. Add an elongated "V" plus a few ticks above the eye and cheek and below the near-side ear for more flowing mane on the horse's face.

Along the mane, add a couple of extra curved lines for more hair definition.

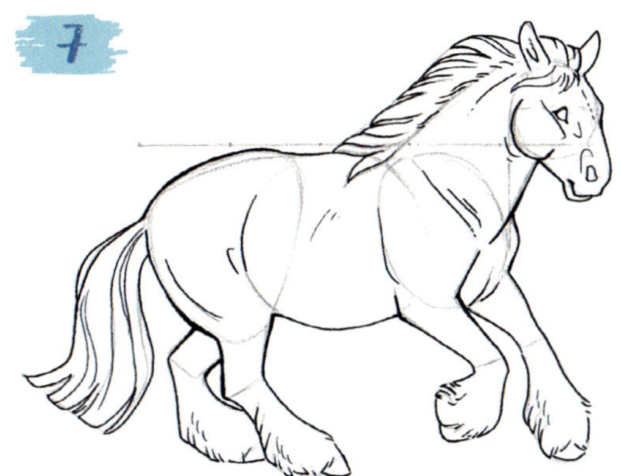

In the neck space, add some muscle and folds of skin. Draw a curved line running parallel to the top neck line, positioned below the top one-third of the line. Then below the cheek "U" shape, add two small curved lines for wrinkles. Using the top of the "L" line for the shoulder drawn in step 4, draw over the middle portion to define the shoulder, then two shorter lines above it to add wrinkles. Draw a line over the middle of the left edge of the shoulder oval to add some muscle definition.

For rib definition, draw two or three tick marks near the middle of the middle circle. Along the right edge of the middle circle, draw a line to show where the ribs finish. Draw over the top left of the shepherd staff shape drawn in step 5, and then over the line defining muscle on the left edge of the hip triangle.

Fill in some extra hair definition by drawing "S" lines that connect the base of the tail to the end. This shows off the flowing tail hair.

Erase the pencil guidelines.

8

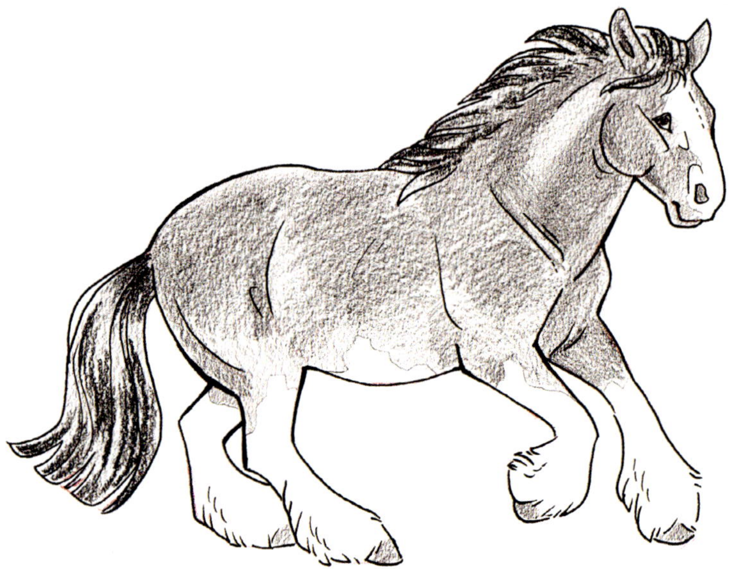

Step 8: Add the shading of your Clydesdale horse (optional).

Fill in the entirety of your horse with a light pencil, except for the areas that will be white. Clydesdales typically have white on their face that runs down the bridge of their nose as well as white socks and a white patch on their tummy. Leave jagged edges along the upper portions of the legs where below them will be white. Add a light, jagged line for a white splotch on the horse's tummy.

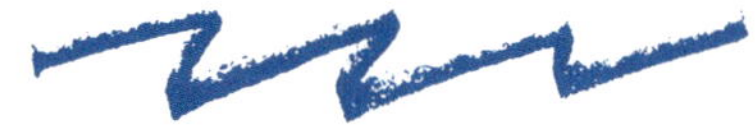

Darken areas of your horse's body with the light pencil. This can be along the top of the neck, along the horse's back and within the top areas of the shoulder and hip space. Also shade in the chest area and in a band from the top of the shoulder "L" area to the cheek "U" shape.

Shade in the tale and mane with a darker pencil. Shade in the direction of the hair growth, leaving bands of lighter hair for the sheen.

Shade in the hooves too.

Fill in the eyes to create the dark iris and the nostril.

For a smoother look, blend together the pencil with your finger or a tissue.

BUCKING BRONCO

For this tutorial, we will go for a horse that has been bucking and playing in a field. This pose is very dynamic, so allowing yourself to do a big drawing will give you plenty of freedom to add detail and not feel confined by working in a small space. I have gone with a paint horse to give you an idea of how to add markings. There will be large areas of darker hair as well as patches of white. Interestingly, the white markings aren't just left white. They get some shading, which will add depth, so that's something to bear in mind. The beauty of paint horses is that you can draw their large splotchy markings however you like. This gives you a lot of flexibility to be creative.

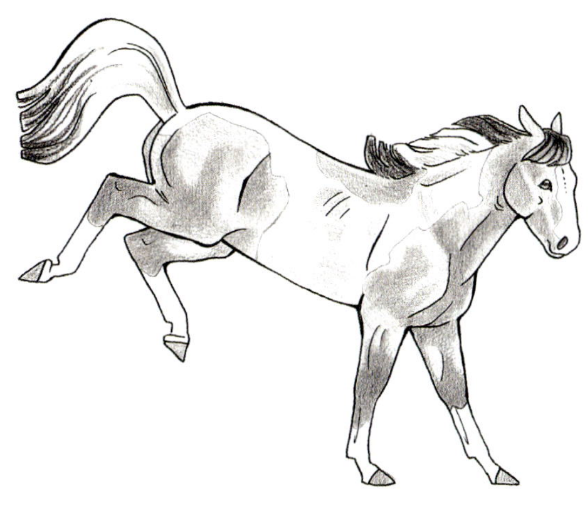

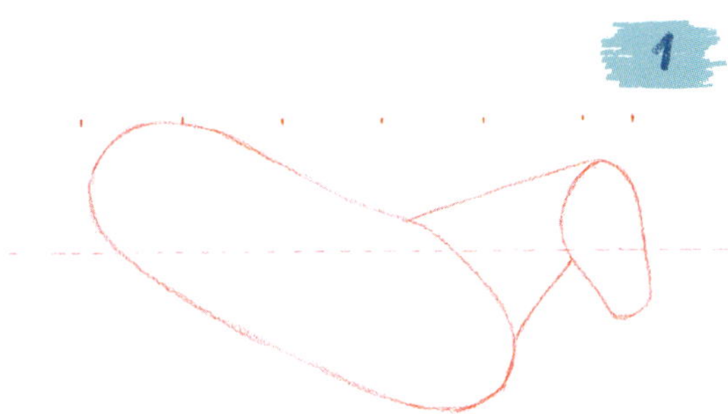

Step 1: Begin by drawing the body, head and neck.

Draw a horizontal guideline across your page two-thirds of the way up. This will help with the placement of your shapes. Then to help with proportions, measure out a series of dashes. These dashes should start one-fourth from the left of the page to leave enough room for the tail and legs. The total distance should be 5½ inches (14 cm) across, with the first six dashes being 1 inch (2.5 cm) apart. This will leave enough room for the tail and legs.

For the main body, draw an elongated sausage-like oval that tilts on an angle with the right end being lower. This shape should be three times as long as it is tall. Half of the shape should be above the horizontal line and the other half below it, creating two shapes that kind of look like teardrops. This body oval should start at the left dash or measurement mark and extend just past the 4-inch (10-cm) mark.

Draw the head to the right of the body oval. The head shape is also like an elongated sausage-like oval that is the same length as the body oval is tall. The head should also be three times as long as it is tall and tilted just shy of vertical with the right edge in line with the 5½-inch (14-cm) mark. Make the shape ever so slightly wider at the top than at the bottom to form the horse's skull shape, and make sure that half of the shape is on either side of the horizontal guideline.

Draw the neck lines. Start with the top neck line by drawing straight from the very top of the head oval and connecting one-third of the way along the body oval, just to the right of the 3-inch (7.5-cm) mark. For the bottom neck line, start a line on the right edge of the head oval just below where the horizontal guideline intersects the head oval. Draw diagonally down to the left until you connect with the body oval just above the right edge.

Step 2: Break the body shape into three sections for the shoulders, middle and thighs, and add the upper portions of the legs.

Divide the body oval into three by drawing two straight lines that run across the body oval. Start the first line at the point where the neck line meets the body oval. Draw it at a 120-degree angle from the top neck line, and draw until you meet the opposite side of the body oval, creating the shoulder section. For the thigh section, divide off the top third of the body oval by starting your line just to the left of the 2-inch (5-cm) mark. Create a 90-degree angle from this edge and draw until you meet the opposite side of the body oval.

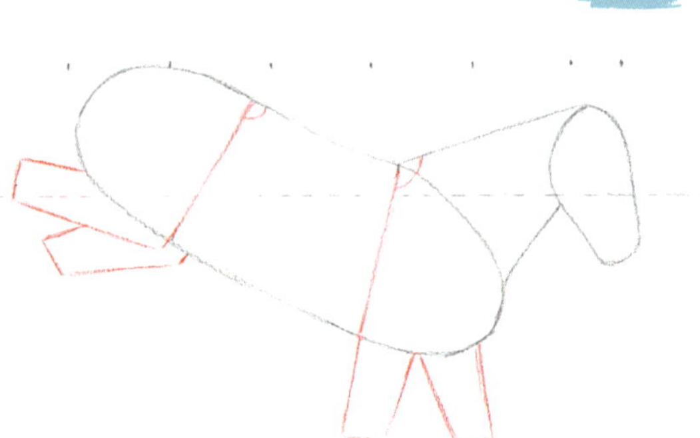

For the upper portions of the legs, start with the near-side front leg, which is the second leg from the right. Extend the line you drew to section off the shoulder and continue it down for 1 inch (2.5 cm). Draw a shorter horizontal line that's one-third of the length of the previous line. Then draw a line that runs parallel to the first line up until you meet the shoulder shape one-third of the way between the shoulder line and bottom neck line.

For the far-side foreleg, start just right of the near-side foreleg, and draw the exact same shape again as you just did for the near-side foreleg. Keep all lines the same length.

For the near-side hind leg, extend the line drawn for the thigh section slightly to create the knee before drawing to the left at a 95-degree angle. This bottom line of the near-side thigh shape should be a bit longer than the lines drawn for the forelegs—1½ inches (4 cm). At the end of the line, create another 90-degree angle and draw a shorter line upwards, one-quarter of the length as the previous line. Then draw a parallel line connecting the previous line to the main body oval.

For the far-side hind leg, start just to the right of the near-side hind leg shape, and draw a little line the same length as you did for the near-side hind leg to form the knee. Then, at a 120-degree angle, draw down to the left creating a line as long as the longest lines drawn for the forelegs. Next, draw a short line aimed up at the end of the near-side hind leg shape, one-third the length of the previous line. Draw a line that connects the shorter line to the middle of the near-side hind leg shape.

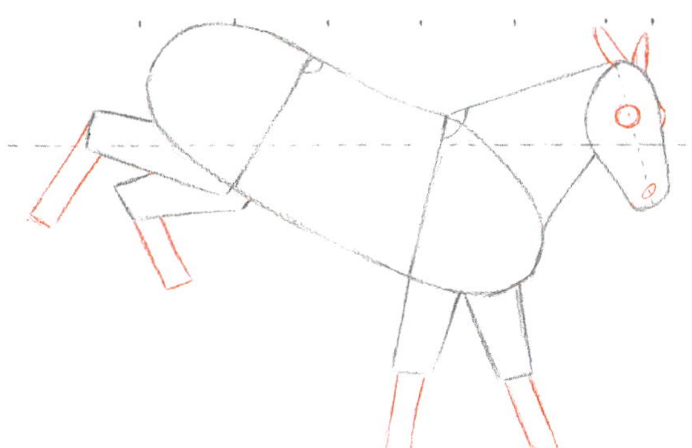

Step 3: Add the ears, eyes, nostrils and lower portions of the legs.

Start with the ears by drawing two upside-down and elongated "U" shapes at the top of the head oval. Draw the near-side ear where the top neck line meets the head oval. The "U" should be three times as long as it is wide, roughly one-quarter the length of the head oval. Then immediately to the right of the shape, duplicate it for the far-side ear.

To add the eyes and nostrils, start by drawing a guideline that connects the left of the near-side ear (where it meets the head oval) down to the center of the opposite end of the head oval. One-third of the way along the guideline, draw a circle that takes up one-third of the width of the head oval, with the guideline running pretty much central. On the right edge of the head oval, level with the near-side eye circle, draw a small backward "C" at the same height as the eye oval for the far-side eye shape. For the nostril, draw a narrow oval one-sixth of the way up from the bottom end of the head oval. The guideline should be centered in this shape too.

Draw the lower portions of the forelegs. Starting with the far-side foreleg, draw a rectangle shape just below the upper portion of the leg. The shape will be slightly narrower but the same length.

Repeat for the near-side foreleg.

For the far-side hind leg, add the same size rectangle as you drew for the forelegs. Draw the bottom edge of this shape as an extension of the short edge on the far-side hind leg. Finish this shape by connecting it one-fifth of the way up from the end of the upper portion of the leg.

For the near-side hind leg, start at the top left corner of the upper portion of the leg and draw diagonally to the left creating an almost 100-degree angle. This shape will be as wide as the other lower leg portion shapes, so taking that distance into account, draw a parallel line to the previous line down from the lower line of the upper leg portion. This second line for the lower leg portion will be the same length as the other three lower leg shapes. Draw a short line to connect the two, and finish the near-side lower leg portion.

Step 4: Draw the mane, forelock, tail and hooves.

Starting with the mane, draw a wavy line that starts where the near-side ear meets the neck and head shape. Have that wave flow up into an arc, down to run parallel with the top neck line and finish by pointing it up away from the main body shape. Now connect the end of that wave to one-quarter of the way from the right of the middle shape of the main body oval.

For the forelock, the section of hair that sits between the ears, draw an arched line starting one-quarter of the way up on the right of the near-side ear shape. Draw this line parallel to the top of the head oval. Before you reach the far-side eye "C" shape, begin drawing to the left in a slightly wavy line over the near-side eye towards the top left of the head oval. Then, just before you meet the left edge of the head oval, return to where you started. This forelock shape should look like a warped triangle.

For the tail shape, draw two highly arched wavy lines from the left end of the main body oval. For the top line, start at the point exactly ½ inch (1.3 cm) from the left. Draw almost vertically upwards, and then create a domed line before drawing back down and sweeping lightly to the left until the line is level with its starting point. For the bottom line, start at the point on the main body oval that is ¼ inch (6 mm) from the left. Draw a similar curved line, but this time, make the dome slightly pointier than the top line. Then run parallel to the left portion of the top line, finishing vertically level with the previous line. Draw a vertical line to connect the two.

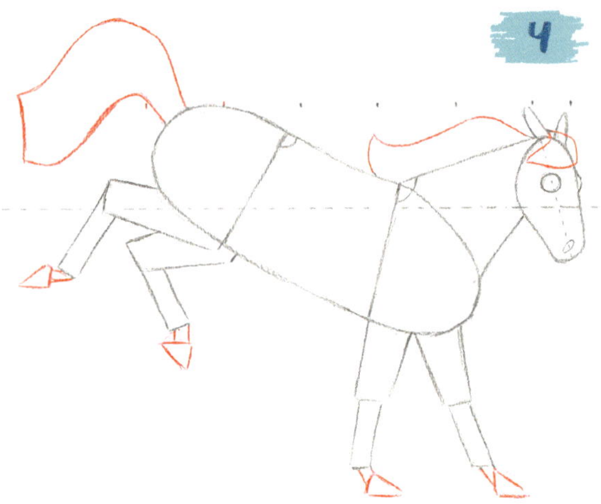

Draw the two foreleg hooves. For the far-side foreleg, draw a triangle just below the right edge of the lower leg. The triangle should be one-third as high as the length of the lower leg, and slightly wider than it is tall. Then connect the top corner to the right line of the lower leg. Draw another line connecting roughly the middle of the left side of the hoof triangle to the middle of the shortest edge of the lower leg.

For the near-side foreleg, draw a triangle the same size as the first one directly level with it and to the left. Position the left edge of the hoof triangle in line with the right edge of the lower leg on the near-side foreleg. Again, draw two short lines that connect the triangle to the lower leg.

For the hind leg hooves, start with the far-side back leg. The hoof triangle will be the same size as the foreleg hoof triangles, with the top right corner placed just below the bottom right corner of the lower leg. The top edge of the triangle should be horizontal with the third corner of the triangle pointing downwards. Again, connect the hoof triangle to the lower leg like you did with the forelegs.

For the near-side hind leg, the hoof triangle will point backwards. This triangle, again, the same size as the other three, should have its bottom edge completely horizontal. The top corner should be level with the bottom left corner of the near-side hind leg's lower portion. Repeat as before, and attach the triangle to the lower leg.

Step 5: Add some definition of muscles plus additional hair lines in the mane and tail.

Starting with the face of the horse, for the eye, draw a small upside-down "U" shape within the eye circle to create the arch of the eyelid. For the horse's cheek, add a "U" shape that extends from the top left of the head oval down along the left edge. Finish the "U" with a notch in the head oval in the center of the left edge.

Add the horse's mouth, which is a light "U" shape at the end of the head oval, just to the left of the nostril.

To add some muscle to the shoulder section, start with a backwards "C" shape connected to the right line of the near-side foreleg. Make this "C" run parallel to the edge of the main body oval between the far-side foreleg and the lower neck line.

Draw the near-side foreleg elbow by adding an inverted "L" shape to the left line of the upper leg portion. Have the long edge of the "L" connect one-third of the way down the left edge of the upper leg portion and just to the left of the shoulder section line. Then run a shorter line parallel to the shoulder section line to finish the elbow.

To add some rib muscle, draw a tick line one-third of the way down from the top-left of the shoulder line.

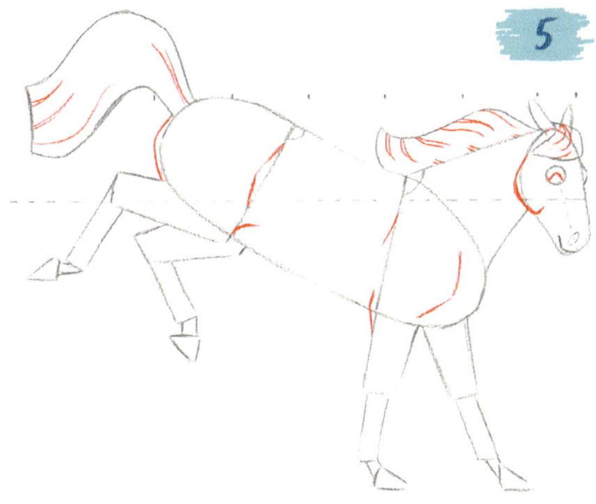

Draw a "C"-like shape to the left of the line separating the hip and the main body oval. Start the top of the "C" just shy of the one-quarter mark, curve out to the left and then meet back at the hip section line one-third of the way up from where the near-side hind leg begins. Now draw a tick mark to the bottom right of the hip section line to create a fold of skin between the near-side knee and tummy.

Just to the left of the main body oval, above the near-side hind leg, add a curve parallel to the main body oval. This will create the far-side buttock of the horse.

Add some curves, tick shapes and "V" shapes within the mane, forelock and tail to define the hair. In the forelock, add a few short curved lines. In the mane along the top neck line, add three pairs of quotation mark-like lines all equally spaced to soften the edge where the hair meets the neck. Along the wavy mane line, add some narrow "V" shapes for where the hair parts in places, plus a few short wavy lines. For the tail, draw some curved lines that meet where the tail attaches to the body oval. At the end of the tail, draw a pair of "V" shapes and a farther wavy line to show off the tail hair.

Step 6: Begin the outline of the horse.

Draw over the outside of the main shapes of the horse with a thicker pen.

Starting with the face, draw over the far-side eye shape, down the bridge of the nose, over the end of the snout and along the jaw. Draw over the cheek and ear shapes.

Add the lower neck line, extending it slightly into the shoulder section to show where the neck meets the chest. Draw over the right edge of the main body shape to create the far-side shoulder and down the front of the far-side foreleg. Make sure you round off the corners for the joints where the upper leg portions meet the lower leg portions.

Draw over the top of the hoof triangles, sectioning off two-thirds to make the actual hoof shape. Follow up around the back of the far-side leg to the chest and repeat for the near-side foreleg.

To the right of the near-side leg, draw partially along the end of the main body oval to add the horse's chest. Draw along the bottom of the main body oval to form the horse's tummy.

Draw over the hind legs. Ensure you section off two-thirds of the hoof triangles to form the actual hooves like you did with the forelegs.

Add the horse's rump and far-side buttock. Leave a little gap where the tail meets the horse's body, and then extend the line over the top of the main body oval for the horse's back.

Draw over the mane, leaving gaps between the prongs of the "V" shapes drawn for hair parting. Then draw over the notches on the top neck line. Do the same for the forelock.

Draw over the tail, again leaving gaps between the prongs of the "V"s to create partings in the hair.

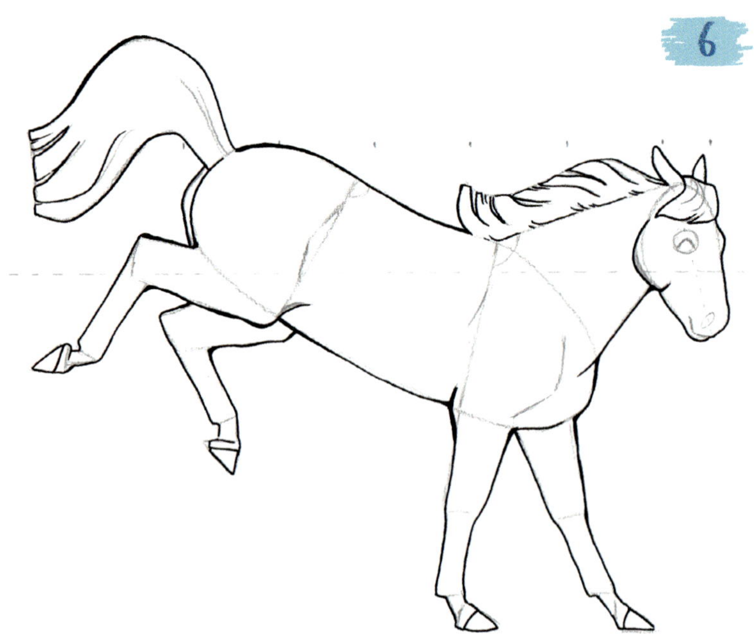

Step 7: **Add the final details of the horse's outline with a thinner pen.**

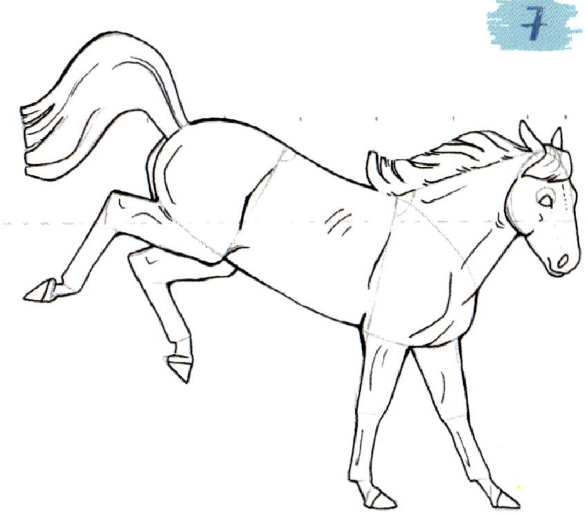

Draw the horse's facial features. Draw over the eye shape, over the nostril shape and over the mouth line. Add a tiny backwards "C" below the eye and above the right edge of the cheek "U." That adds bone structure to the cheek. Draw a line of dots exactly in the middle between the two eye shapes for the center of the horse's forehead.

Add some more muscle to the horse's neck by drawing a "J" just below the left half of the top neck line. Then add a line that runs parallel to the lower neck line between the bottom of the cheek "U" and right of the shoulder "C" shape. Draw two small "V"s below the cheek "U" shape for folds of skin on the horse's neck.

Draw over the horse's shoulder "C" shape and the short line of muscle drawn to the left of the shoulder section line. Add a line that runs up from the chest line drawn in step 6, creating muscle definition.

For the forelegs, draw a few lines that run vertically down the upper and lower leg portions for muscle and bone structure.

Add definition within the horse's body. In the middle section of the main body oval, draw three short and evenly spaced lines in the middle right of the shape to define the ribs. Draw over the "C" shape guide drawn to the right of the hip section line to add volume to the ribs and middle of the horse. Also draw the little fold of skin to the right of the near-side hind leg knee. Then, draw a curved line within the horse's hip section that runs parallel to the left end of the main body oval. This adds muscle to the buttock area of the horse. Using the main body oval as a guide, draw a pair of lines on the top left section of the near-side hind leg for folds of skin.

Add two "U" shapes at the end of the upper portion of the hind legs to create a definition of the horse's ankles.

Finally, add the hair lines drawn in step 6 within the tail for further hair definition.

Erase all of the pencil lines.

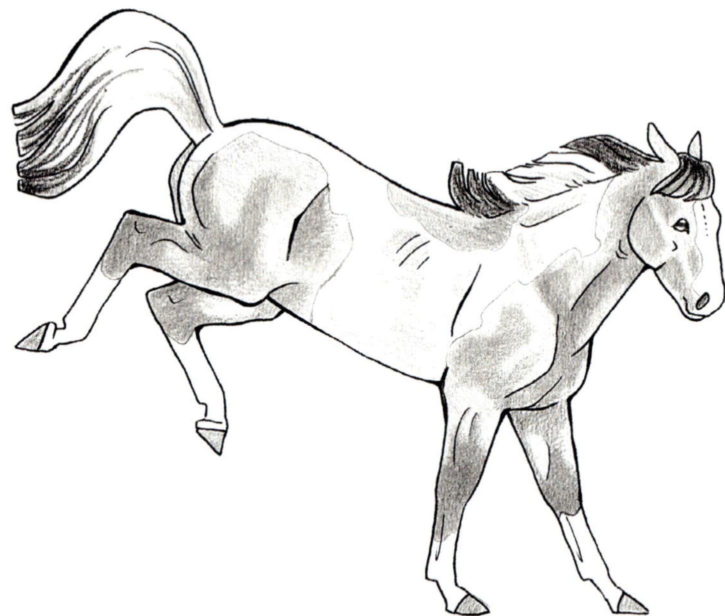

8

Step 8: Add the shading and markings for your horse (optional).

For this horse, we'll go with the classic paint horse markings. The best thing about this is that they can be however you'd like them to be.

Take your lighter pencil and draw splotches for your paint markings. I gave this horse sock markings and left the lower sections of the horses leg's white. I drew jagged edges to shape the stockings. Then, I drew from the horse's elbow up to the top right of the horse's neck. I added a section for the shoulders and a portion of the horse's back. I left the right edge of the horse's face white as well. I drew a large splotch from just below the horse's tail, over the thigh and hips, and then finished just right of the knees.

Using the lighter pencil, fill in these shapes. Continue to use the lighter pencil to add shading in the splotches such as around the horse's joints, within the cheek, along the neck muscle line and over the horse's facial structure. In the hip shape, fill in a band of shadow to the right of the buttock guideline and within the center of the hips for additional muscle definition. Also, shade in the hooves.

Add very light shading within the white areas on the horse's body, such as along the belly and over the three lines for the ribs.

With a darker pencil, add dark hair for the mane and tail. Black hair grows where the body splotches meet the mane, so fill in these portions of the mane. Draw in the direction that the hair grows. For the tail, darken the very end of the tail, but add some fainter lines for where the hair is left white.

ZEN-LIKE ZEBRA

With their distinctive black and white stripes, these striking members of the horse family are super charismatic. As they're so similar to horses, I thought it would be fun to include zebras alongside their domesticated family members. I've chosen a pose that you'd also find horses in: lounging and snoozing on the ground. Feel free to use this tutorial as a basis to draw domestic horses too. For now, we will focus on drawing a peaceful and Zen-like zebra.

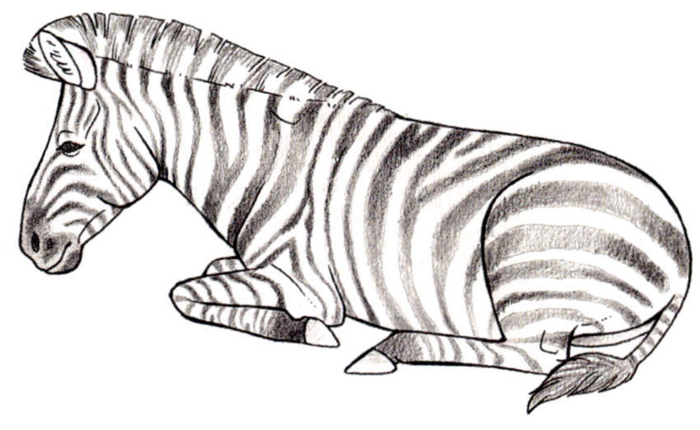

Tip: Zebra markings can be tricky to get right. You might not think it, especially as they appear like just simple black and white stripes, but there's a knack to it. To get them looking realistic and have depth as they wrap around the shape of the zebra, it's worth taking your time when you reach that stage of this tutorial.

1

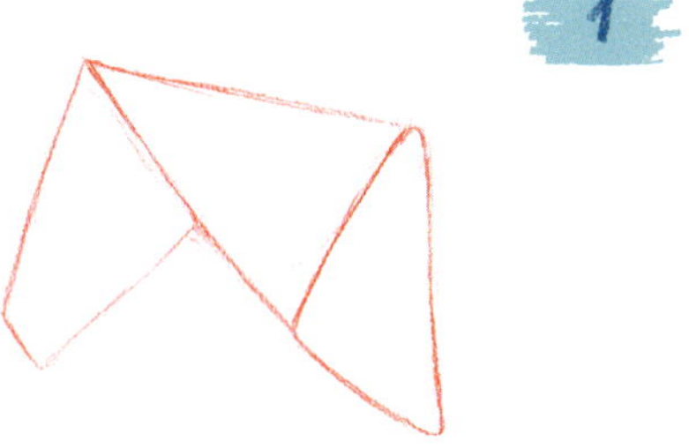

Step 1: Draw the zebra's head, neck and shoulders.

The zebra's head has four sides, but think of it as a triangle with the bottom tip cut off. Begin by drawing the left edge on the middle of the left side of your page. This line should aim down diagonally just left of vertical. For size to help you with proportions, make this line 2 inches (5 cm) long. Then draw the righthand edge, creating a 45-degree angle in the top corner. This line is shorter than the first, 1⅜ inches (3.5 cm). Draw the third line diagonally down to the left, creating a 90-degree angle from the second line. Make the third line 1½ inches (4 cm). Draw a short line connecting the end of the third line to the end of the first line to create your head shape.

Draw the triangle shape for the neck. Start with the top neck line by creating a 90-degree angle to the first line drawn for the head shape. This line is a little longer than that first headline, 2⅜ inches (6 cm). Next, draw the bottom neck line for the throat. Extend the right line of the head shape down, doubling the length of that line. Connect the two neck lines.

Draw the shoulder shape by extending that throat line again, therefore tripling the length of the line that runs from the top corner of the head shape down to the bottom right corner of the shoulder shape. Connect the end of that line to the end of the top neck line.

Step 2: Draw the ears, facial features, upper portion of the foreleg and the main body.

Draw the zebra's chin as a narrow "U" shape at the bottom left corner of the head shape. The right side of the "U" should connect one-quarter of the way along the lower line of the head shape. The "U" should be three times as wide as it is deep.

Add the nostril. This is a little oval shape with its bottom end level with the middle of the shortest line on the head shape. The oval should be two times as tall as it is wide and finish one-tenth of the way along the top head line.

For the eye, draw a circle that's one-eighth of the length of the first head line in diameter. In this case, 1/4 inch (6 mm) across. Place it one-third of the way down the first head line from the top corner of the head shape. Leave a small gap so the eye circle isn't touching the head shape.

Draw the ear shape. This shape is a narrow oval, three times as long as it is wide. Make this shape twice the length of the eye diameter, in this case 1/2 inch (1.3 cm) long. Place it one-fifth of the way down from the top corner and one-quarter below the top head line and three-quarters above it.

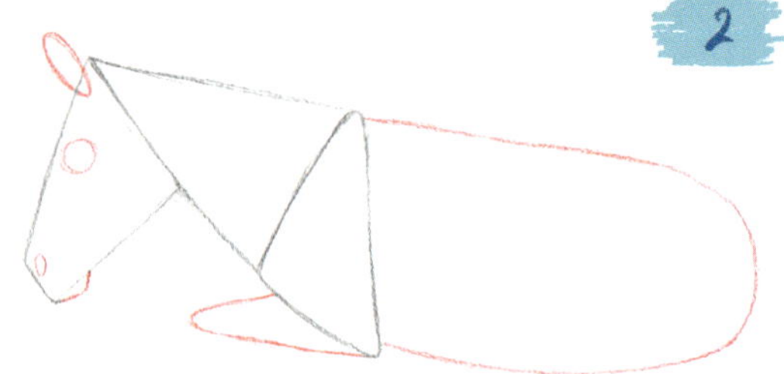

For the foreleg, draw a sideways narrow "U" shape with the prongs of the "U" attached to the shoulder shape. The bottom line, which will be the back of the foreleg, will be almost twice as long as the top line. Anchor the bottom line to the bottom right corner of the shoulder shape and draw horizontally towards the zebra's chin. Make this line four-fifths the length of the first head line, in this case just over 1½ inches (4 cm). Round off the "U" shape and connect to the shoulder shape, one-fifth of the way down from the corner where the shoulder shape meets the neck shape.

Draw the main body shape, which is a large "U" shape extending from the right side of the shoulder shape. This "U" should be sideways and a little less than twice as long as it is tall. The height of it should also be the same distance as the length of the first line drawn for the head shape. So, in this case, the "U" should be 3½ inches (9 cm) long and 2 inches (5 cm) tall. Connect the top of the sideways "U" to the top corner of the shoulder shape. Connect the bottom of the "U" just above the bottom right corner of the shoulder shape. This then forms an elbow joint for the foreleg.

Step 3: Add the zebra's mouth, eyelid, back of the ear, mane and thigh shape.

For the mouth, draw a small "S" shape starting at the bottom corner of the head shape. Run along the bottom of the head shape and finish it in line with the chin shape.

For the eyelid, draw a curved line from the eight o'clock to the four o'clock mark of the eye circle. Don't make the dome too steep. The zebra's eye is only slightly open because it is sleeping.

Finish off the ear by drawing a backwards "C" shape connecting the very bottom of the ear oval around the righthand side to one-third of the way down from the tip of the ear.

Draw the mane guideline, starting with the portion just in front of the ear. Draw a straight line at a 90-degree angle from the top of the zebra's head where the left side of the ear meets it. Make this line the same length as the upper portion of the initial ear oval. Then draw a short curved line connecting the start of the mane to the tip of the ear.

Finish the mane guideline by extending the line you just drew to the zebra's ear tip in a gentle curve down the zebra's neck. Stop once you meet the main body "U" one-sixth of the way down the main body oval.

Draw the thigh shape by adding a curved line from the top right of the main body shape to the bottom middle. The curve should start just before the one-quarter point from the right end of the main body "U." Curve down diagonally and to the left until you're in the very middle of the main body shape before drawing down towards the bottom edge of the main body "U."

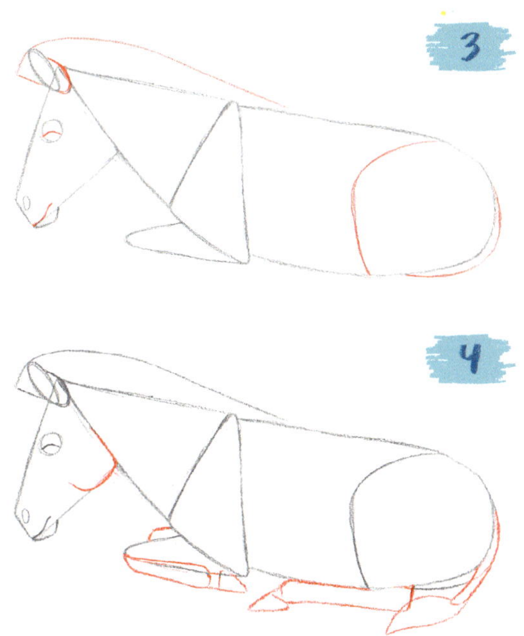

Add the far-side buttock of the zebra with a line that connects one-third of the bottom of the "U" from the right and runs parallel along the right edge of the "U." Finish this line just above the right edge of the main body "U" shape.

Step 4: Draw the zebra's cheek, finish the legs and add the tail.

Add the cheek by drawing a "U" shape along the edge of the zebra's head shape that meets the neck triangle. The right edge of the "U" should start halfway down the back of the head shape and continue down and along the bottom edge of the head shape. Just over one-third from the right, draw the curve for the left edge of the cheek "U."

Add the far-side foreleg by drawing a small "L" shape that starts just below the left corner of the shoulder triangle and connects with the top line of the upper leg portion halfway along.

Draw the lower portion of the near-side foreleg. This shape is going to be a sausage with its left end being a point at the joint of the foreleg. The bottom line of this lower portion should be two-thirds the length of the bottom line of the upper leg and run parallel to that line. Then draw a line from where the previous line meets the upper leg portion and run it just above the lower line of the upper leg portion. Once the two lines are the same length, round off the end for the lower portion.

Add the near-side foreleg hoof. Draw a small triangle shape to the right of the end of the near-side foreleg, leaving a slight gap for now. The bottom edge of the triangle should be in line with the bottom edge of the lower portion foreleg and the tip of the triangle should overlap the initial foreleg shape from step 2 (page 90). Now draw a short line to connect the bottom left of the hoof triangle to the bottom edge of the lower near-side foreleg.

Draw the near-side hind leg, starting with a horizontal line from the point where the thigh shape meets the bottom of the main body "U" shape. This line should be as long as the lower portion of the foreleg drawn previously. Now draw the bottom line as an "L" shape that starts a little to the right of the point where the buttock line meets the lower part of the main body "U." Draw down vertically initially, and then add a 90-degree angle before running parallel until you are level with the point where the top line ends. Round off this shape and connect the two lines.

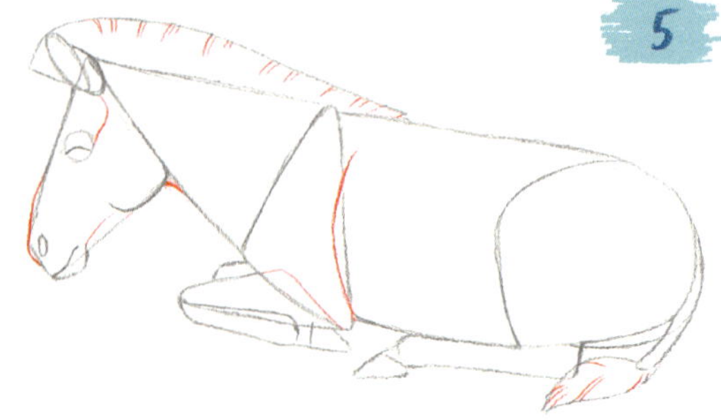

Add the near-side hoof by drawing a triangle shape. The top corner should be level with the bottom of the foreleg hoof. Have the bottom edge just below the bottom of the hind leg shape. Make the triangle twice as wide as it is tall.

Add the tail shape, using the far-side buttock line as a guide. The width of the tail should be the same as the width of the buttock shape. Around the center of the buttock shape, extend the line down and create a narrow "U" shape for the tail. Make this shape half the length on the left as the right. At the end of this shape, add the tail hair by drawing a curved line that connects to the left side of the tail "U" and extends below the hind leg shape. Then draw a wavy line from the right edge of the tail "U" and connect to the end of the previous curved line.

Step 5: Add definition to the zebra's face and hair to the mane and tail.

Draw the bridge of the nose. This will add an extra bit of depth to the zebra's face. Start at the middle of the initial head line and curve down along the face, before finishing just below the bottom end of the zebra's nostril.

Add bone definition along the jaw by drawing a curved line that begins where the right side of the chin shape meets the head shape. Keep the line level with the mouth line and draw until you reach the cheek "U" shape.

Draw a little curved line for the throat. Make this a very short curve from the right of the cheek "U" shape to the zebra's bottom neck line.

Add the bone structure behind the eye. Draw a short wavy line that starts just above the right end of the eyelid line. Make this wavy line run parallel to the initial head line, curving up to meet the very bottom of the back of the ear line.

Draw the fold of skin above the near-side foreleg. Think of this as a sideways "L" shape, with the short edge an extension of the top line of the upper leg portion. Make the short edge of the "L" one-third of the length of the long end. Once you've drawn the short end of the "L," arc back down and draw the long end down to the zebra's elbow.

Add a curve for the front of the zebra's ribs behind the shoulders. Start at the point where the bottom of the main body "U" meets the right edge of the shoulder shape, and curve that line up to the left. Continue that curve until you intersect the right line of the shoulder shape, one-third of the way from the top. Finish just to the right of the shoulder shape, making sure you don't draw all of the way to the top.

Draw the hair definition for the zebra's mane by doing a series of double lines all the way down the top edge of the mane.

For the tail, add some curved lines from the edges inwards. This creates definition for the tail hair.

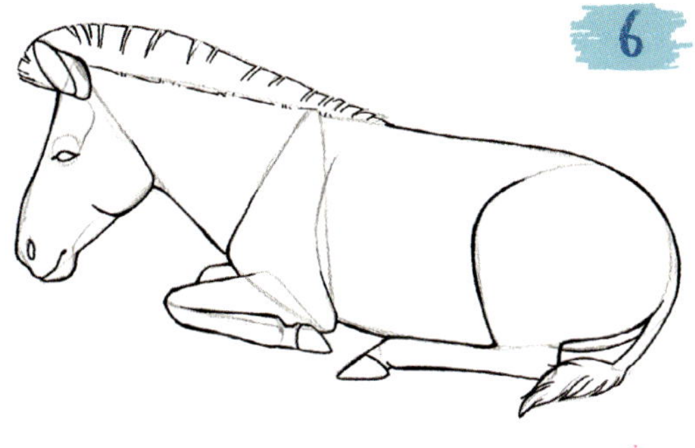

Step 6: Draw the main outline for the zebra using a thicker pen.

Start with the face. Draw over the ear oval and the back of the ear line. Then draw along the initial head line, over the bridge of the nose and over the mouth, chin and cheek shape.

Draw over the eyelid and over the bottom of the eye circle to create the sleepy eye. Draw over the nostril too.

Draw along the throat line and bottom neck line. When you meet the shoulder, draw over half of the top left line of the shoulder triangle and down until you meet the top of the near-side foreleg.

Draw over the near-side foreleg starting with the top line of the upper leg, down over the lower leg and over the hoof. Round off that triangle for the hoof where it meets the leg. Draw over the far-side foreleg line.

Round off the zebra's elbow and draw partially over the rib curve. One-third of that line will do. Draw between the elbow to the joint of the near-side leg.

Draw over a portion of the thigh, leaving the top one-third of the curve blank. Draw over the lower portion of the near-side leg, adding the hoof. Next, draw over the buttock and tail, leaving the attachment point of the tail to the body "U" blank. Draw over the tail hair, leaving some breaks in the line between the hair definition to soften the look.

Add the back line by drawing over the top of the body "U" shape. Stop the line when you meet where the end of the mane connects to the body. Draw a broken line along the top of the neck where the mane attaches. This broken line of dots and apostrophes softens the growth points of the mane. Finally, draw along the top of the mane, going over the quotation mark guidelines. Leave a gap between the two dashes of each of the quotation marks to show partings in the fur. Make sure you do this for the portion of the mane to the left of the ear.

Step 7: Finish the zebra's outline using a thinner pen.

Add more definitions to the mane. Add some tick marks from the top neck line towards the edge of the mane.

Add some inner ear fur by drawing a series of sideways "V" shapes inside the ear oval.

Add more definition to the face. Draw an arch over the top of the eye using the eye circle as a guide. Also add a small curved line below the eye to show the lower eyelid. Draw partially over the bone structure behind the eye and the jawline. Add two tiny sideways "V" shapes between the nostril and mouth line for some muzzle wrinkles.

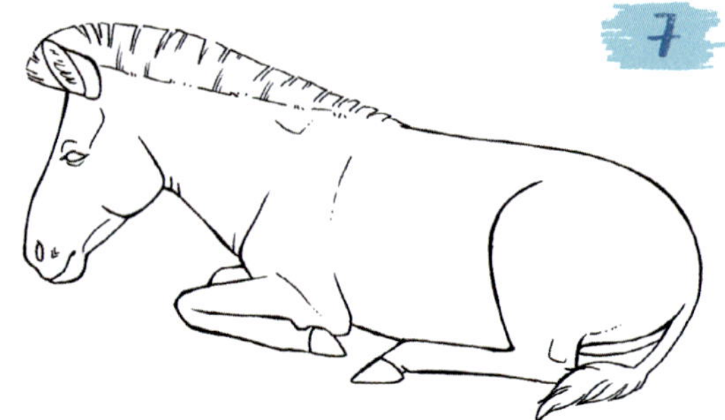

Add some definition to the throat by drawing two lines to the right of the cheek and one line to the left of the shoulder. This creates skin wrinkles. At the top of the neck where the top line meets the shoulder, draw a backwards "J" to create a well where the muscle sits on the neck.

Draw partially over the fold of the leg drawn in step 5 (page 93). Add some dots towards the right end to soften the line. Also extend that rib curve guide and draw some dashes along the right of the shoulder shape.

Add some definition to the hind leg. Draw a "C" shape on the right side of the lower portion of the hind leg to emphasize the bone structure. Then draw some dashes and dots in a line parallel to the bottom edge of the body "U" for further definition to the buttocks.

Erase your pencil guidelines.

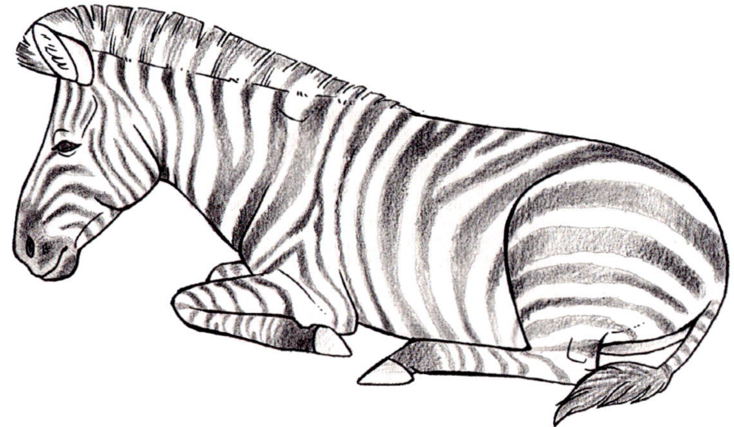

8

Step 8: Draw the famous zebra stripe markings.

Make the bits where the markings meet the outline darker with your darker pencil. Leave the middle parts of the markings lighter. This helps create volume and shadow while you create your markings.

Start with the mane. All along the top edge of the mane add a strip of darker hair. Then alternate with bands of dark while leaving equally sized areas of white between them.

Shade the muzzle of the zebra, arching over the mouth, nostrils and one-third of the way up the face along the bridge of the nose. Extend some stripes from the muzzle shading, arching back over towards the jaw, with the lower stripes meeting the jawline.

For the cheek, draw stripes directly up from the bottom edge of the "U" towards the eye and ear. On the zebra's forehead, shade in stripes from the ear towards the eye.

For the neck stripes, extend the bands of darker hair of the mane down into the neck space. Make these stripes into gentle waves until they meet the neck line. One stripe could be a "Y" shape.

In the shoulder space, turn a stripe into a reverse "Y" by starting one line at the mane stripe before splitting and finishing either side of the upper foreleg.

For the legs, darken the area just next to the hooves, and then do bands of stripes across the leg shapes.

Draw the stripes for the main body, making sure they are all curved like "C" shapes. This curve also helps build up volume on the zebra's body. You can also do a "Y"-shaped stripe in the middle. Add a short stripe between the two top prongs of the "Y." Make them thicker in places to add interest.

Add stripes to the thigh shape and tail. The stripes across the thigh should be perpendicular to the stripes drawn on the body. So, think of them as horizontal stripes instead of vertical ones. Stack them until you've filled the thigh space. Last of all, shade in the tail hair area, drawing in the same direction of the flow of fur, and add bands of stripes along the main tail.

Feel free to blend the stripes with your finger or a tissue for a smoother look, being careful not to lose the definition.

An Arabian Alternative

Using the Pony Portrait tutorial (page 66) as a base, it's possible to make a few adjustments to create an entirely different breed of horse. The pony is a generic horse, so here, we will look at a much more distinct breed: the Arabian. Arabians typically have narrower muzzles, tall, pointed ears and large nostrils. Their manes start much lower on their necks, and their necks are also distinctly arched.

So, let's look at the adjustments you can make to create an Arabian horse portrait.

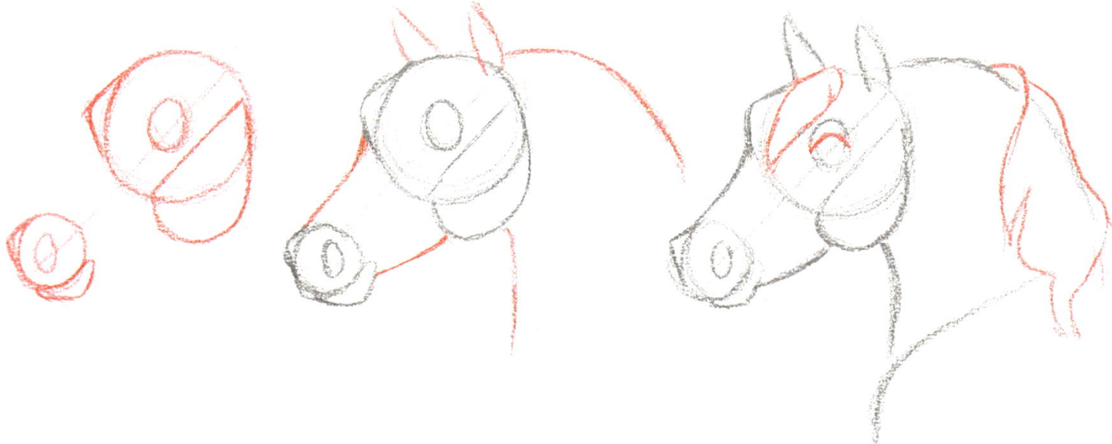

The head and mouth shapes that you drew in step 1 (page 66) of the Pony Portrait tutorial should be rounder. Make them circles rather than ovals.

When adding the eye circle and far-side eye "C" shapes like in step 2 (page 67) of the Pony Portrait, make these shapes much larger in comparison. With the head circle as a guide, make the near-side eye circle one-quarter of the size of the head circle and place it centrally within the head circle. The far-side eye "C" shape should meet the head circle at the ten o'clock and eight o'clock marks.

Place the nostril oval a little lower down to the left along the diagonal guideline drawn in step 1 of the Pony Portrait.

The cheek structure is an additional shape instead of the "L" drawn in step 3 (page 67) of the Pony Portrait. For the Arabian's cheek shape you will create a teardrop-like shape. Start with a diagonal line that runs from the three o'clock mark of the head circle to the six o'clock mark. Then draw a curved line that creates a gap one-third of the diameter of the head circle. Continue the curve upward until you connect with the three o'clock mark of the head circle, making sure the last section of the line on the right is almost vertical and flush with the head circle.

To create the bridge of the muzzle, as their faces are more concave along the upper face line, draw a curved line instead of a straight one. The line will connect from just above where the bottom of the far-side eye shape connects to the head circle down to the far-side nostril. Have the line dip slightly in the upper one-third of the line to create that concave appearance.

Make the ears tilt diagonally to the left and be more pointed than the ears drawn in step 2 (page 67) of the Pony Portrait.

For the top neck line, draw almost horizontally away from the right edge of the near-side ear shape. Where the neck line drawn in step 2 of the Pony Portrait is more like a lightly curved line, the Arabian's neck is much more domed.

The throat line will start centrally in the cheek shape. Start with a little curve that goes to the right of the cheek shape before drawing down vertically to finish the throat.

Draw the curved line within the eye circle like step 3 of the Pony Portrait. As the eye circle is larger, this will naturally make the eye shape larger on the Arabian.

Draw the forelock just like step 4 (page 69) of the Pony Portrait. However, the forelock for the Arabian should be narrower and sit centrally on its forehead above the near-side eye. Create almost a leaf-like shape.

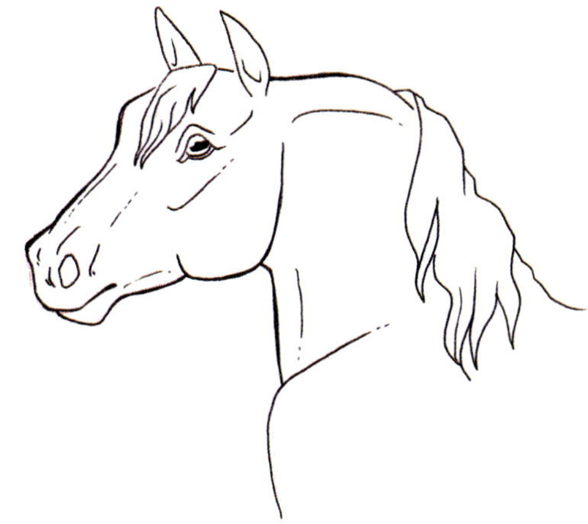

The mane should start one-third down the top neck line. Start with an "S" shape that connects to the top neck line and then goes up in a small dome before flowing downwards into the neck shape. The little dome at the top left of the mane shape will make it appear like the hair is flopping over to the side. Finish the mane shape with a flowing wavy line that runs along the lower section of the top neck line. Draw some more waves and "V" shapes to show the structure of the fur.

Outline the Arabian, like you did in steps 6 and 7 (pages 70 and 71) of the Pony Portrait. You can also shade it if you like.

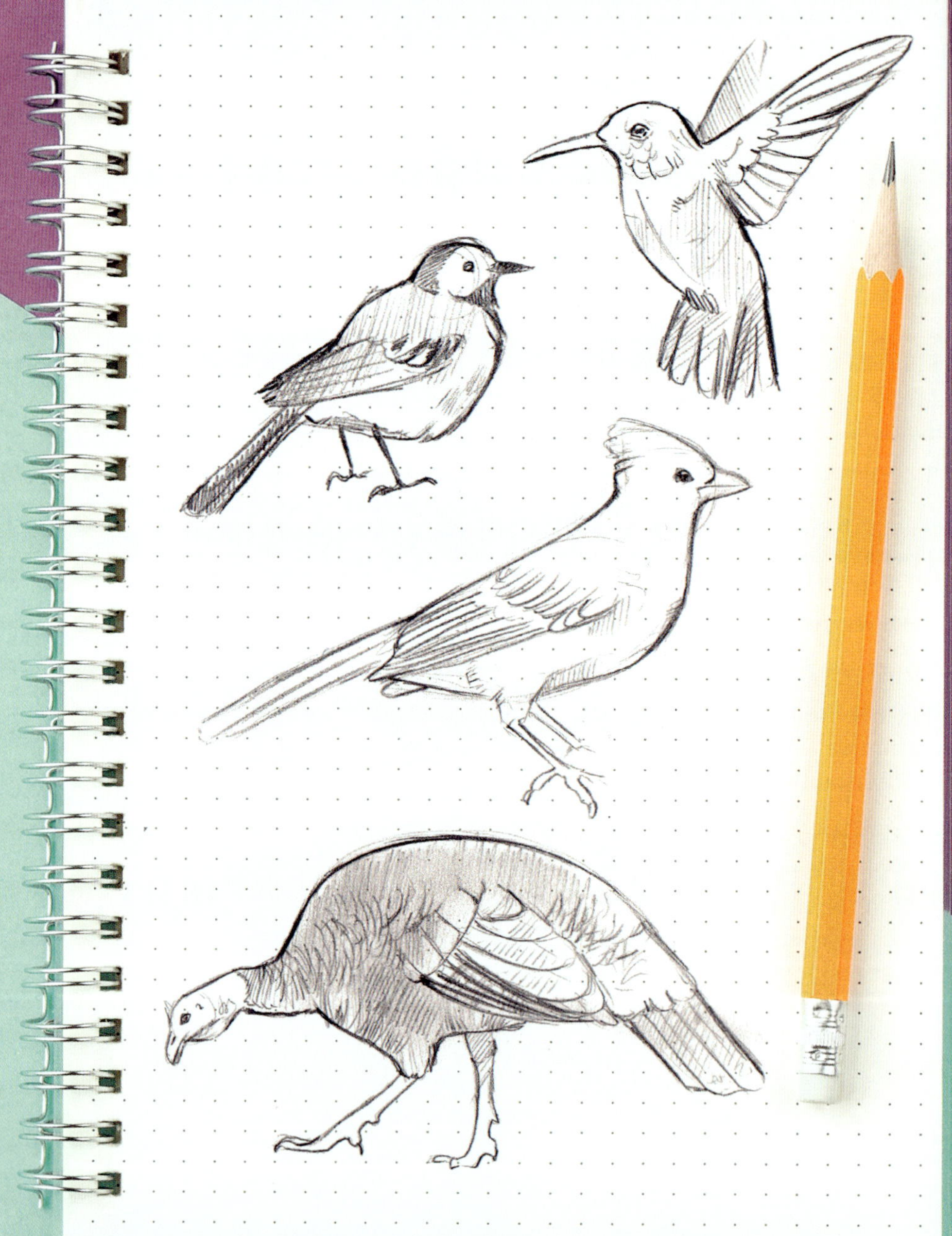

Breaking Down BIRDS

Birds come in all sizes and shapes, so naturally, they can be a very versatile drawing subject. Even bird wings alone can vary wildly depending on the purpose they serve, and that's something we will explore at the end of this chapter.

Drawing birds that are stationary can be very straightforward. The sizes and shapes that make up a bird's head and body are pretty simple, as you'll see. However, the tricky part can come when drawing a bird in flight. As a result, this can be intimidating for some artists, especially when you consider that wings are not just one large shape, but instead, several. They actually have the exact same joints in their wings as you do in your arm. That might help you understand as you work on drawing the flying birds in this chapter.

To start, we will look at a pair of small common and charismatic birds: the northern cardinal and pileated woodpecker—both of which will be in simple, stationery poses. Then, we will look at a less common, but no less charming bird, the bald eagle in flight. Finally, we will look at the adjustments you can make to draw a selection of other birds in flight: a gull, pigeon and cardinal.

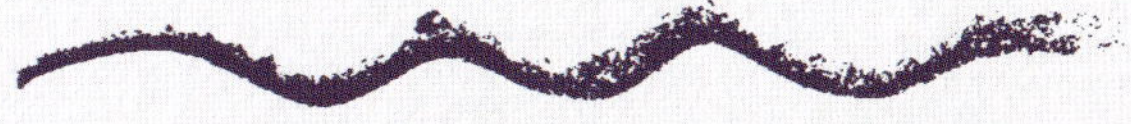

PERCHING CARDINAL

For this tutorial, you will draw a black-and-white illustration of the northern cardinal. They're normally bright red, so adding color is optional and will be something we explore in Adding Color (page 149). Meanwhile, without color, this illustration could be either a male or female northern cardinal. While females don't possess the full bright red coloration that the males have, they're the same size and shape. They have a dark face mask too.

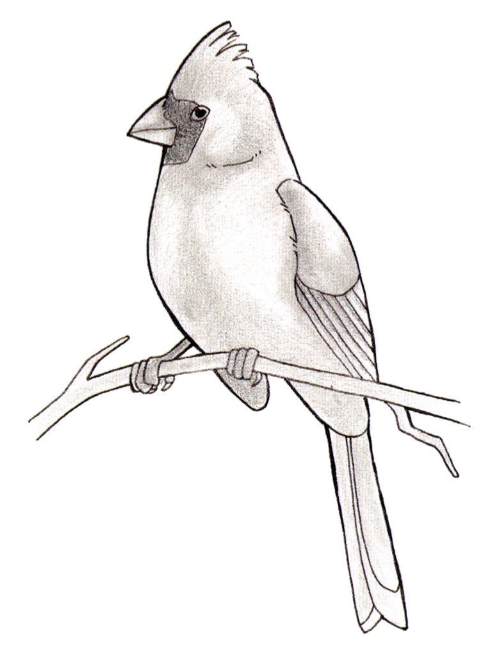

Tip: When drawing the wing feathers, you will be adding a series of straight lines. Go as slowly as you need to keep these lines straight and parallel to each other.

1

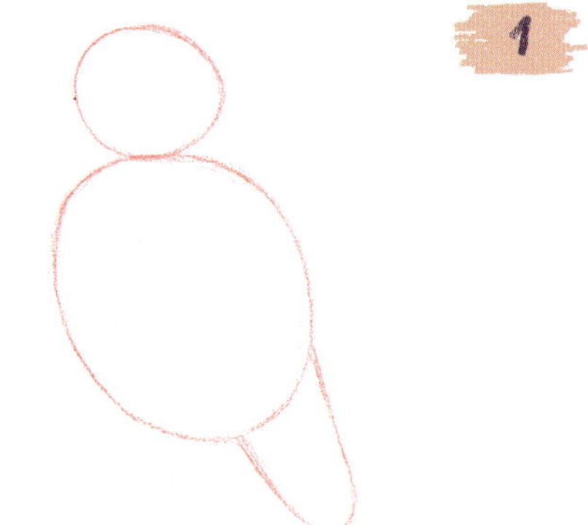

Step 1: **Draw the head, body, and base of the tail shapes.**

Start with the head by drawing a circle in the top quarter of your page. The size of this shape will help construct the proportions of the remainder of the illustration. If you want a good reference size, make the diameter of the circle 1 inch (2.5 cm).

Draw the main body by adding a large oval just below the head circle. This oval should be one and one-half times as wide as the head circle and twice the height. This oval should be tilted very slightly to the right.

Draw the base of the tail by adding a "U" shape at the bottom right of the main body oval. If the main body oval was a circle, the tail base "U" would attach at four o'clock on the right edge and just right of six o'clock for the left. The "U" should be pointing in the five o'clock direction, and the right edge should be slightly longer than the left. The left edge should be the same as the diameter for the head circle.

Step 2: **Draw the crest, neck and tail feathers.**

Starting with the crest, add an upside-down "V" shape on top of the head circle. The prongs of the "V" should meet the head circle at the ten o'clock and two o'clock marks. The distance from the top of the head circle and the point of the "V" should be half the diameter of the head circle, so ½ inch (1.3 cm).

Draw the neck by connecting the left and right edges of the head circle to the main body oval. Draw the left line of the neck from the eight o'clock point on the head circle just left of vertical until it meets the main body oval between the ten o'clock and eleven o'clock marks. Draw the right line of the neck from the three o'clock mark of the head circle until it meets the main body between the one o'clock and two o'clock marks.

Draw the tail feathers by adding a long and slender shape at the bottom of the base of the tail "U." This shape should start with two parallel lines running just right of vertical. The distance between the two parallel lines should be the same as the base of the "U." The length of the two lines should be a little over five times as long as they are apart. Then, where the two lines end, draw a small upside-down "V" shape to create the parting of the tail feathers. This "V" should be half as tall as it is wide.

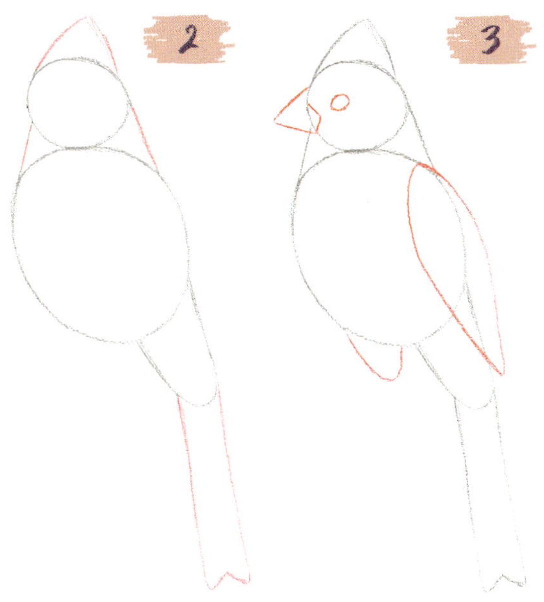

Step 3: **Draw the beak shape, eye and wings.**

To draw the beak, start with a sideways "V" shape pointing in the nine o'clock direction that leaves the left of the head circle. Make the top of the beak shape connect at the ten o'clock mark on the head circle. Connect the bottom of the beak shape at the eight o'clock mark on the head circle. Finish the beak shape by drawing a smaller "V" shape in the inside of the head circle, pointing towards the three o'clock direction. The bottom of the smaller "V" should connect to the eight o'clock mark and the top of the "V" should connect to the nine o'clock mark. The lines of the smaller "V" shape should be one-third the length of the larger "V."

Draw the eye shape by adding a small oval within the head shape. The oval should be one and one-half times as wide as it is tall. The left end of the "V" should sit one-quarter of the way across the head circle from the nine o'clock mark. So, the eye should appear to sit just left of center within the head circle.

Start the wings by drawing the end of the feathers on the far-side wing. The majority of the wing isn't visible, so it'll just appear as the tips of the feathers beneath the main body shape. Add a small "U" shape just to the left of the base of the tail "U." The wing feathers "U" should be half the size of the base of the tail "U," and the right edge should meet the body oval at the six o'clock mark.

Draw the near-side wing by adding a shape that looks like an upside-down water droplet to the right edge of the main body and base of the tail "U" shape. Start by drawing the left edge of the wing shape. Draw a curved line that starts just to the left of the right neck line. Continue this curved line almost parallel to the left edge of the main body oval until it intersects the main body oval one-third of the way from the right between the two ends of the base of the tail "U." Continue this line, intersecting the right edge of the tail "U" two-thirds from the top, and finish when the line is level with the bottom of the far-side wing "U."

Finish the near-side wing shape by drawing the right edge as almost a mirror of the left line. Draw just shy of vertically upwards from the bottom end of the left line, curve lightly to the left and draw along the top of the main body oval between the right neck line and the start of the left line for the wing shape. Finish when you meet the start of the left line for the near-side wing.

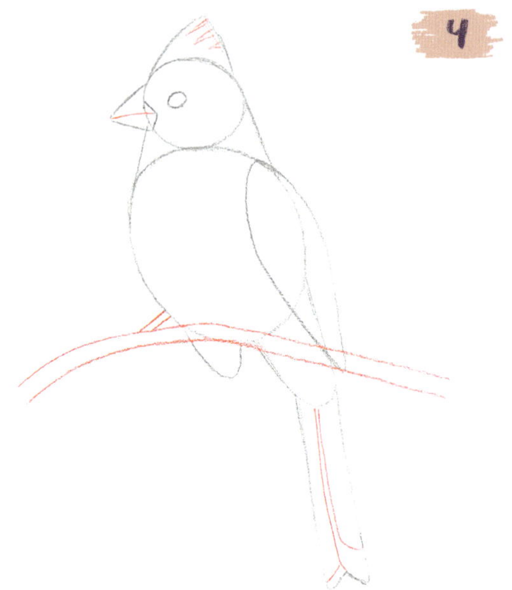

Step 4: Draw the crest feathers, mouth, branch, leg and tail feathers.

Along the right edge of the crest "V" draw three narrow sideways "V" shapes to create the partings in the crest feathers. The "V"s should get progressively smaller from the top to the bottom.

Draw the line for the mouth within the beak shape by connecting the points of the two "V" shapes drawn in step 3 (page 101). This will create a horizontal line for the mouth.

Add the branch by drawing two parallel lines that run across the drawing. Place the branch at the bottom of the main body shape. The length of the branch lines should be twice the width of the space that the cardinal takes up on the page. Start by drawing the bottom line for the branch from left to right, beginning just above level with the bottom of the base of the tail "U." Arch the line upwards until it runs along the bottom of the main body oval and down in line with the tip of the near-side wing shape. Extend the bottom line of the branch a little to the right. Repeat this same line for the top of the branch directly above the bottom line. Make sure it runs parallel to the first line with a distance that's equal to the width of the cardinal's eye shape.

Draw the far-side leg by adding two parallel diagonal lines from the bottom left of the main body oval. The two lines should point in the eight o'clock direction and leave the main body oval between the seven o'clock and eight o'clock marks. The distance between these two lines should be half the distance of the branch lines.

Add the tail feathers. Start at the inverted "V" at the end of the tail feather shape. Draw from the tip of the "V" towards the left slightly, extending the right edge of the inverted "V." When you're one-third of the way across the shape from the left edge, bend the line and draw parallel to the long edge of the tail shape until the line meets the bottom of the base of the tail "U." Returning to the end of the tail feather shape, draw a short parallel line from the bend in the previous line down to the end of the left edge of the tail shape. Draw an additional feather within the right feather shape created by the first line. Draw a smaller version of that shape created by drawing diagonally in the ten o'clock direction from the right edge of the tail shape, one-fifth of the way up from the bottom. Stop the short diagonal line before you reach the first tail feather line, then draw parallel upwards until you reach the bottom of the tail "U."

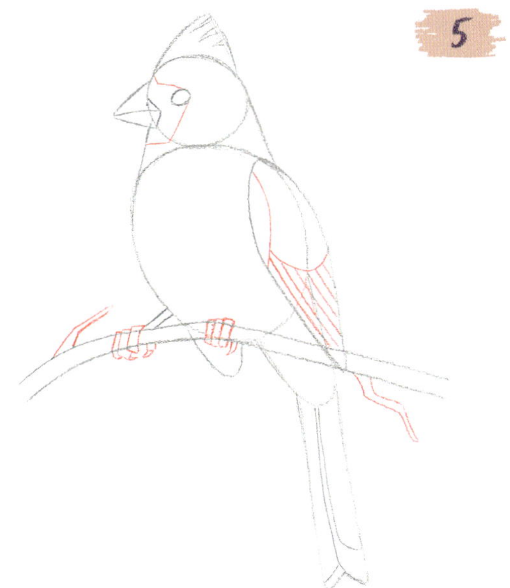

Step 5: **Add the cardinal's mask, wing feathers, feet and branch details.**

Starting with the mask shape, create two backward "L" shapes on the left edge of the cardinal's head. The first "L" will lay horizontally above the eye shape. Draw the short edge of the "L" down from the bottom of the left edge of the crest in a five o'clock direction. When the line is just above level with the eye shape, draw the long edge of the "L" towards the eye until it meets the top. Draw the bottom line of the mask by attaching the long edge of the bottom backward "L" to the right end of the eye oval. Draw down in a seven o'clock direction until it meets the seven o'clock point of the head circle. Add a short horizontal line running just above the middle of the left neck line to finish the mask shape.

For the wing feathers, create the body feathers that overlap the top of the wing by drawing a curved line just below the top of the left edge of the wing shape down to the middle of the wing shape. The curve should look like a reverse "C" shape and create a willow leaf-like shape on the left edge of the wing.

Draw a curved line in the wing shape that creates the separation between the small feathers and the longer feathers. Draw this curved like a flattened "U" from the middle of the right edge of the wing shape. The left of this curved line should meet one-fifth up from the bottom of the curve drawn for the overlapping body feathers. Then, draw the long wing feathers by drawing six equally spaced lines that run parallel to the bottom left of the wing shape. The lines should get shorter as they go towards the right.

Add the shapes for the feet. This step might appear complicated, so take it steady. Start by drawing two sets of three rectangular shapes that will create two separate sets of toes. Draw the left set of toes or three rectangles immediately to the left of where the top line of the leg meets the top line of the branch. The rectangle shapes should be three times as tall as they are wide, be no thicker than the leg shape and sit with the top and bottom edges on either side of the branch lines. For the left foot, make the middle rectangle the tallest, and at the very bottom end, draw a tiny "V" shape for the claw. Opposite of where the leg line meets the branch, underneath the bottom line for the branch, draw a small square that's the same width and height as the width of the toe rectangles, and attach a tiny "V" to the bottom edge. This creates the fourth hidden toe. Repeat the three toe rectangle shapes where the far-side wing feathers meet the body shape. Draw the hidden fourth toe for the right leg by adding a small "V" for the claw just to the right of the right toe.

Add a couple of small twigs off the main branch. On the top left line of the branch, halfway between the left foot and the end of the branch, draw two "L" shapes that come to a point in the direction of the body. This can be as long and thick as you like. Then, on the bottom right of the branch, below the bottom edge to the right of the tip of the near-side wing shape, draw two zigzag lines that also come to a point away from the cardinal. Again, this can be as thick and long as you like. However, make these twigs thinner than the main branch.

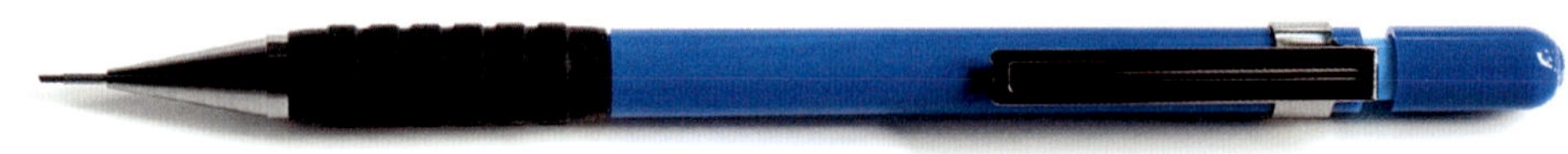

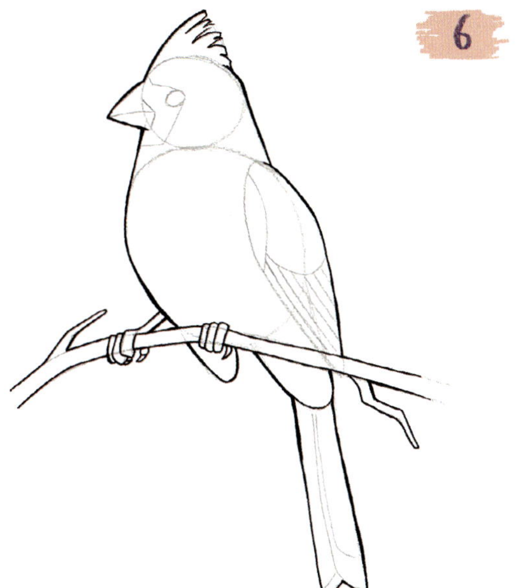

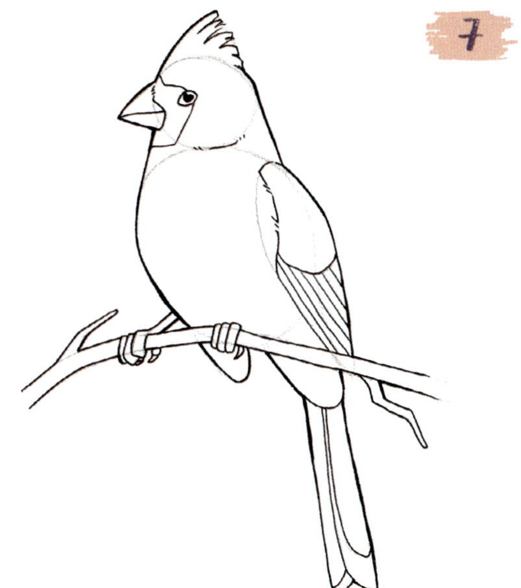

Step 6: Draw the outline of your cardinal illustration.

With a thicker pen, start at the top of the crest, run along the left edge and over the left "V" of the beak shape. Continue down over the left of the main body, over the leg line and left toes. Draw over the right toes, the far-side wing tip "U" shape, the base of the tail "U" and down over the outside of the tail shape. The near-side wing tip of the cardinal will be tucked behind the branch, so don't draw over this part. Go over the edge of the wing shape, up over the right side of the neck and then along the right edge of the crest. Make sure to draw over the "V" shapes, with a few extra tick marks added for the parting in the crest feathers.

Draw over the branch shapes last. Go over the branch lines, including the twigs.

Step 7: Draw the details of the cardinal.

With a thinner pen draw the inner edge of the beak and mouth. Along the top of the beak where the left "V" meets the head circle, draw a broken line with dashes to create feathers. Draw over the smaller right "V" for the beak with a solid line. Then draw along the horizontal mouth line.

Draw over the mask shape and eye oval. Add a pupil by drawing a circle within the eye oval, leaving the top right blank for the eye shine.

Along the bottom of the head circle, add a tick line with a set of quotation marks at each end for the feathers.

Draw over the overlapping feathers from the main body on the wing shape, using a series of ticks and apostrophe marks to soften the look. Then draw over the wing feathers including the curved line and the feather lines. Draw over the tail feather guidelines.

Erase all of the pencil lines.

Step 8: Shade your cardinal (optional).

Fill in the entirety of the cardinal, including the branch, with your lighter pencil.

Add darker areas for the shadow. Start with the cardinal's mask by taking a darker pencil and filling in the whole shape of the mask. On males, this shape is completely black, so if you're drawing a male make this shape as dark as you want.

With your lighter pencil, go back over areas within the cardinal that will be darker. Creating layers with a lighter pencil will make the shading softer. Good areas to darken are within the crest, along the right of the head, below the head shape and down the middle of the cardinal's body. Also darken the left edge of the wing shape, down each of the wing feathers, the tail shapes and the legs and toes. The far-side wing tips should also be darker.

For a soft finish, go over the shading with your finger or a tissue to blend together the pencil.

8

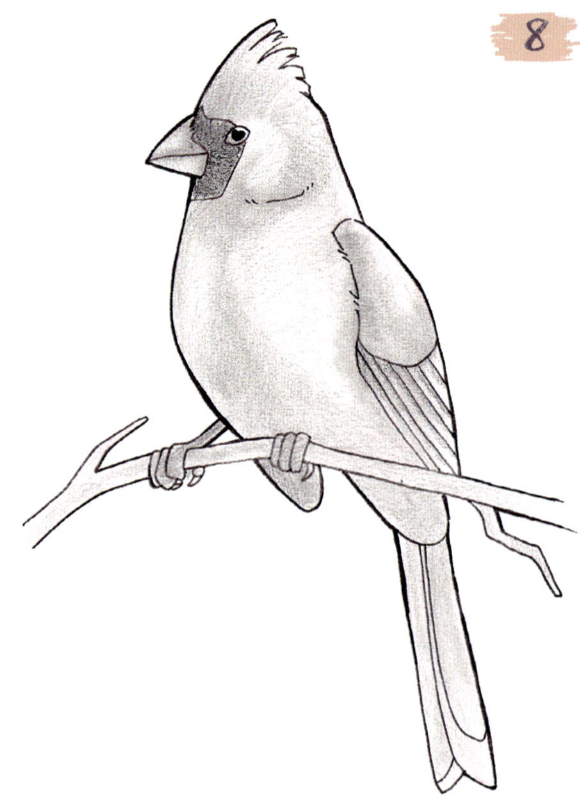

WOODPECKER CLIMBING

While some woodpeckers are colorful, for this tutorial we will draw a pileated woodpecker, which is mostly black and white. The males and females are similar but do differ in the red feathers on their heads. Adding the bright coloration is optional and can be explored in Adding Color (page 149). Like the Perching Cardinal tutorial (page 100), this could be either a male or a female pileated woodpecker. Furthermore, you could actually use this same tutorial to draw a whole host of different woodpecker species.

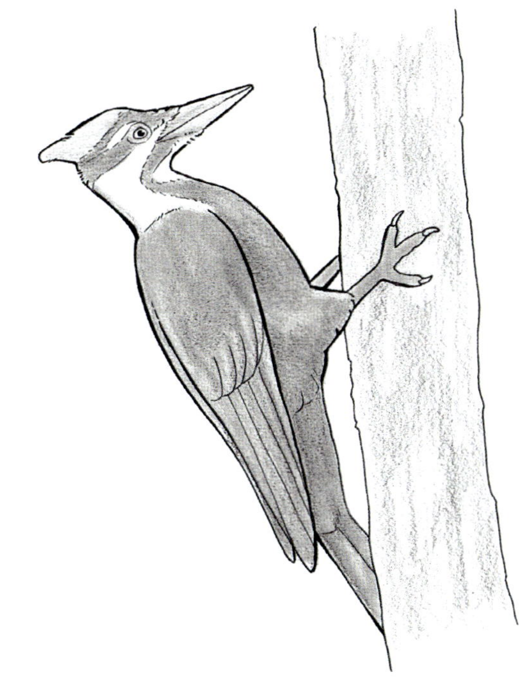

Tip: The markings on this pileated woodpecker's head are pretty complex. The tutorial details just how to draw them, but do take your time. These shapes don't need to be perfect to capture the essence of your woodpecker illustration.

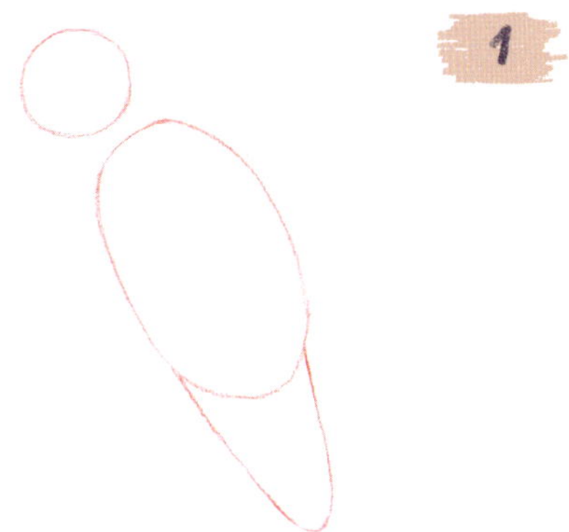

Step 1: Draw the head, body and base of the tail.

Draw a circle for the head in the upper left section of the page, three-quarters of the way up. Make this circle 1 inch (2.5 cm) in diameter to help with proportions for the rest of the bird.

Draw the body by adding a large oval shape to the bottom right of the head circle. The oval should be tilted slightly with the top edge pointing towards the head circle in an eleven o'clock direction, while the bottom of the oval should point down in a five o'clock direction. Make the body oval one and one-half times as wide as the head oval and two and one-half times as tall. Therefore, the oval should be 1½ inches (4 cm) wide and 2½ inches (6.5 cm) tall.

Add the base of the tail by drawing a "U" on the bottom end of the main body oval. Draw the left edge of the "U" partway along the left edge of the main body oval, creating one straight line from the left edge of the oval down to the bottom of the "U" shape. The right edge of the "U" should attach just shy of the right edge of the main body oval. The base of the tail "U" should point also in the five o'clock direction. Make the left edge of the oval twice the length of the head diameter, so 2 inches (5 cm).

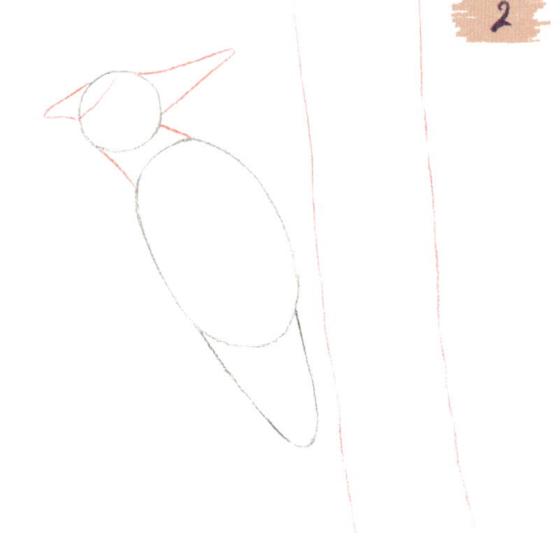

Step 2: Draw the beak, crest, neck and tree.

Draw the beak shape by adding a sideways "V" shape starting from the top right of the head circle at the one o'clock mark. The bottom edge of the beak should attach at the three o'clock mark. The point of the "V" should be in the two o'clock direction. Make the tip of the beak the same distance from the edge of the head circle as the diameter of the head circle, so 1 inch (2.5 cm) long.

Draw the crest, starting with a "V" shape from the left edge of the head circle. The top of the crest "V" should leave the head circle halfway between the ten o'clock and eleven o'clock marks and point downwards in an eight o'clock direction. The bottom line of the crest should leave the head circle at the nine o'clock mark and be roughly horizontal. The distance between the tip of the crest "V" and the head circle should be one-third of the diameter of the head shape. Finish the head crest by drawing a curved line inside the head circle from the nine o'clock mark of the head and circling up to the twelve o'clock mark.

Draw the neck lines, starting with the right line for the throat. Draw a line from the four o'clock mark on the head circle down towards the main body oval in a four o'clock direction until it meets the body. Draw the left neck line by drawing in a five o'clock direction from the seven o'clock mark of the head circle until the line meets the main body oval.

Draw the trunk of the tree to the right of the woodpecker. The wonderful thing about the trunk is that it can be drawn however you like. The only important thing is making sure it's not too far away from the woodpecker's body. For a guide, draw two vertical lines that run parallel, the same distance apart as the thickness of the main body of the woodpecker. These lines don't need to be straight as they'll help represent the bark of the tree. The left line should run parallel to the bottom of the woodpecker, leaving a gap of one-quarter the width of the top of the tail "U."

Step 3: **Draw the wing, base of the leg and tail feather shape.**

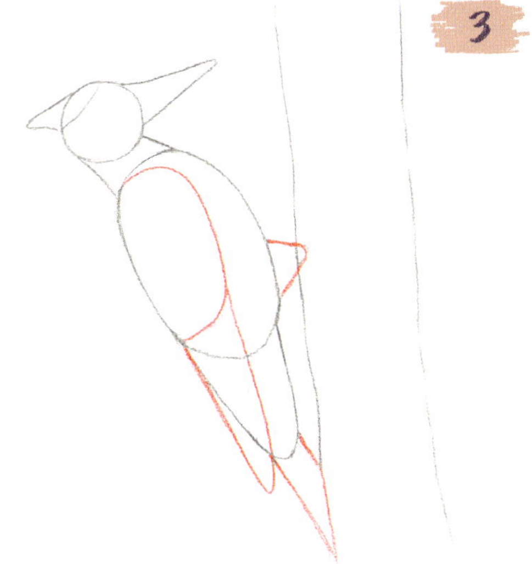

Draw the wing by adding a backward "C" shape within the main body oval. Draw the top of the "C" from the point where the back neck line meets the main body oval. Draw in the two o'clock direction initially until level with the bottom of the throat line, and then draw downwards, just shy of vertical. Once the line is two-thirds of the way down the body length, curve towards the eight o'clock direction and draw until the line meets the point where the left of the base of the tail "U" meets the main body oval.

Add the tip of the wing by drawing a tall "V" shape at the bottom of the backward "C" we just drew. Attach the left edge of the wing "V" to the point where the "C" meets the main body oval and draw downwards between the five o'clock and six o'clock direction. Attach the right edge of the wing "V" to the right of the backward "C" shape, creating one long continuous line. Connect the bottom of the right end of the wing "V" to the bottom of the left end. The tip of the wing "V" should stop a little lower than the tip of the base of the tail "U" and be the same length as the backward "C."

Draw the base of the leg by adding a sideways "V" shape to the right edge of the body oval. The top of the "V" should attach just below the middle and stick out to the right almost horizontally. The bottom edge of the leg "V" should leave the body one-fifth up from the bottom and point between the one o'clock and two o'clock direction. The point of the leg "V" should sit half the distance away from the main body as the width of the upper wing "C" shape.

Draw the tail shape by adding two parallel lines from the end of the base of the tail "U" shape. Both lines should point in a five o'clock direction. The bottom line should start at the point where the right edge of the wing "V" intersects with the bottom of the base of the tail "U." Draw this line until it meets the tree trunk. Then draw the top line from the right edge of the base of the tail "U." The two lines should be one-third of the distance apart as the width of the upper wing "C" shape.

Step 4: Draw the mouth, eye, feet and individual wing and tail feathers.

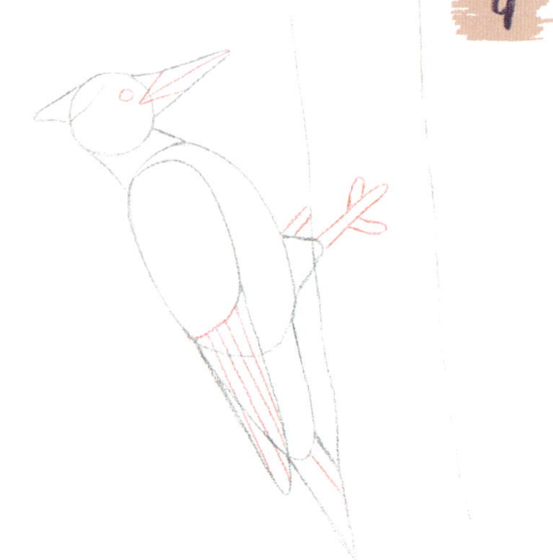

Starting with the mouth and the beak, draw a sideways "V" opposite to the initial beak "V" that's half the size and pointing downwards in an eight o'clock direction. The top of the smaller "V" should meet the top of the initial beak "V," one-quarter away from the head circle. The bottom of the smaller "V" should meet the bottom of the initial beak "V" one-third of the way along from the head circle. Now draw the mouth by adding a line that runs between the two "V" points.

Draw the eye by adding a small oval shape just up and to the left of the point of the smaller mouth and beak "V." This oval should be a little over one-eighth of the diameter of the head circle.

Draw the legs and feet to help the woodpecker attach to the trunk, starting with the far-side leg. Draw two parallel lines that leave the top edge of the leg "V" added in step 3 (page 109). The lines should point up between the one o'clock and two o'clock directions. The left line should start where the leg "V" meets the main body. The distance between the two lines should be one-third of the distance between the tip of the leg "V" and the main body.

For the near-side leg, draw a long sausage shape that starts at the tip of the leg "V." Point it between the one o'clock and two o'clock directions. The width of this shape should be the same as the far-side leg's. Make the length of this shape the same as the width of the upper wing created by the backward "C" from step 3. The sausage shape will be part leg and part toe. Draw the first toe by adding a small inverted "U" that's the same width but one-quarter the length of the initial sausage shape. The left of the first toe should attach at the middle of the top edge of the initial sausage, and the "U" should be pointing just shy of twelve o'clock. Now add the third toe, which will be a "U" of the same width and one-third the length of the initial sausage shape. Set it centrally on the bottom edge of the initial sausage shape and point it just below the three o'clock direction.

Draw the individual feathers within the wing "V" shape. Create five distinct feathers by adding four equally spaced lines that all run parallel from the bottom edge of the upper "C" shape to the bottom of the "V" shape.

Add a line within the tail shape to create a distinct feather shape. Draw a diagonal line from the bottom of the base of the tail "U" to the trunk of the tree, parallel to the two lines drawn in step 3. It should create two smaller shapes, the bottom of which is almost twice the width as the top.

Step 5: **Draw the far-side wing, upper wing feathers, claws and facial markings.**

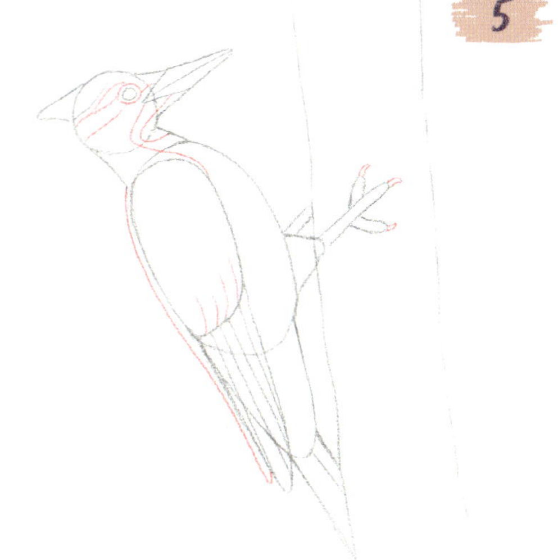

Draw the far-side wing by creating a sliver of a shape running all the way along the left edge of the woodpecker. Start the line just at the base of the neck shape, above where the left neck line meets the main body shape. Run the line parallel to the left edge of the main body shape and down the left edge of the wing "V" shape. Make sure the far-side wing shape is very narrow.

Draw the upper wing feathers on the near-side wing along the bottom edge of the backwards "C" drawn for the wing. Add four equally spaced "J" shapes along the bottom edge. The tall end of the "J" should be one-quarter the length of the upper wing shape.

Draw the claws by adding a "V" to the end of each of the toes on the near-side leg. The "V"s should be narrower than the toes.

Draw the facial markings. This step creates quite a few complex shapes, so take your time with this. Draw a ring over the eye shape to create the eyelids. From the three o'clock mark of the outer ring of the eye, draw a short line in the two o'clock direction to the center of the top line of the smaller mouth and beak "V" from step 4. Draw two parallel lines from the bottom left of the outer eye ring to the back of the head. These lines should be slightly wavy. The top line should connect between the nine o'clock of the eye ring to the nine o'clock of the head circle. The bottom line should run from the seven o'clock of the eye ring to the eight o'clock of the head circle. Then, add a willow leaf-like shape above the two parallel lines by drawing a curved line from the twelve o'clock mark of the eye ring to just left of the middle of the top wavy line.

Finally, draw two lines to create a band of dark feathers from the bottom of the beak to the chest. From the middle of the bottom line of the small "V" of the mouth and beak, draw from the eight o'clock direction, and curve your line down to connect with the four o'clock mark of the head circle before curving back and meeting the middle of the throat line. Then draw an "S" shape from the tip of the smaller beak "V" that starts parallel to the previous line. Curve down to the five o'clock mark of the head circle, and then run it down in a four o'clock direction until it meets one-quarter of the way down the wing "C" shape.

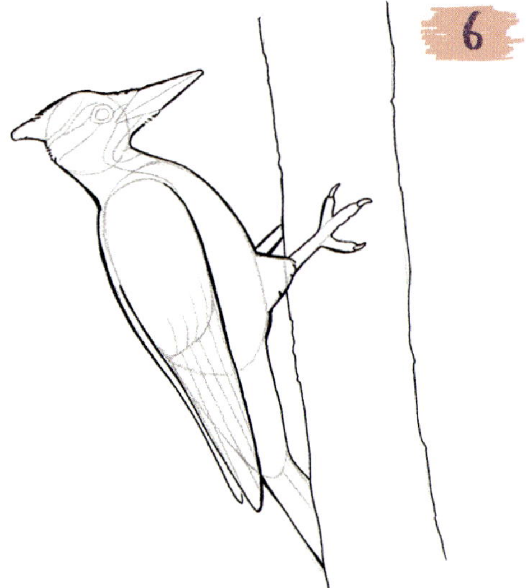

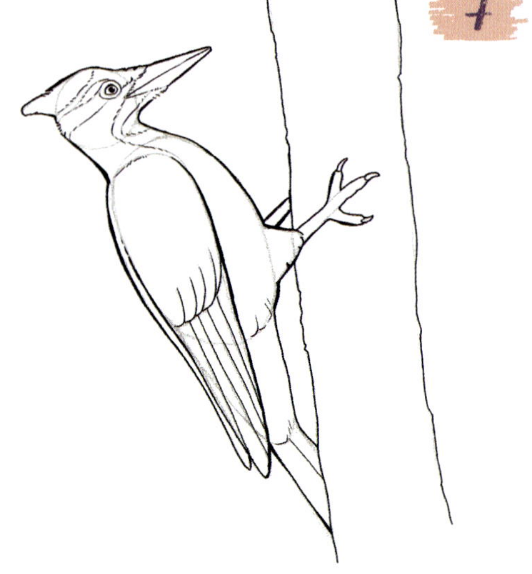

Step 6: Draw the outline.

With a thicker pen, draw along the initial beak "V" shape with a solid line until it meets the points of the smaller beak "V." Between the top end of the smaller beak "V" and the top of the head circle, draw a zigzag for feathers. Then draw over the top of the head to the crest, adding a few ticks and a gap in the line for the parting in the crest feathers. Draw around the back of the crest "V," down the back of the head, and make sure there are a few apostrophe marks just below the crest for feathers.

Draw down along the neck, over the far-side wing, and partially over the left edge of the near-side wing. Draw along the right edge of the near-side wing shape. Leave the top edge of the wing shape down to the middle of the left edge free of pen. Draw over the outside of the tail shape, along the right of the base of the tail "U" and over the leg "V." On the lower edge of the leg "V," add a few notches for feathers.

Draw over the woodpecker's feet and claws. Then draw along the top right of the body shape, along the throat and up to the feathers below the beak.

Draw along the trunk of the tree, keeping the lines sort of jagged for the tree's bark.

Step 7: Add the details.

With a thinner pen, draw along the mouth line. Draw ticks and apostrophes for the feathers along both edges of the smaller beak "V." Draw over the eye shape and the ring around the eye. Add a pupil by drawing a small circle within the eye shape, leaving the top right blank for the eye shine.

Draw over the markings guidelines from step 5 (page 111), but make sure the pen lines are broken. Drawing a series of ticks, dashes and apostrophes along the marking lines creates the appearance of feathers. Do the same for the bottom curved line of the crest. Also add dashed lines on the top edge of the near-side wing "C," a couple of dashes from the left tip of the near-side wing outline, and a few ticks along the guide of where the main body meets the tail "U" shape. Also, draw a few ticks at the bottom end of the "U" where it meets the tail feathers.

Draw over the bottom edge of the wing "C" shape, but instead of drawing one single line, use the "J" shapes from step 5 (page 111) as a guide. Essentially, draw four "J" shapes side by side, and a short curved line from the bottom of the right "J" to the right edge of the wing. Then draw over all the individual wing tip feathers within the wing "V" shape and along the diagonal line drawn for the individual feathers in the tail shape.

Erase your pencil lines.

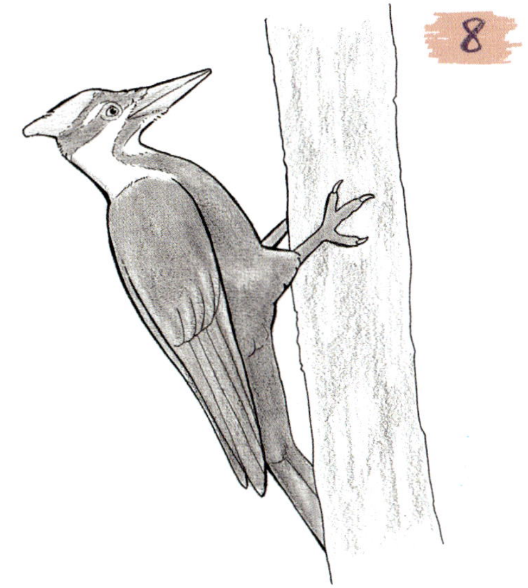

Step 8: Shade your woodpecker drawing (optional).

With your lighter pencil, fill in the entire tree trunk and woodpecker. Some of the marking shapes added in step 5 will be left white. These shapes are on the throat below the beak, the large section that runs from the back of the head to the beak and the small willow leaf shape above the eye.

With your darker pencil, add the darker feathers. Pileated woodpeckers are almost black, except for the head crest. Leave the crest shape lighter, as well as the beak. Go over the facial markings that are not being left white, and then shade the rest of the bird in a darker pencil. Leave a few patches a little lighter to account for the shine on the feathers. For example, the top of the leg "V," the inside sections of the feathers and the top right of the main body where the chest is are good places to leave a little lighter.

Add some texture to the tree with a darker pencil. This can be as you please, but add patches that are wonky and darker, leaving some sections lighter. If your paper is textured, this can be a great way to add some roughness to the tree. Try to sketch in the same direction and parallel to the trunk lines.

Soften the shading on the woodpecker by blending the pencil with your finger or a tissue.

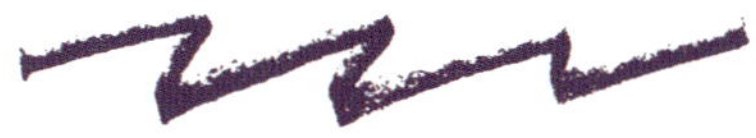

EAGLE IN FLIGHT

For this tutorial, we are going to draw a magnificent bald eagle in flight. The focus of the illustration is the wings as they're so big, especially when compared to the eagle's body. This means we will look at the structure of the wings, including the individual feathers that allow these impressive birds to take flight.

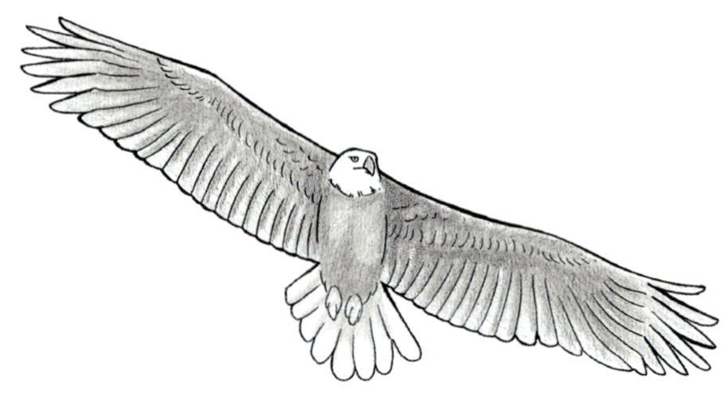

Tip: Drawing the individual wing feathers can be tricky, so go slow. Drawing smooth lines will really help. Pay attention to which direction the lines curve to show off how they overlap each other.

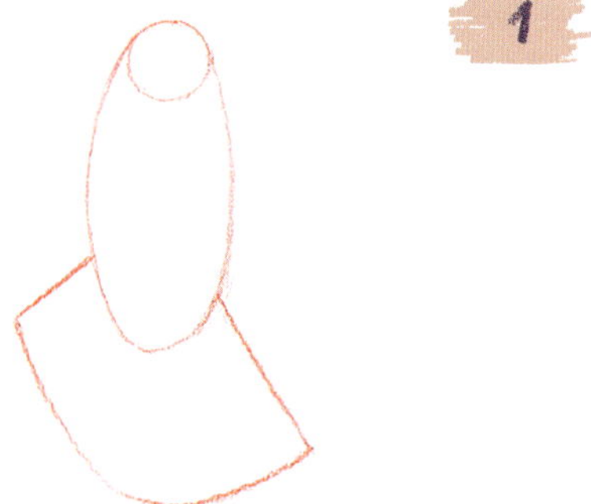

Step 1: Draw the body, head and tail structure.

For the body shape, draw a narrow oval in the middle of the page. Make sure to leave plenty of space on either side of the body for the wings. This oval should be vertical and to help with proportions, make the oval 1½ inches (4 cm) tall and ½ inch (1.3 cm) at the widest point.

At the very top end of the body oval, draw a small circle for the head. This circle will help structure the rest of the facial features. If the body is ½ x 1½ inches (1 x 4 cm), draw the circle ⅓ inch (8 mm) in diameter.

Draw the tail shape, starting with the left and right edges. Draw the left edge of the tail by drawing diagonally down between the seven o'clock and eight o'clock direction from one-quarter of the way up from the bottom of the body oval on the left side. Draw the right edge of the tail by drawing a diagonal line from one-fifth of the way up from the bottom of the body oval on the right. The right edge of the tail should point in a five o'clock direction and be twice as long as the left edge.

Finish the tail shape by drawing a shallow "U" between the ends of the left and right edges of the tail. The distance between the bottom of the "U" and the bottom of the body oval should be half of the body shape's height.

Step 2: Draw the eye, beak and feet and start the wings.

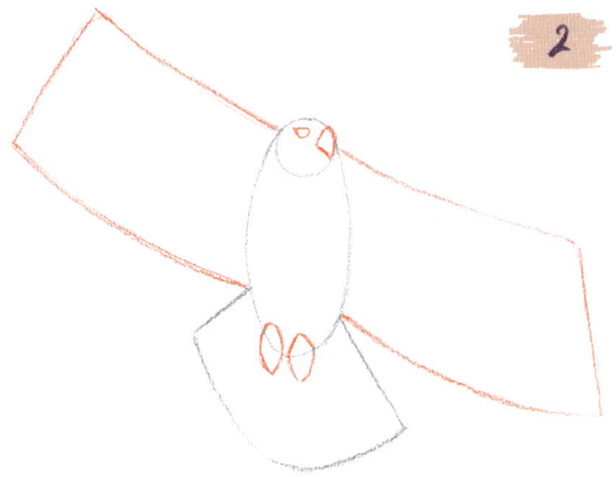

Add the eye by drawing a tiny oval shape in the top of the head circle. This circle should be just left of the vertical midline and in the top one-third of the head circle.

Draw the beak by adding a triangle shape to the top right of the head circle. The top right edge should run along the top right of the head circle. Draw the top left edge of the beak by drawing diagonally down to the left from between the one o'clock and two o'clock marks of the head circle. Draw the bottom edge of the beak from the four o'clock mark of the head circle in a diagonal line towards the eye shape and stop where the left and bottom edges of the beak meet to form the beak shape.

Draw the feet by adding two small petal shapes on the bottom edge of the body oval, exactly in the middle between the left and right edges of the tail shape. These petal shapes should be twice as tall as they are wide and be separated by a tiny gap. The top of the petal shapes should sit above the bottom line of the body oval, and the bottom of the petal shapes should sit below the bottom line of the body oval.

Begin drawing the wings, starting with the top lines of each wing. The top edge of the left wing should extend from the ten o'clock mark of the head circle and point in a ten o'clock direction. This line should be the same length as the main body is tall, so 1½ inches (4 cm). Then draw the top edge of the right wing from the three o'clock mark of the head circle and draw down in a four o'clock direction. This line should be a little longer than the top line of the left wing due to perspective, roughly 1¾ inches (4.5 cm).

Draw the bottom line of each wing, starting with the left wing. Draw up in a ten o'clock direction from the point where the left edge of the tail meets the main body oval. Make this line the same length as the top line for the right wing, again 1¾ inches (4.5 cm) long. Draw the bottom edge for the right wing from the point where the right edge of the tail meets the body shape. Draw down in a four o'clock direction, curving slightly upwards in a very flattened "U" shape. Make this line the same length as the top right wing line.

Finish this stage of the wing shape by connecting the end of the top line to the bottom line for both wings.

Step 3: Add the forehead, mouth and head feathers and complete the base wing structure.

To draw the eagle's forehead, draw a tiny sideways "J" shape on the top right of the head circle.

Draw the mouth by adding a very short line from the left corner of the beak triangle. The line should point slightly diagonally down to the left. It should be no longer than the width of the eye shape and extend to below the middle of the eye.

Draw the white head feathers shape by adding a flattened "V" just below the head circle. The left line should point down in a rough four o'clock direction and the right line should point down in an eight o'clock direction. The point of the "V" should be directly below the end of the mouth line.

Add the remaining structure of the wings, starting with the ends of the wings. For this, draw the top edges of the ends of the wings first. Extend the top left corner of the left wing with a line that points just below the ten o'clock direction, creating an angle at the joint of 170 degrees. This line should be three-quarters the length of the top edge of the left wing. Draw the same length line from the top right corner of the right wing pointing in the four o'clock direction. Draw the bottom edges of the ends of the wings, starting with the left wing. This line should be slightly curved and extend from the bottom left corner of the wing shape. Point this line in the ten o'clock direction, and make it half as long as the top line of the left wing. Draw the same length line pointing in a four o'clock direction from the bottom right corner of the right wing shape. Finish these shapes by drawing a line connecting the ends of the lines for both the left and right wing end shapes.

Draw the wing structures, which essentially form the eagle's arms within the wing shapes. Start with the left wing by drawing a diagonal line that starts exactly midway between the top and bottom lines of the initial wing shape from the left edge of the body oval. Extend that line into the wing end shape and curve it up to meet the middle of the top line of the wing end shape. Do the opposite for the right wing, starting midway between the inner wing shape from the right edge of the body oval. Extend the line into the right wing end shape, curving up to meet the middle of the top line of the right wing end shape.

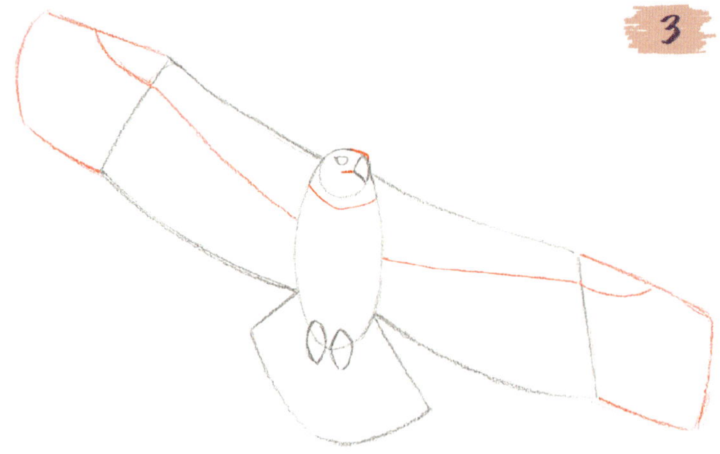

Step 4: Draw the tail and wing tip feathers.

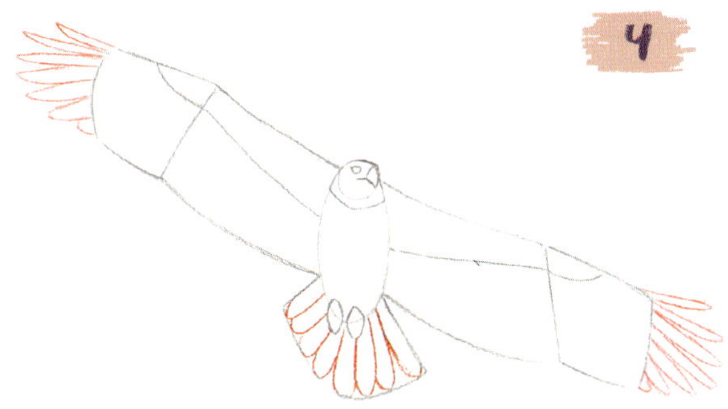

Start with the tail feathers by adding a series of "U" shapes to the tail shape. To make it easier, draw the left tail feather first by creating the base of the "U" against the curved end of the tail. Do the same for the right tail feather with the long edge of the feather running parallel to the right edge of the tail shape. Draw a feather for the middle of the tail. Then, using the left feather as a guide, draw three feather shapes between the left feather and the middle feather. Then add two feathers between the right feather and the middle feather. The bottom curve of the feathers should sit on the curve of the tail shape from step 1, and the long edge of the feathers should point towards and connect with the bottom edge of the body oval.

Draw the wing tip feathers, starting with the left wing. You'll be adding a series of slender and regular "V" shapes along the left edge of the wing—seven feathers in all. The top two feathers should point in a ten o'clock direction and the bottom five in more of a nine o'clock direction. Start with the top feather. Make it half the length of the top edge of the end of the wing shape. The second feather from the top should be the same width as the top feather, one and one-half times as long. The third feather from the top should be a little wider than the first two but the same length as the second. The fourth feather from the top should the same length as the previous two, but twice as thick. The fifth feather should be as thick as the fourth, but a little shorter. Then the sixth feather should be as thick and a little shorter again. The bottom feather should be the shortest feather.

Now add the feathers for the right wing tip. Again, there will be seven feathers created by narrow "V" shapes, all attached to the right edge of the right wing end. Due to the perspective of the wing, all these feathers will be the same width as the top three feathers on the left wing. The top feather should be half the length of the top edge of the right wing end shape. The second feather from the top should be one and one-half times as long as the first and point towards four o'clock. The third feather should be the same length, also pointing in a four o'clock direction. Then the fourth feather from the top should be the same length and pointing between the four o'clock and five o'clock direction. The fifth feather from the top should be a little shorter, pointing more towards five o'clock. The sixth feather from the tip should be a little shorter again and pointing towards five o'clock. The bottom feather should be the shortest, also pointing in the five o'clock direction.

Step 5: Draw the claws of the feet and the wing feathers.

For the claws, draw two short curved lines within each of the feet petal shapes from step 2 (page 115). They should run from the bottom end of the feet shapes to the middle. Point the toe lines towards the left slightly within the left foot and slightly to the right for the right foot.

Draw the wing feathers, starting with the left wing end shape. Draw curved lines from the left edge partially towards the smaller shape drawn at the top right of the wing end. The lines should all point toward the wing joint. Draw from the points where the bottom edges of the feathers meet the left edge of the wing end, which should lead to six curved lines initially. Then, along the bottom edge of the wing end shape, draw some additional "J" shapes side by side, equally spaced and with the tops all pointing towards the wing joint.

Move to the right end of the wing, again adding curved lines from the bottom edges of the wing tip feathers towards the wing joint. These should look more like backwards "J" shapes. Once the bottom edge of the bottom wingtip feather has been added, draw an additional backwards "J" shape from the bottom edge of the right wing end shape towards the wing joint.

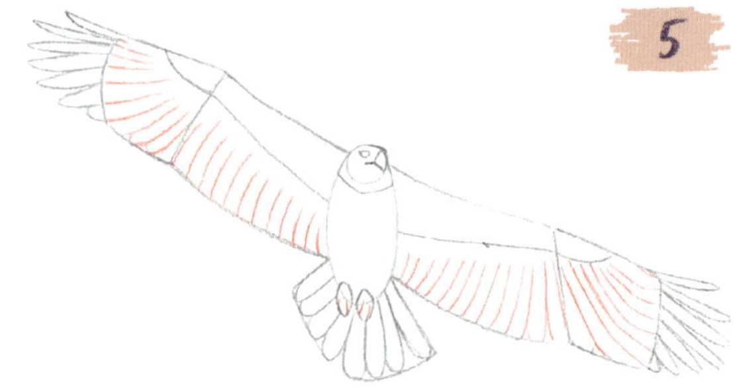

Draw the feathers that run along the lower edge of the wing shape. Add a series of equally spaced curved lines that point from the bottom edge of the wing shape to the top edge. Keep these feathers the same distance apart as the curved lines drawn on the ends of the wing shapes you just drew. These curved lines should be partial and not fill the entire space. The lines should curve parallel to the edges of the body shape, so the left wing feathers should look like backwards "J" shapes and the right feathers should look like regular "J" shapes.

Step 6: Draw the outline.

With a thicker pen, draw over the eagle's forehead and continue over the right and left edges of the main body, finishing before you reach the head feather guideline from step 3. Then draw over the tops of the wings in one solid, flowing line all the way to the tips of the wing feathers. Draw over the wing tip feathers.

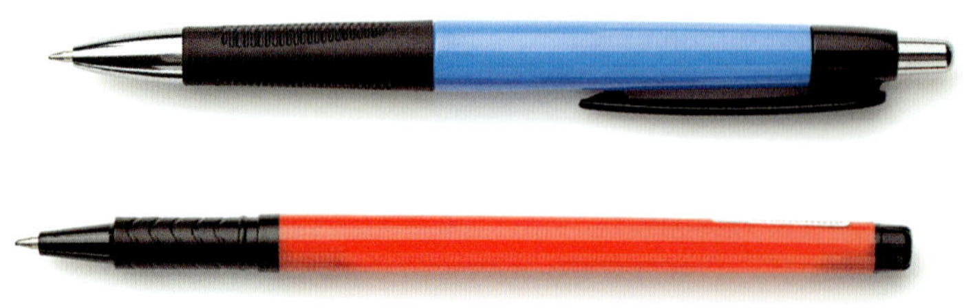

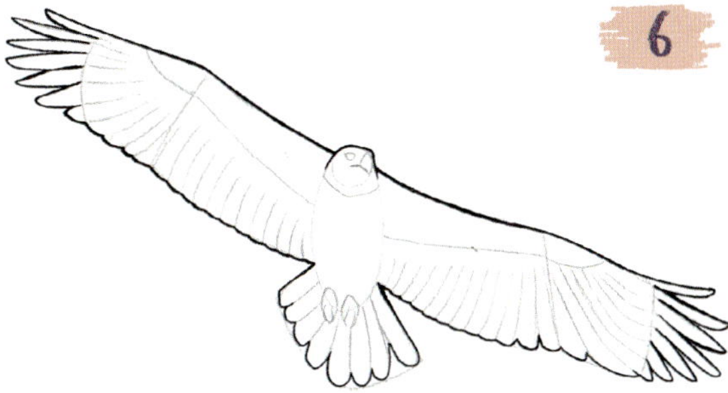

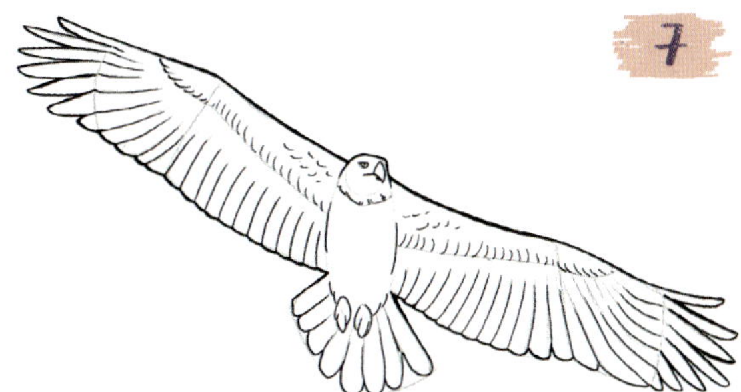

For the lower edge of the wings, use the individual feather marks to guide you. Instead of drawing along the straight edges of the wing guide shapes, draw a line that almost looks like the waves on top of a calm sea along the bottom end of each feather. The peaks of the "waves" should be where the lines from step 5 meet the bottom edges of the wings. This creates the appearance of individual feathers.

Draw over the tail shape, starting with the left and right edges. Then draw over the ends of the individual feathers.

Step 7: Finish the outline by adding the details.

With a thinner pen, draw over the eye shape, making sure the top edge is flat to create the eagle's frown. Draw a singular dot in the middle of the top edge of the eye for the pupil. Draw over the beak triangle and mouth, and add a little mark just above the bottom tip of the beak triangle to create the lower part of the beak. Draw along the flattened "V" shape for the head feathers using ticks and dashes to create the individual head feathers.

Draw over the eagle's feet, including the toes, then over parts of the body shape. Draw a line along the middle section of the left and right of the body shape, leaving gaps above and below to soften the edge. Then, between the feet and the edges of the tail, draw a couple of ticks to add smaller feathers and soften the end of the body shape.

Draw over the individual tail feathers from step 4 (page 117) and all along the wing feathers added in step 5. Last, for the wings where the arm shapes were added in step 3 (page 116), draw all along the guidelines using short ticks. This adds the smaller feathers found on the underwing. Then draw a few more ticks and dashes in the space between the top of the wings nearest the body and the arm lines.

Erase your pencil lines.

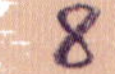

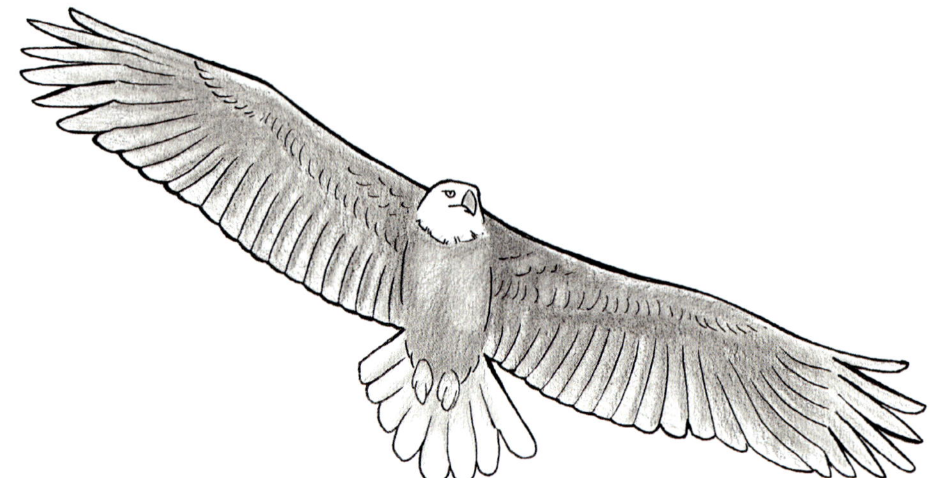

Step 8: Shade your eagle (optional).

With a lighter pencil, fill in the entirety of the bird, leaving the head and tail blank. Bald eagles are mostly dark brown, except for their white head and tail. Lightly add a bit of shadow between the tail feathers where they meet the body, but make it very faint.

Add shadow for depth with a darker pencil. Shade in the sections of the wings closest to the body and along the arm shapes. Then shade between each of the wing feathers, leaving the section of the feathers on the side of the body slightly paler. Within the main body, darken the edge below the head feathers. Also, darken the bottom of the body oval. Add narrow, darker sections along the left end to the right of the body shape and directly up the middle for the chest.

Finally, for a smoother finish, blend the pencil shading with your finger or a tissue.

A Word on Wings

As I mentioned at the beginning of this chapter, birds come in a variety of shapes and sizes. I also mentioned their wings and how they differ depending on what they're used for. For this final section of the chapter, I will show you three mini-tutorials with variations of flying birds that you can draw: the gull, pigeon and cardinal.

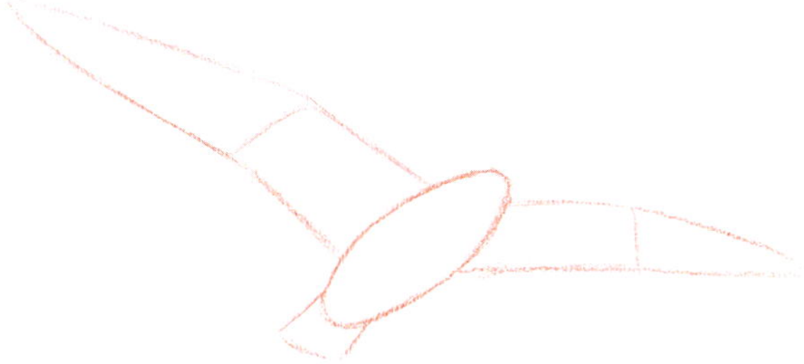

THE GULL

Gull wings are quite different from an eagle's. The eagle has long, thin and separate wing tip feathers, while the gull's wing tip feathers gather to a point. Gull wings are also much narrower and appear like the wings of a plane in that they're slender and aerodynamic. Keep this in mind as you adapt the Eagle in Flight tutorial (page 114) to draw the gull.

To draw a gull, start with the slender oval for the body like step 1 of the Eagle in Flight tutorial. Tilt the oval between the two o'clock and eight o'clock direction, and make the oval three times as long as it is wide.

Add the tail shape, again like step 1 of Eagle in Flight, but this time, make it narrow for the gull. The gull's tail should be closer to rectangular. The tail of the gull should be short too, with the middle of the tail shape only one-eighth of the length of the body oval away from the bottom end of the body.

Draw the wing shapes by adding the sections closest to the body, like in step 2 (page 115) of Eagle in Flight. For the left wing of the gull, draw two parallel lines in the ten o'clock direction from the left edge, one-quarter from the bottom end of the body oval and one-quarter from the top end of the body oval. Make these lines three-quarters the length of the body oval. Draw a line between the two ends to finish the left wing. The right wing, due to perspective, will appear narrower than the left wing. Draw two parallel lines in the three o'clock direction—one that is one-eighth of the way down from the top of the body, and the other halfway up from the bottom end of the body. Make the top line half the length of the body oval and the bottom line three-quarters the length of the body. Draw a line to connect the two ends.

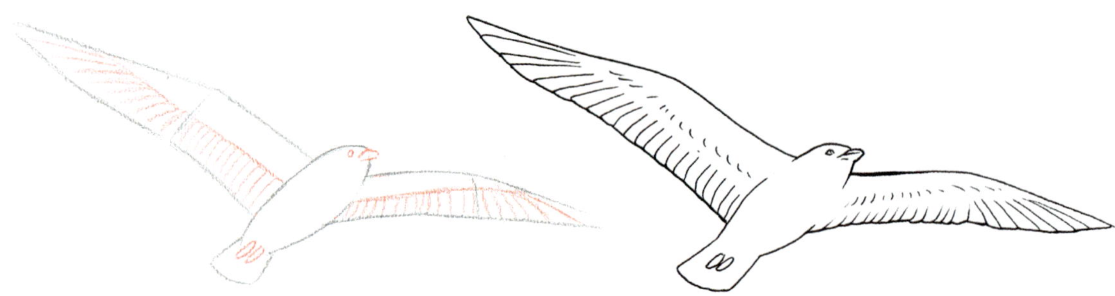

Draw the wing tips by adding triangle shapes at the end of the base wing shapes just drawn. For the left wing, continue the bottom edge of the base wing shape, just shy of ten o'clock, which will create a soft angle for the joint. Make this line one and a quarter times as long as the body shape. Draw the top edge of the wing tip by connecting the end of the lower line of the wing tip to the top left corner of the base wing shape. Add the triangle for the right wing shape by continuing the bottom line for the base wing shape in the three o'clock direction. Make the bottom line of the right wing tip shape two-thirds the length of the body oval. Connect the end of the bottom line for the right wing tip to the top right corner of the base wing shape, forming the wing tip triangle.

Draw the beak, eye, and feet. Add the beak by drawing a small triangle at the very top end of the body oval. Then add a tiny oval just to the left of the beak triangle. For the feet, add two tiny ovals side by side on the bottom edge of the main body oval, between the points where the tail lines connect to the body. Make them the same size as the beak triangle.

Create the gull's arm shape by drawing a line that runs through the horizontal middle of the base wing shapes to the top edge of the wing tip triangles. On the left wing, draw the arm line until it meets the middle of the top edge of the left wing tip triangle. For the right arm, draw it until it's one-third of the way along from the top right corner of the base wing shape.

Add the feather shapes. For the base wing shapes, draw all of the feathers from the bottom edge pointing towards the top edge. For the wing tips, draw from the bottom edge of the wing triangles and point them towards the joint of the wing at the top corner of the wing tip triangle.

Draw the outline. Make sure to add an undulating line along the bottom edges of the wings to add a bit of definition to each of the flight feathers. Also, along the gull's arm shapes, draw little ticks for the smaller under-wing feathers.

THE PIGEON

Pigeon wings are also slender and come to a point like a gull's, but aren't quite as long. So, you can draw their wings in one long shape rather than the two separate shapes used for the Eagle in Flight (page 114) and The Gull (page 121). Using these two tutorials as a guide, it's time to draw a pigeon.

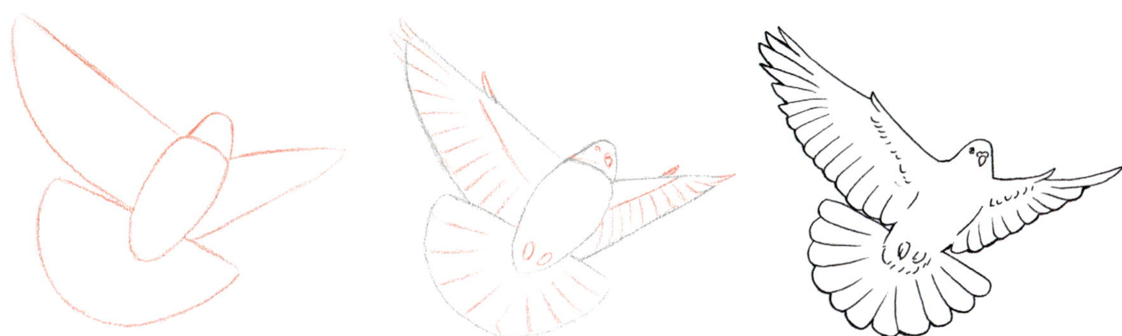

Draw an oval-like shape for the body. The pigeon's body oval will be flattened at the top end and tilted between the one o'clock and seven o'clock directions. The body shape should be twice as long as it is wide.

Draw an upside-down "U" shape on the flattened top end of the body oval to create the head. This shape should be as wide at the base as it is tall.

Add the tail by creating a semicircle shape at the bottom end of the body oval. The flat edges of the semicircle should start one-third of the way up from the bottom end of the body oval. The left edge should point towards ten o'clock, and the right edge should point towards four o'clock. Make the left line a little longer than the width of the body oval, and the right line the same width as the body oval. Connect the two ends of the lines with a large "U" shape to finish the tail semicircle.

Drawing the wings will start with two sideways "V" shapes that attach to the sides of the body oval between the head and the tail shape. For the left wing, draw the top edge of the sideways "V" from where the left of the head "U" meets the body. Draw between a ten o'clock and eleven o'clock direction and make the line the same as the distance between the top of the head shape and the base of the "U" for the tail shape. Draw the bottom edge of the left wing "V" as a gentle curve from the end of the top edge down to where the top left of the tail meets the body. For the right wing, draw the top of the "V" just above the three o'clock direction from the base of the head shape, making the line two-thirds as long as the top line of the left wing. Connect the end of the top line for the right wing down in a straight line to where the top right of the tail meets the body.

Draw the arm shapes by adding a diagonal line from the main body to the top edge of the wing shapes. For the left wing, draw the line from the middle of where the left wing "V" meets the body to the middle of the top wing line. For the right wing, draw from one-third of the way down from where the top of the "V" meets the body and draw just to the right of the middle of the top of the wing "V."

Draw the feathers, starting with the "thumb" feathers and wing tip feathers. For the "thumb" feathers, draw two inverted "V"s along the top edge of the wing shapes. The left "thumb" feather should sit just right of where the arm line meets the top of the wing and point in an eleven o'clock direction. The right "thumb" feather should sit just left of where the arm meets the top of the wing and point in a two o'clock direction.

On the left wing, draw two or three tiny sideways "V"s that are no bigger than the "thumb" feather shape, pointing between a ten o'clock and eleven o'clock direction. They should sit on the bottom line of the wing, just below where the bottom line meets the top line. For the right wing, draw one tiny "V" shape pointed in a three o'clock direction for the wing tip feather. All along the bottom edge of the wing shapes, draw the lines for the feathers. The four feather lines closest to the ends of the wings should point toward the "thumb" feathers. The rest should point towards the top edge of the wing shape.

Add the feathers for the tail by drawing a series of equally spaced lines that run from the "U" edge of the tail towards the body. The feathers should therefore appear wider at the tip and narrower as they get closer to the body.

Draw two tiny almond shapes for the feet below the top left and top right edges of the tail shape. Make sure the feet ovals point towards nearly the bottom end of the body "U." Then add a tiny circle for the eye just left of the middle of the head "U" shape, and a tiny, inverted triangle for the beak in the right half of the head "U."

Draw the outline. Add the nostrils by drawing a small "3" shape lying on its side above the beak triangle. Also, when drawing along the edges of both the wing feathers and tail feathers, add an undulating line that connects each of the individual feather lines. This will give some rounded definition for tips of each of the feathers.

THE CARDINAL

We started this chapter with a cardinal perching in a tree, so we will end with a cardinal in flight. Their wings are short compared to their body, so bear this in mind for the proportions. They're also quite rounded compared to the other wings we've drawn so far. Like The Pigeon tutorial (page 122), you can draw the base shape of the cardinal's wing with one shape.

Start with the main body oval, with a slightly flattened top edge. The width of the body oval should be two-thirds its length and should tilt between the two o'clock and eight o'clock directions. On the top edge of the body oval shape, add an inverted "U" shape, which should be half the size of the body oval.

Draw the tail shape. This shape will be similar to the tail in Eagle in Flight (page 114), but proportionally larger. Start with two lines leaving the bottom end of the body oval shape, one-quarter of the way from the bottom. The left edge of the tail should point just below the nine o'clock direction and be as long as the cardinal's body oval. The right edge of the tail should point just left of the six o'clock mark and be two-thirds the length of the left edge. Join the ends of the left and right edge of the tail with a gentle curve.

Draw the wings by adding a pair of sideways "U" shapes between the head and tail shapes. The left wing "U" shape should be twice as long as it is wide and appear almost upside down. The long edges of the "U"

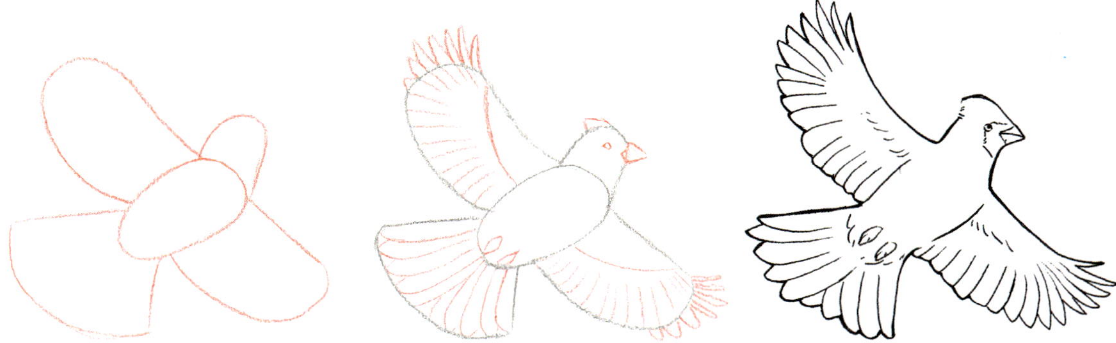

shape should be parallel and point between the ten o'clock and eleven o'clock directions. Connect the top of the left sideways "U" to the point where the left of the head "U" meets the body. Connect the bottom of the left wing "U" to where the left edge of the tail shape meets the body. The bottom edge should be slightly curved. Draw this exact same shape mirrored for the right wing with the long edge of the "U" pointing more towards the four o'clock direction. The left edge of the right wing "U" should meet where the right of the tail shape connects to the body and the right edge of the "U" should meet where the right of the head shape meets the body.

Draw the arm shapes of the wing, starting with the left wing. Draw a curved line from the middle of where the left "U" meets the body oval up to the top edge of the "U," two-thirds of the way along from where the "U" meets the head shape. Draw the arm for the right wing, again from the middle of where the right "U" meets the body. Draw the arm line to two-thirds of the way along from where the top of the right "U" meets the head.

Add wing tip feathers, like step 4 (page 117) in Eagle in Flight. Create a series of "V" shapes along the bottom curves of both wings' "U" shapes, with the four feathers closer to the top of the wings being roughly the same size. The bottom three feathers closer to the bottom edges of the wings should get progressively smaller as they get nearer to the bottom. The feathers should point in the same direction as the wing they are connected to.

Draw the tail feathers, similar to the tail feathers from step 4 of in Eagle in Flight. Make the cardinal tail feathers more pointed at the tips. The fifth feather from the top left edge should overlap the fifth tail feather from the right.

Draw the feet by adding two oval shapes to the bottom edge of the body oval. The left leg should be centered. The right leg should be in the middle between the left leg and where the right edge of the tail meets the body.

Draw the crest, eye and beak shape. Recreate the shapes from step 2 (page 101) and step 3 (page 101) of Perching Cardinal, only on the opposite side of the head.

Outline the cardinal. Don't forget to add the mouth and mask shapes from the Perching Cardinal (page 103).

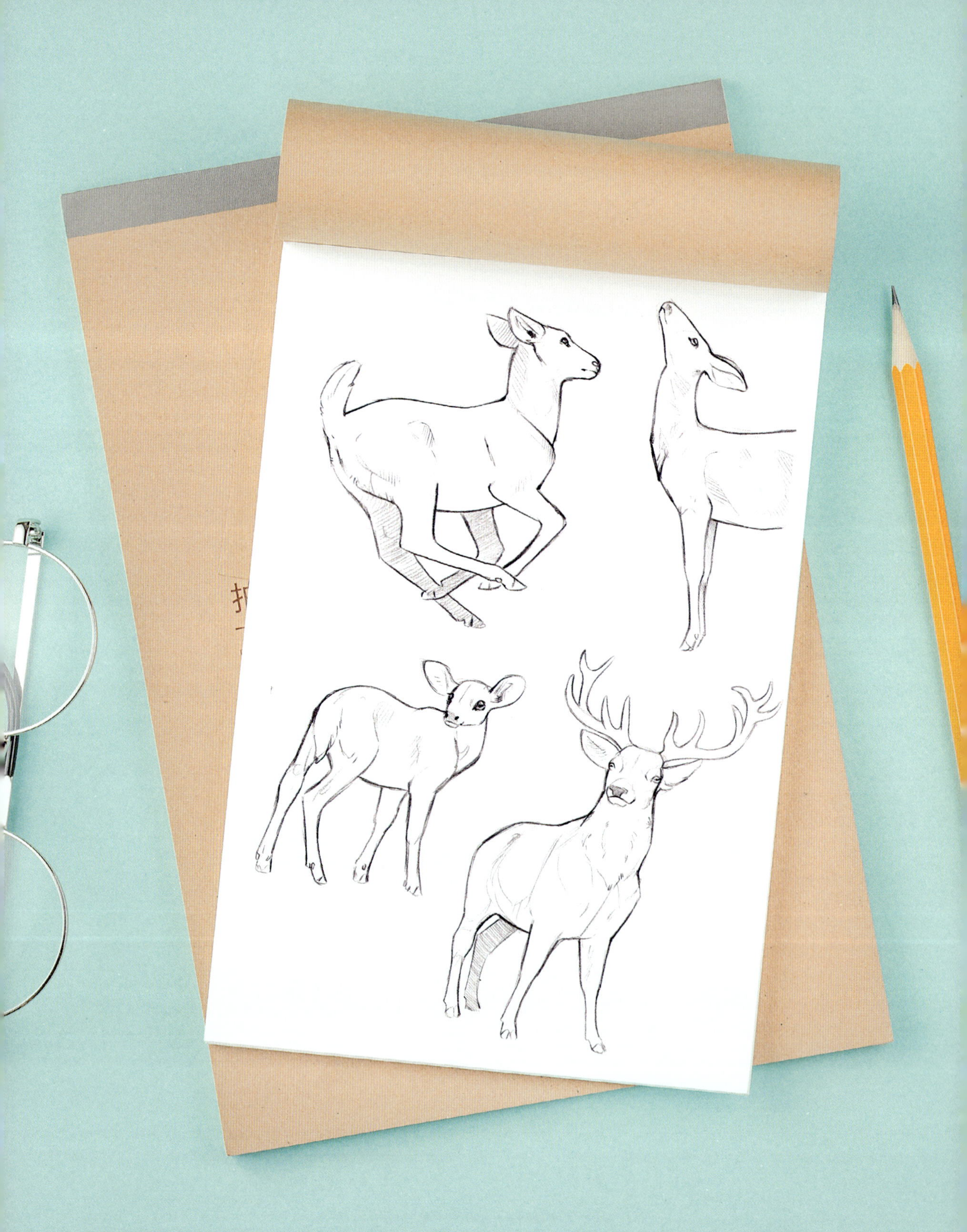

Depicting DEER

Deer are very enigmatic creatures that often attract artists to drawing them. Structurally, they are similar to horses. Their main body doesn't flex much, so a lot of their movement comes from their shoulders and limbs.

Male deer wield antlers, and that is something that will be covered with three of the four tutorials in this section. It's worth noting that antler structure can be quite complicated. When you reach these sections, go with care to follow the instructions. Antler shapes are very different for each deer species. However, although antlers within a species follow similar shapes and formats, they can look different between individual males. This means it's okay if the length of antlers, prongs or even prong count end up being different than what's in the tutorials. Nothing is perfect in nature.

Lastly, with Dainty Doe (page 142), we will draw a female deer. She won't be wielding antlers, but that doesn't mean she is any less beautiful.

WHITETAIL RUNNING

For this tutorial, we will look at a dynamic pose for the whitetail deer. This male will be mid-run, showing off the upright white tail that they are famous for. As he's alert and on the run, his head will be carried quite high, so take that into consideration. The interesting thing about the antlers here is that all of the prongs point up and forward. Plus, the prongs that grow off the main section of the antlers are all situated on the top edge.

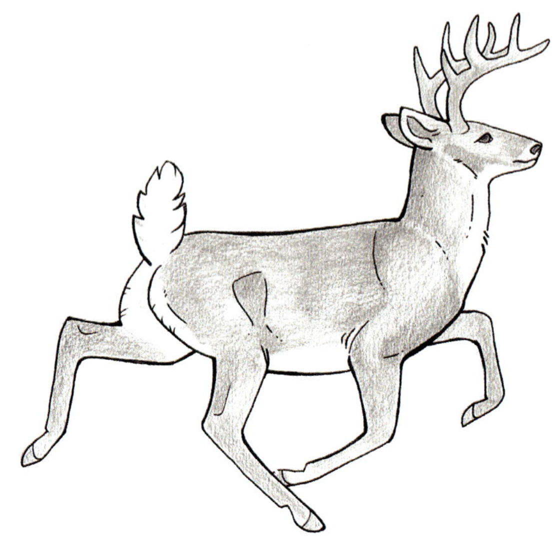

1

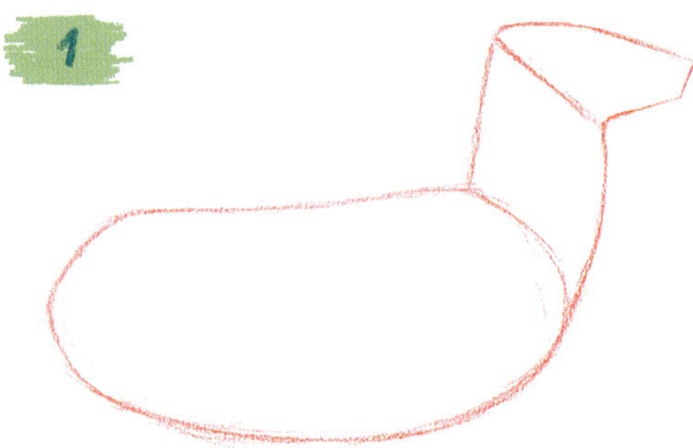

Step 1: Draw the main body, neck and head.

Draw a sausage-like shape in the middle of the page for the body. This shape should be twice as long as it is wide. If it helps with proportions, make the shape 3 inches (7.5 cm) long and 1½ inches (4 cm) tall.

Draw the neck by creating a diamond-like shape on the far right end of the main body sausage. Start with a lightly curved line that begins in the middle of the body sausage on the right edge. This will create the deer's throat. This line should be almost vertical and one-third of the length of the main body sausage. So, in this case, a little over 1 inch (2.5 cm) long. Draw the back of the deer's neck by drawing a straight line, again, 1 inch (2.5 cm) long, parallel to the throat line. This neck line should connect one-sixth of the way along the main body sausage from the right, which is ½ inch (1.3 cm) over. Connect the two top ends of the neck and throat line with a diagonal line. You'll know if you've got the shape right if this diagonal line is also 1 inch (2.5 cm) long.

To draw the head shape, start with the top edge of the head, which connects to the top corner of the neck diamond shape. Draw horizontally to the right before curving downwards slightly to where the nose will be. This line will be just over one-third the length of the main body sausage, in this case 1¼ inches (3 cm) long. Then draw the chin line by drawing up from the right corner of the neck diamond. This line should be almost half the length of the top line, ½ inch (1.3 cm) long. Connect the two right ends of the lines with a short diagonal line to finish the head shape.

Step 2: Section the main body, begin the near-side legs, draw the near-side ear and start the near-side antler.

Divide the main body into the rump, middle and shoulder sections. Draw a diagonal line that connects one-quarter from the left on the top edge of the main body sausage, in this case, ¾ inch (2 cm) along the top. Draw diagonally to the right until you're just right of the one-third mark from the left along the bottom edge of the main body sausage. For the shoulder section, start one-quarter from the right of the body sausage and draw diagonally to the left until you're just left of the two-third mark from the left along the bottom edge of the main body sausage. This should create a middle section for the main body.

Draw the upper portions of the near-side legs. Start by creating a rectangle for the back leg on the left of the drawing. This shape should be twice as tall as it is wide, in this case, ¾ inch (2 cm) tall and ⅓ inch (8 mm) wide. The right edge of the rectangle should connect to where the rump section line meets the bottom of the main body sausage. The rectangle should aim slightly diagonal to the left.

For the near-side front leg, draw a "U" with the left edge meeting where the shoulder section line meets the bottom edge of the main body sausage. The "U" shape should be the same height as the back leg rectangle and slightly to the right. The section of the "U" that attaches to the bottom of

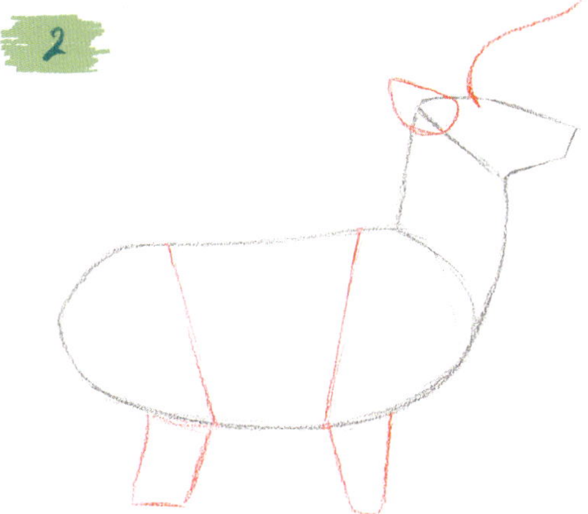

the main body sausage should be the same width as the hind leg rectangle. The bottom of the "U" should narrow to two-thirds of the width of the top.

Draw the near-side ear shape, starting with the point where the ear attaches to the head shape. For this, draw a backwards "C" shape from the top head line to where the head meets the neck shape. This "C" should meet one-third of the way along the edge of the neck shape and one-fifth along from the left of the top head line. Extend the bottom of the backwards "C" to the left until you're just past the back of the neck. Then extend the top of the backwards "C" parallel to the bottom ear line. The bottom ear line should be two-thirds the length of the top line. Connect the two left ends of the ear lines together to form the ear shape.

Start the guideline of the near-side antler by drawing a backwards "S" shape, starting one-third of the way from the left of the top head line. Start the line just below the top head line, curve initially towards the ear and then up to the right. The antler line should finish level with the nose of the deer.

Step 3: Add the far-side rump, the far-side legs, the far-side ear and the remainder of the near-side antler.

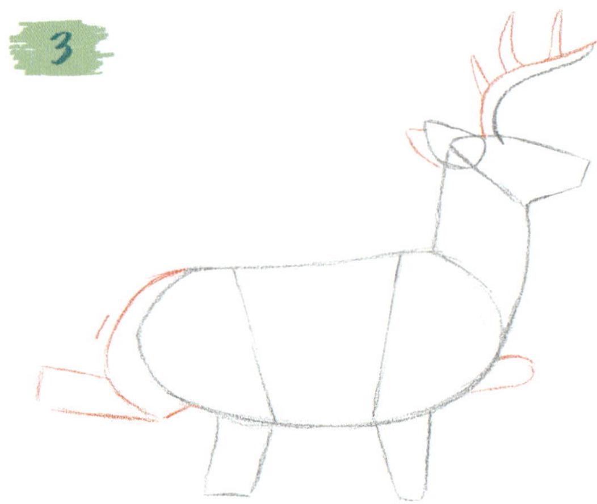

Draw the far-side rump. To do this, draw a "C" shape that connects to the top edge of the main body sausage. Draw the "C" shape around the end of the main body shape and connect it to the bottom edge of the main body sausage, just to the left of the near-side hind leg rectangle. This will create a crescent shape, forming the far-side rump shape.

Draw the upper leg section for the far-side back leg. Draw the top line of the leg out from the "C" shape you just drew, two-thirds of the way down. This line should be as long as the near-side hind leg upper portion is tall. At the left end of the line, draw down creating a 90-degree angle. Make this line as long as the near-side hind leg upper portion is wide. Finish by drawing a parallel line from the end of the previous line until it connects to the "C" shape for the rump.

Draw the far-side front leg by adding a sideways "U" shape to the right edge of the shoulder section. Begin with the bottom edge of the "U" by drawing almost horizontally to the right from a point that is two-thirds of the way between the shoulder section line and the throat line. Then when you're level with the curve of the throat line, curve the "U" shape back until you meet just below where the throat connects to the main body shape.

Draw the far-side ear by attaching a "V" shape to the left edge of the near-side ear. Start the "V" just below the top left corner of the near-side ear. Then attach the bottom of the "V" just below where the near-side ear intersects the back neck line. This should make a small triangle for the far-side ear.

Finish the near-side antler by first drawing a second "S" shape from the top head line, just to the left of the initial "S," repeating the same shape as before. Connect the two "S" shapes at the right ends to create the point of the antler. Now, along the new "S" shape, which has become the top of the antler, draw three upside-down "V" shapes for the additional points of the antler. Each point should be fairly equally spaced along the top edge of the antler and be narrower than the main section of the antler. Make the two right "V" shapes one-third the length of the main section of the antler. Make the bottom prong a little shorter than the other two.

Step 4: Draw the tail, lower sections of the legs and far-side antler.

Create a large oval shape for the tail that sits at the top of the deer's rump. This oval should be twice as tall as it is wide.

Draw the lower portions of the legs, starting with the far-side hind leg. Draw an elongated "U" shape that's four times as tall as it is wide from the end of the upper leg section of the far-side hind leg. The width of this shape should be half of the near-side hind leg upper portion. Draw this shape at 90 degrees to the far-side upper leg portion. At the end of this elongated "U" shape, draw a smaller "U" for the hoof, making it slightly narrower than the lower portion you just drew. This smaller "U" should point diagonally down and to the left and be three times as tall as it is wide.

For the near-side hind leg, add the same two "U" shapes from the bottom of the far-side hind leg lower portion. The first "U" for the lower leg portion will be a little longer than the far-side hind leg lower portion and start out a bit wider as it connects to the bottom corners of the upper portion. Create an approximate 45-degree angle to the right with this lower leg section. Attach the smaller "U" for the hoof at the same angle on the end of the previous "U" shape, again slightly narrower and three times as long as it is wide.

For the near-side front leg, draw the first "U" shape 80 degrees out and to the left from the upper leg portion. Make this "U" pretty much identical in size to the "U" drawn for the far-side hind leg. Again, add a smaller, narrower "U" at the end of the leg shape so that it overlaps the near-side hind leg.

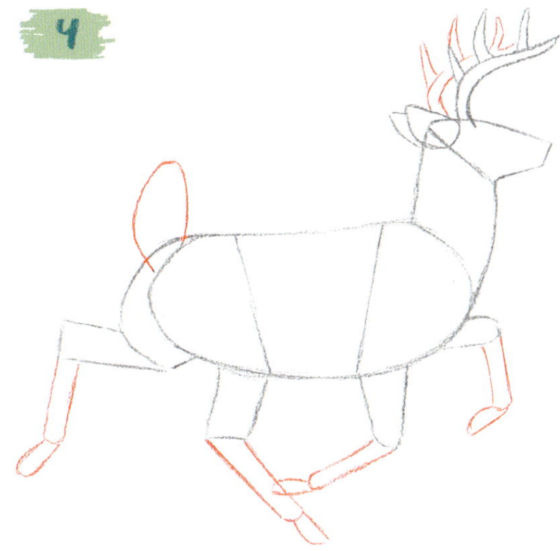

For the far-side front leg, repeat the same two "U" shapes. Have the first "U" extend at approximately 90 degrees down from the end of the upper portion. Then add the smaller "U" for the hoof at the end of the previous "U" shape, aiming down in the same direction as the lower portion of the near-side front leg.

For the far-side antler, repeat the shape you drew for the near-side antler. Start by drawing the main antler portion with the same width and curve as the antler on the near side. The bottom line will only be visible up to the left edge of the left "V" on the near-side antler. The top line of the far-side antler will disappear behind the "V"s and reappear between them. Draw three upside-down "V"s along the top edge with the two right "V"s appearing between the near-side antler prongs.

Step 5: Refine the fur of the tail and add the hooves, muscle definition and facial features.

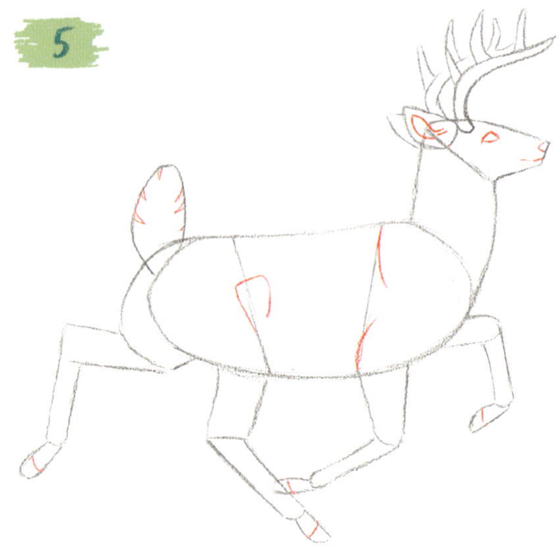

Along the top edge of the tail oval, place five to six "V" shapes to create gaps in the fur of the tail. Place them as you like.

Just below the halfway point of the hoof "U" shapes, draw a line directly across to create the toes of the hooves.

Draw some muscle definition of the main body, starting with an upside-down "U" in the middle third of the rump section line. Draw from one-third of the way up, out diagonally to the left and then curve up and over to the right. Finish by continuing the curve until you're level with the middle point of the rump section line, leaving a gap between that line and the end of the "U" just drawn.

Add some muscles for the shoulder shape by drawing two light curves along the shoulder section line in the main body sausage shape. Draw the first line down from the top, run along the shoulder section line initially and then curve in towards the shoulder shape. Do the same from the bottom of the shoulder section line. Each little curved line should be a little longer than one-third of the length of the shoulder section line.

Draw the facial features by starting with the inner ear. Draw a line on the inside of the near-side ear that runs parallel to the left and bottom edges of the ear shape. Then draw a small "S" shape from the top left of the inner ear line and connect it to the right of the top corner of the neck diamond. Draw a pair of ticks where the "S" shape meets the neck to define the fur.

Draw the eye shape by drawing an almond shape, directly level with where the throat meets the head shape. Make sure to leave a small gap between the top of the almond shape and the top head line. The almond shape should be one-eighth the length of the top head line.

Draw the nose at the right end of the head shape where it narrows for the muzzle. Draw a small "V" to create the nose shape. Connect it to just left of the top right corner of the end of the muzzle and one-third of the way down the short right line of the head shape.

Add the mouth by drawing a flattened "U" shape that starts one-third of the way up from the bottom right corner of the head shape. Extend it into the head shape, and make it three times as long as the "V" drawn for the nose shape.

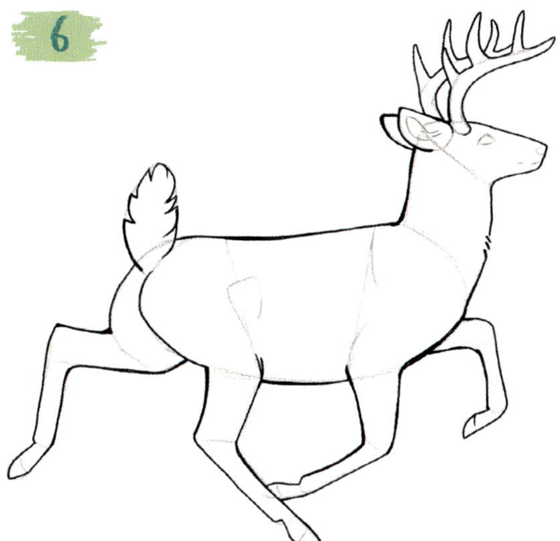

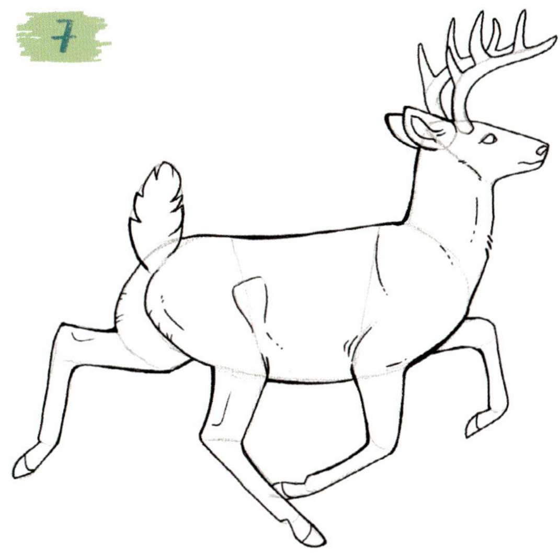

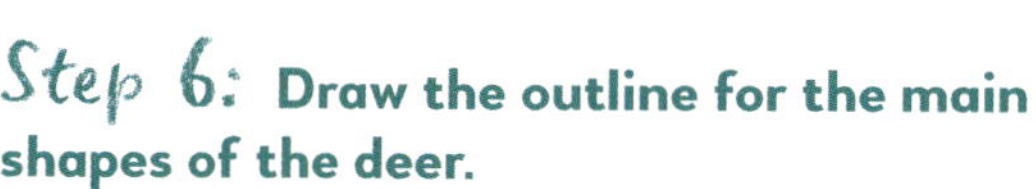

Step 6: Draw the outline for the main shapes of the deer.

With a thicker pen, draw over the outside of the antler shapes, along the ears and over the outside of the head. Leave a gap for a more seamless look where the ear connects to the head.

Draw down the throat line, adding a few ticks and apostrophes for some fur in the middle. Draw the back of the neck and extend that line along the back.

Draw over the tail and the "V"s for the fur. Leave gaps between the prongs of the "V"s for the parting of the fur.

Go over the back of the rump, drawing over the outside of the hind legs. Keep the lines smooth and curvy. When drawing the near-side hind leg, at the right edge where the upper portion meets the tummy, draw two small lines to add folds of skin at the knee point of the deer.

Draw over the bottom edge of the main body between the two near-side legs for the tummy.

Draw over the near-side front leg. Create the deer's elbow by drawing partially over the bottom curve for muscle definition. Round the right edge of the near-side front leg and draw along the bottom right of the main body sausage to create the shoulder. Draw over the far-side front leg.

Step 7: Draw the finer detail with a thinner pen.

Draw over the eye, nose, mouth and inner ear. Go over the muscle guides drawn within the main body shape. To soften the ends of this muscle definition, draw dots at the ends, instead of drawing solid lines. This makes the lines for the muscle less harsh.

Add the hooves by drawing over the hoof "U" shapes.

Add some additional definition for fur and muscle. Draw some ticks and apostrophes along the top neck line where the head sits. Also add some dots and dashes parallel to the throat and the top left edge of the main body sausage shape where the neck sits. Add some folds of skin behind the elbow on the near-side by drawing a pair of ticks to the left of the lower muscle curve line. Along the rump lines, draw some ticks pointing toward the body for extra fur. Add a line and some dots running parallel to the near-side rump line for more muscle definition. Then along the backs of the upper portions of the hind legs, draw two "J" shapes. This defines where the tendons are, creating the ankles of the deer.

Erase your pencil lines.

Step 8: Shade your drawing (optional).

With your lighter pencil, fill in the entire deer, but leave the white markings blank. The white areas are as follows: the tail, which gives this species of deer its name; the crescent space of the far-side rump shape; along the edge of the rump; along the tummy between the two near-side legs; and along the throat and bottom of the head shape.

Darken the eye and the nose completely. Deer eyes are very dark, so this shape can be almost black.

Add some shadows using either your lighter pencil again or a darker pencil. Whitetail deer are quite light in color, so the shadows don't need to be too dark. Good places to shade are along the back of the neck, the top of the shoulders and along the back. Shade within the upside-down "U" drawn for the muscle definition on the rump section line. You can also add light shading in the bottom of the shoulder shape.

For a smoother finish, blend the pencil together using your finger or a tissue.

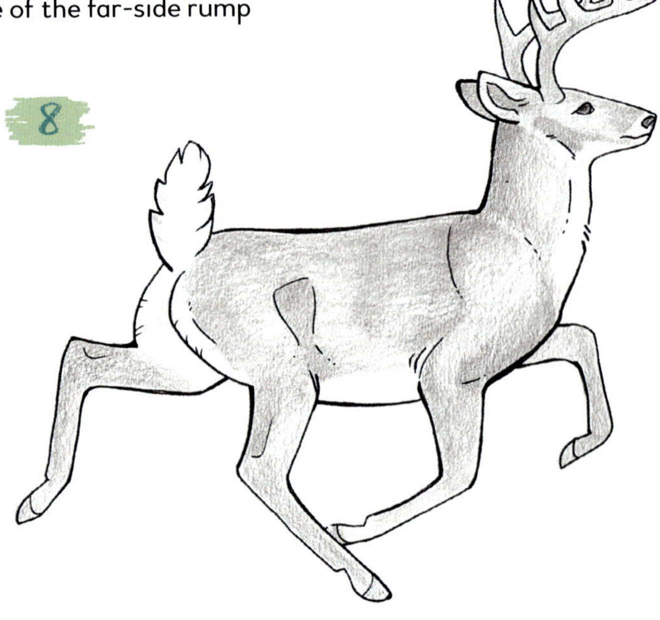

MALE MOOSE

Unlike other deer species who have thin antlers that branch out like sticks, moose antlers are more like shields with slender prongs along the outside edge. To help you better understand the proportions of a moose, it's worth noting that they are quite stocky. So, their bodies are fairly short in length and are very tall at the shoulder. This is for the neck muscles that support the heavy antlers. These animals also tend to be fairly steady going, so I've opted for a nice stationery pose to allow you to capture their lumbering personality.

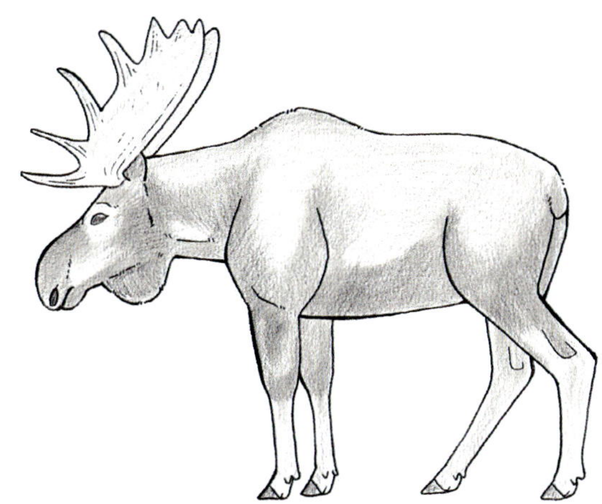

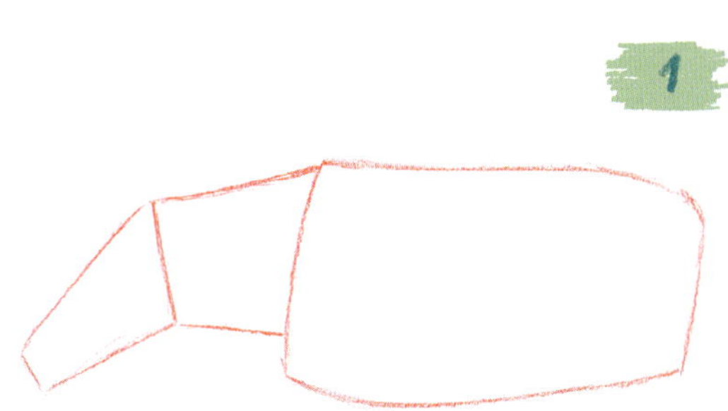

Step 1: Start with the body, neck and head of the moose.

Draw a large rectangle for the body. Place it just right of the center of your page. This shape should be twice as long as it is tall. For the long edges of the shape, make them ever so slightly curved rather than straight. Make the top line curve down one-third of the way from the short edge. Make the bottom line curve upwards one-third of the way from the short edge.

Draw the neck by adding two lines to the left of the body rectangle. Draw the throat line one-sixth of the way up on the left short edge of the body rectangle. Make it completely horizontal and one-quarter as long as the long edge of the main body rectangle. Draw the top neck line by attaching it to the top left corner of the body rectangle and draw slightly diagonally downwards, just between the eight o'clock and nine o'clock direction. Make this line a bit over one-third the length of the long edge of the body rectangle. This should make the neck narrow towards where the head will go.

Draw the head by first connecting the two ends of the neck lines you just drew. This line should be the same length as the throat line. Add the top line for the head by drawing from the top left corner of the neck shape. This line will be the same length as the top neck line. Angle it down to the left between the eight o'clock and seven o'clock direction. Add the bottom head line by drawing from the bottom left corner of the neck shape. Aim this line towards the eight o'clock direction and make it a little shorter than the top head line. Connect the two ends with a short line.

Step 2: Begin the near-side antler and the legs.

For the base of the near-side antler, draw a large diagonal oval along the top edge of the head shape. The bottom end of the oval should align with the top one-third of the top head line. This oval should then extend to the right over the neck shape with three-quarters of the shape positioned away from the head. This oval should be four times as long as it is wide.

Draw the upper portions of the legs, beginning with the near-side foreleg. Draw a "U" shape with the left edge of the "U" starting at the bottom left corner of the body rectangle. This "U" should be two-thirds the length of the short edges of the body rectangle and twice as tall as it is wide.

Draw the far-side foreleg by drawing a "J" shape to the right of the previous "U." Make the long edge of the "J" the same length as the height of the "U." As the "J" is the far-side foreleg, the left edge is hidden behind the other leg. As a result, make the inside space of the far-side leg three-quarters the width of the near-side foreleg.

Draw the near-side hind leg by adding a tilted "U" shape to the right end of the body rectangle. Make the upper portion

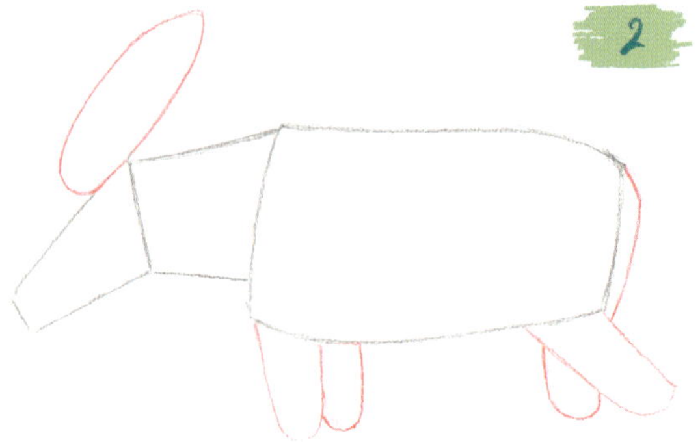

tilt towards the four o'clock direction. This "U" shape will be a fraction wider than the near-side foreleg and one-quarter longer. With this "U" tilted and a little longer than the foreleg "U," both bottoms of the two "U" shapes will actually be level.

Add the far-side hind leg, starting with the rump. Draw a curved line that starts at the top right corner of the body rectangle and runs almost parallel to the short edge of the body rectangle. End the curved line for the rump when it meets the back or right edge of the near-side hind leg "U" shape, one-eighth of the way along from where the "U" meets the main body.

To create the upper portion of the far-side leg, add a backwards "J" shape on the front or left edge of the near-side hind leg "U." Start the long edge of the backwards "J" one-fifth of the way down along the near-side "U" shape. Make the curve of the "J" run level with the bottom edges of the upper leg portions already drawn, and then connect the short end of the "J" one-third of the way up from the end of the near-side hind leg "U" shape.

Step 3: Add the antler prongs, nose structure, dewlap and shoulder ridge.

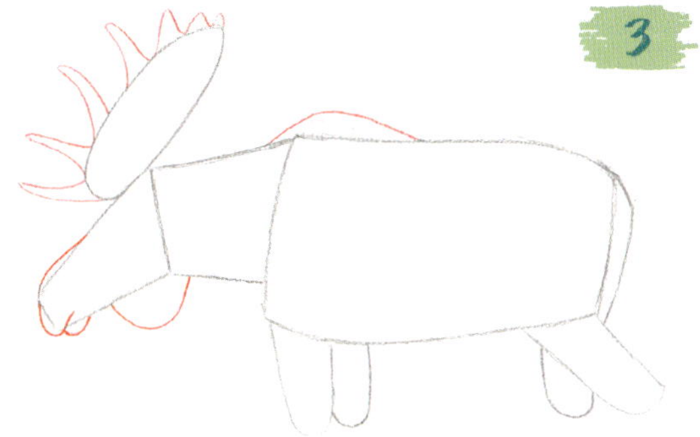

Start with the antler prongs by drawing seven inverted "V" shapes that run along the top edge of the antler oval. Begin the first prong at the bottom by drawing a "V" that's lying horizontally at the bottom of the oval. The length of this prong should be one-third of the length of the antler oval. The prongs of the "V" should be fairly narrow at one-quarter apart as the "V" is long.

Draw the second and third prongs immediately next to the first one. This should look like three inverted "V"s all connected at the points where the "V"s meet the main oval of the antler. Make the second and third prongs the same size as the first with the second prong pointing a little above the nine o'clock direction and the third prong more towards the eleven o'clock direction.

Draw the remaining prongs, leaving a gap of one-eighth the size of the antler oval between the third and fourth prongs. The fourth prong should be a little wider and shorter than the previous three prongs and also pointing in the eleven o'clock direction. For the fifth, sixth and seventh prongs, draw three inverted "V" shapes, each getting progressively smaller. These smaller prongs should all point towards the twelve o'clock mark, and the points of the "V" should all be level with each other.

For the dome of the bridge of the nose, draw a curved line that starts in the middle of the top head line and connects to the top left corner of the head shape. This dome shouldn't be too high and it should create a shape that looks like a slender willow leaf.

Add the end of the proboscis, which is the name for the droopy nostrils that moose have. Do this by drawing a small "U" at the short edge of the head shape. Start in the top left corner of the head shape and curve around and up through the bottom left corner of the head shape. This will create a mouth shape as well.

Draw the chin by adding a second "U" to the right of the proboscis "U." Have the curve of the chin "U" slightly lower than the curve of the proboscis "U."

Draw the dewlap, which is the flap of skin that hangs below the moose's jaw. This will be a larger "U" shape starting halfway along the bottom line of the head shape and connecting one-fifth of the way along the throat line. The bottom of this "U" should be level with the bottom of the chin "U."

Add the shoulder ridge by drawing an arched curve line from four-fifths of the way along the top neck line to one-third along the top edge of the body rectangle. The peak of this arch should be one-twelfth of the way along the top edge of the main body rectangle and the height should be one-fifth of the length of the ridge.

Step 4: Draw the eye, nostril, near-side antler attachment point, far-side antler and lower leg shapes.

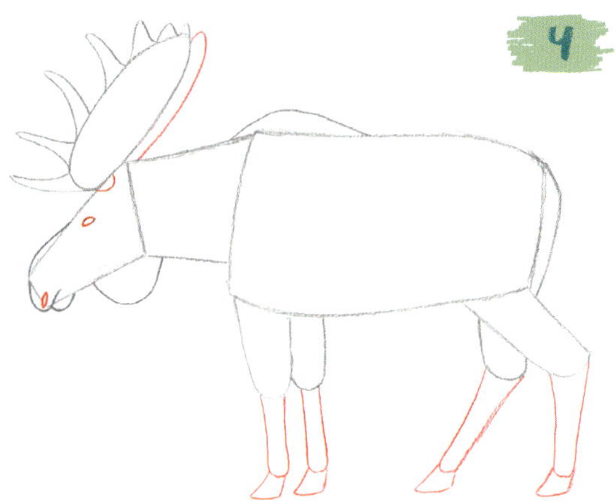

Start with the eye and nostril by drawing two almond shapes in the moose's head. The left end of the eye almond shape should be below the center point of the top head line, and the right end of the eye almond should be in line with the point where the main antler oval meets the top head line. For the nostril almond, draw a shape narrower than the eye almond in the middle of the proboscis "U."

Add the attachment point for the near-side antler. This is a little "U" shape. The left of the "U" should meet where the antler oval meets the head line. The right of the "U" should connect halfway between left of the "U" and the top right corner of the head shape. Make sure the "U" is half as tall as it is wide.

Draw the far-side antler by drawing an upside-down "J" that starts at the top of the near-side antler oval. Draw the long edge of the tick parallel to the bottom edge of the near-side antler oval until it meets with the top neck line.

Draw the lower leg portions, starting with the forelegs. Begin with a "U" shape on the end of the upper portion of the near-side foreleg that is the same length and half the width of the upper portion. At the bottom end of the lower "U," add the hoof shape by drawing first a "V" shape with the left edge angled towards the eight o'clock direction and the right edge horizontally flush with the ground. Then draw a short line that connects the end of the horizontal edge of the "V" to the end of the right line of the lower leg "U." The hoof shape should be one-third the height of the lower portion of the foreleg "U" shape. Repeat this "U" and hoof shape for the far-side foreleg.

For the lower portion of far-side hind leg, draw a narrow "U" shape that's the same length and half the width of the "U" drawn for the upper portion. Have this section of the leg aimed down towards the seven o'clock direction. Add the same hoof shape that you drew for the forelegs.

For the near-side hind leg, draw the same sized "U" as the lower portion of the far-side hind leg. This time, angle the end of the "U" towards the six o'clock direction. Add the hoof shape as before.

Step 5: Draw the ear base, shoulder base, knee, tail and hoof details.

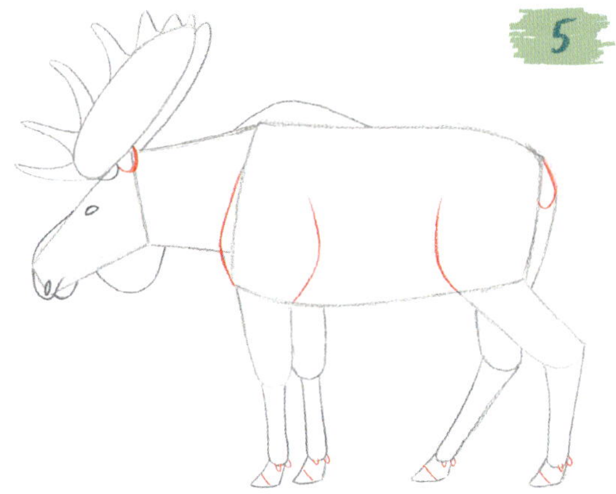

For the base of the ear, draw a "U" shape to the right of where the antler attachment "U" sits. The ear "U" should be the same width as the antler attachment point, but slightly bigger, and connect one-third of the way along the antler oval.

Define the shoulders by drawing two curves opposite each other that are attached to the top of the "U" drawn for the upper portion of the near-side foreleg. Start the left curve at the bottom left corner of the body rectangle and connect one-third of the way down along the right short edge of the body rectangle. Create a long and slender willow leaf-like shape. For the back of the shoulder, mirror the previous curved line. Start it at the right edge where the upper leg meets the bottom long edge of the body rectangle. Make this line a fraction shorter than the previous curve.

Draw a curve for the knee. Start the curve at the point where the left edge of the near-side hind leg meets the bottom long edge of the body rectangle. This curve should be the same as the first shoulder curve but as long as the second shoulder curve.

Draw the tail by creating a small teardrop shape at the right end of the body rectangle. Start the tip of the teardrop at the top right corner of the body rectangle, draw partially over the top one-quarter of the far-side rump line. Then draw the curve of the teardrop until you meet one-third of the way down along the right edge of the main body rectangle.

For the hooves, add the dewclaws and hoof nail section. You will repeat this process for all four hooves. Start with the near-side foreleg by creating the nail section of the hoof. Do this by drawing a diagonal line from halfway along the left edge of the hoof "V" to halfway along the horizontal edge of the "V." For the dewclaws, draw two tiny "U" shapes, one in the middle of the curve of the lower leg "U," and one just above where the right of the hoof shape meets the lower leg "U." Repeat for the remaining legs.

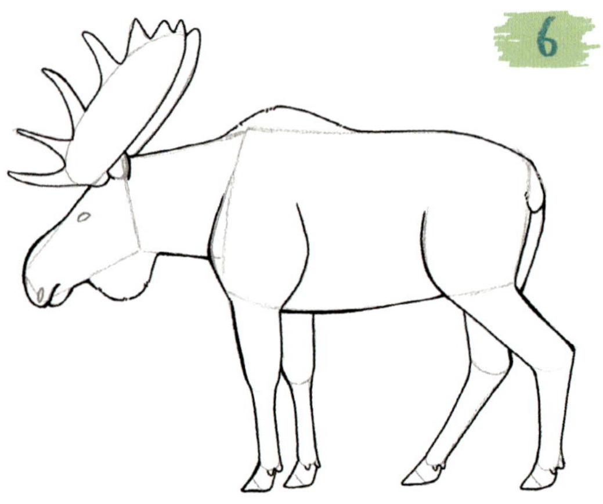

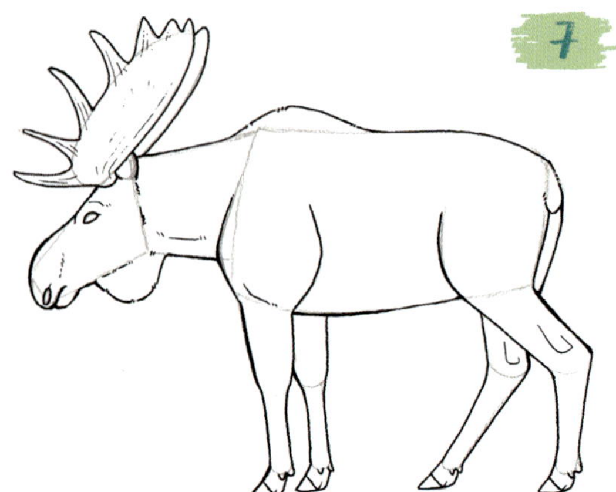

Step 6: With a thicker pen, begin drawing the outline of the moose.

Start with the moose's head. Draw down from the base of the antler, over the bridge of the nose and down over the proboscis and mouth.

Draw over the antler shapes. Go over the "U" attachment point of the antler, along the bottom edge of the oval and over each of the prongs on the near-side antler. Draw over the far-side antler tick shape and then the ear, leaving the bottom of the ear "U" blank to soften the look.

Draw over the top edge of the neck, over the shoulder ridge and along the moose's back. Over the shoulder ridge, break the outline up slightly with some apostrophe marks for the fur. Go over the tail, also breaking up the line to add some fur. Then draw over the rump and down the back of the near-side hind leg. Draw over the tiny "U"s for the dewclaws, along the outside of the hoof and up the front of the leg and the knee curve. Repeat for the far-side hind leg.

Draw over the bottom edge of the body rectangle to create the tummy. Then draw over the forelegs, repeating the process you did for the hind legs. Last, draw along the shoulder curves and over the throat line and then complete the dewlap. Break the line up with apostrophe marks for fur.

Step 7: With a thinner pen, add the finer details.

Draw over the eye almonds. Add definition to the face by doing a row of dots to frame the proboscis. Draw these dots from between the nostril and the mouth shapes, aiming up towards the center of the top of the moose's head. Also add the eyebrow ridge by doing a curved line that runs over the eye almond at the same distance as the eye is to the top of the moose's head.

Add some fur definition along the bottom and right edge of the head shape where they meet the dewlap and neck. Draw a series of small ticks and apostrophes. This creates definition but keeps the look soft.

Add some fur to the lower section of the neck. One-fifth of the way up from the throat line, draw a short line with a set of quotation marks at each end. This again softens the line and adds fur definition.

Draw some ridges along the near-side antler. Run a few very faint broken lines parallel to the bottom edge of the antler oval. Also draw a few lines within each of the prongs to create ridges. Less is more here.

Add a bit of muscle definition to the shoulder shape. Along the section of body rectangle that sits between the shoulder curve lines, draw a tick and set of quotation marks for soft muscle definition.

Draw the recess of the tendons on the hind legs by adding two "U" shapes within the bottom half of the upper "U" shapes. Add one for each leg. These "U" shapes should be taller on the left than the right, and the edges should run parallel with the right edges of the upper leg "U" shapes.

Finish the hooves by drawing over the short diagonal line added for the hoof toe sections. Add a small tick mark that points upwards where the diagonal line meets the horizontal edge of the "V." This will create a tiny backwards "J" shape, creating the definition between the moose's toes. Repeat for all four hooves.

Erase your pencil lines.

Step 8: Shade your moose (optional).

With your lighter pencil, fill in the entirety of your moose.

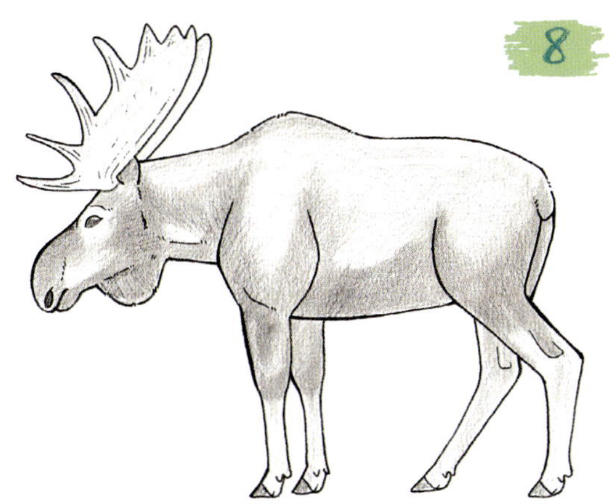

8

Go over the areas for the shadows and markings with either the light or dark pencil. Leave the sections of the leg below the moose's joints light, and only add darker areas to the hooves. This is because the lower sections of moose legs are typically pale.

Add shadow to the snout. Shade in over the proboscis and chin, along the bottom edge of the head shape and up around the right edge for the cheek. Darken the nostrils, eye and ear shape.

Shade the dewlap and lower edge of the neck shape, and add a band of shadow along the horizontal middle of the neck shape. Leave the top edge and just above the neck fur definition lighter to add depth to the neck muscles.

Add shadow along the shoulder curves and upper portion of all of the legs. Also add shadow along the tummy, knees and rump curves. Leave the top edge of the moose lighter, as well as the middle sections of the shoulder, tummy and thigh.

For a smoother finish, blend your shading using your finger or a tissue.

DAINTY DOE

Female deer are often smaller and can appear slenderer, especially around the neck. They don't need as much muscle strength as males need to support antlers, so take that into consideration. This tutorial could be used for a wide variety of deer species, as does tend to look pretty similar no matter what. An interesting thing to note is that as this doe is standing still, the pose shows off how a deer's back legs are often longer than their front ones. This causes their rump to be much higher than their shoulders.

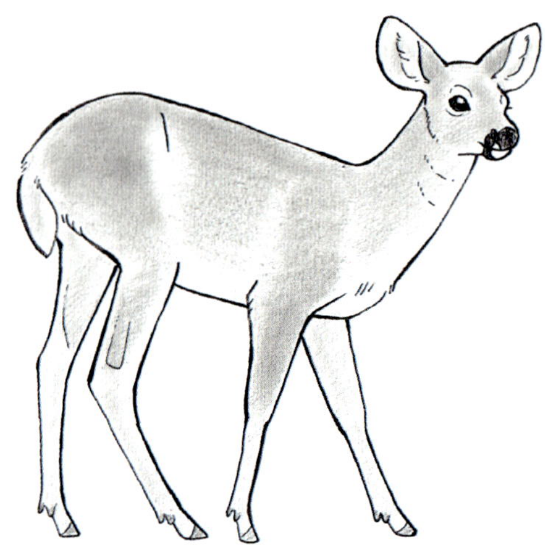

1

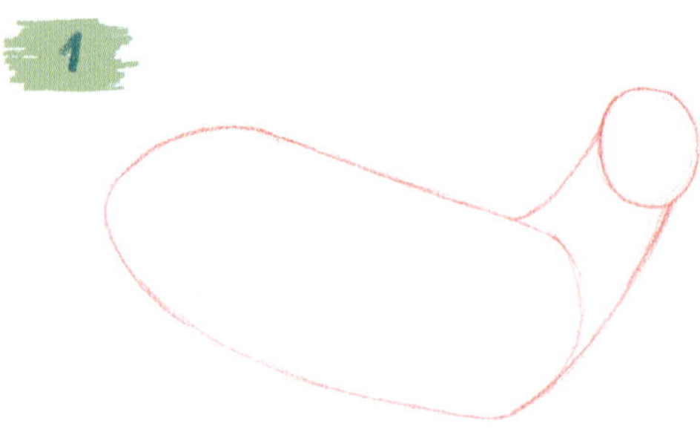

Step 1: Draw the main body, head and neck.

For the main body shape place a rounded rectangle or sausage-like shape in the middle of your page. This shape should be tilted with the left end pointing towards the ten o'clock direction and the right end more towards the four o'clock direction. For the left end of the shape, make it rounded like the end of a sausage. For the right end, make it a little flatter with rounded top and bottom corners. This will make the right edge a curve, the middle of the curve slightly farther to the right than the corners of the main shape. This shape should be twice as long as it is tall, so as a good guide, make the shape 3 inches (7.5 cm) long from end to end and 1½ inches (4 cm) tall.

Add the head by drawing an oval to the right of the main body shape. For proportions, if the body is 3 inches (7.5 cm) long, make the head ⅔ inch (1.7 cm) wide and ¾ inch (2 cm) tall. Place the head oval with the bottom edge just above level with the top right corner of the main body shape and the left edge of the head oval just to the right of level with the middle of the curve of the right edge of the main body shape.

Draw the neck by attaching the head oval to the main body shape with two lightly curved lines. For the top line of the neck, attach it just above the nine o'clock mark on the head oval. Curve it down in a seven o'clock direction and meet the top edge of the main body shape one-sixth of the way along, ½ inch (1.3 cm) from the middle curve of the right edge. For the bottom line of the neck, start it just right of the six o'clock mark of the head oval. Curve it down in a seven o'clock direction until you meet the right edge just below the middle. This lower neck line should run smoothly into the lower curve of the right edge of the main body shape.

Step 2: Draw the ears, muzzle, shoulder and thigh shape.

Draw the ears by adding two inverted shapes that are a cross between a "U" and a "V." The length of the ears should be almost the same as the width of the head oval. Attach the left ear with the right edge leaving the eleven o'clock mark of the head oval and the left edge leaving where the top neck line meets the head oval. The right line should be almost straight and aimed up to the left in a ten o'clock direction. The bottom should be curved with the one-third closest to the head being almost horizontal before curving up to meet the end of the top line. For the right ear, draw the opposite shape of the left ear with the left edge leaving from the one o'clock mark and the bottom edge leaving from the two o'clock mark.

Draw the muzzle by adding a smaller oval at the bottom right of the head oval. The muzzle oval should be one-quarter the size of the head oval. The muzzle oval should overlap the head oval with the twelve

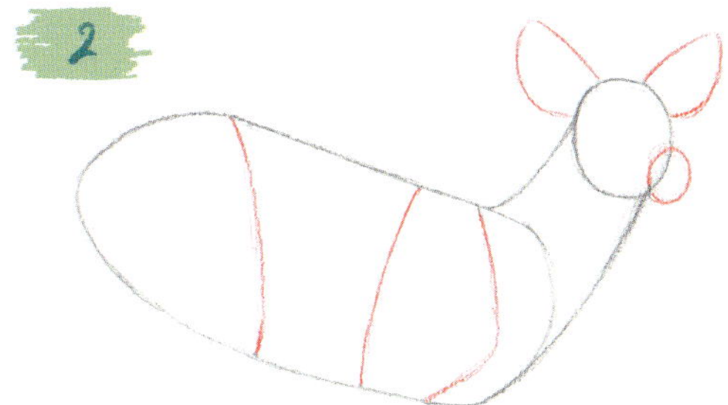

o'clock of the muzzle oval sitting on the three o'clock of the head oval. The eight o'clock of the muzzle oval should sit on the five o'clock mark of the head oval.

Start the shoulder shape by drawing a line that connects the top line of the main body shape to the bottom line. This line should connect one-third from the right on both of the long lines of the main body shape. Create the front of the shoulder by adding a curved line to the right of the first shoulder line. This line should be like a backwards "L" with the short edge of the "L" being half the length of the long edge. The bend in the "L" should be 110 degrees. Draw the top end of the backwards "L" just to the left of where the top neck line meets the main body shape. Make the bend of the "L" level with where the bottom neck line meets the main body shape. Attach the end of the short section of the backwards "L" halfway between the end of the first shoulder line and the bottom right corner of the main body shape.

Draw a line to create the thigh shape, which will then look like a guitar pick. Draw a slightly curved line from the top of the main body shape, one-quarter of the way along from the left point of the main body shape. Then, draw it to the middle of the bottom edge of the main body shape.

Step 3: Draw the facial features and start the legs.

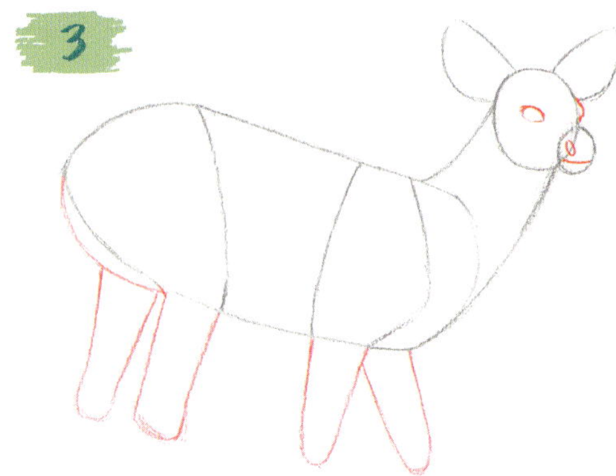

Draw the eye shapes. For the far-side eye, draw a small backwards "C" shape between the base of the right ear and the top of the muzzle oval that's twice as tall as it is wide.

Draw the near-side eye within the head oval. Create an almond shape that is the same height as the far-side eye "C" shape. Make this almond twice as wide as it is tall and place it just left of the exact center of the head oval.

Draw the nostril by placing a very small almond shape in the top quarter of the muzzle oval. Have this small almond shape tilted just shy of vertical, pointing in the eleven o'clock direction.

Add the mouth by drawing a gently curved horizontal line across the bottom quarter of the muzzle oval.

Begin the upper portions of the legs with the near-side foreleg. Draw a narrow "U" shape that is four times as tall as it is wide, narrowing at the bottom to half the width of the top. Extend the top of the "U" down from the points where the two shoulder lines meet the bottom of the main body shape. Have this "U" pointing just to the left of the six o'clock direction.

Draw the upper portion of the far-side foreleg, by repeating the "U" drawn for the near-side foreleg. This "U" shape should be the same width and length as the upper portion for the near-side "U," this time angled towards the five o'clock direction. Have the top left end of the far-side "U" meet one-sixth the way down on the right of the near-side foreleg upper portion.

Draw the near-side hind leg, by adding another "U" shape. This "U" doesn't narrow but remains the same thickness all the way down, which is the same thickness as the top of the upper portion of the near-side foreleg. Make the right edge of the near-side hind leg extend down from the point where the thigh line meets the bottom edge of the main body shape. Have this "U" pointing in the same direction as the upper portion of the near-side foreleg.

Draw the far-side hind leg, beginning with the rump. For this, draw a curved line that leaves from the very left tip of the main body shape. Curve this line down until it meets the point where the left of the upper portion of the near-side hind leg meets the main body shape. This rump shape should appear narrow, almost like a willow leaf.

Add a "U" shape for the upper portion of the far-side hind leg. This "U" should be similar to the "U"s drawn for the upper portions of the forelegs, only a little bit longer. Have this "U" point in the same direction as the upper portions of the two near-side legs. Connect this "U" to the rump line, leaving a tiny gap between it and the near-side hind leg.

Step 4: Draw the folds of the ears, the tail and the lower portions of the legs.

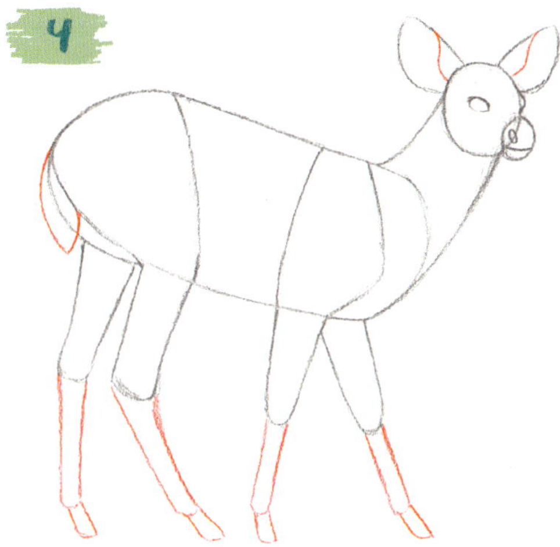

For the right ear, draw an "S" shape from the top edge down to the head oval. Start the "S" one-third of the way along from the tip of the ear. End the "S" halfway between the two points where the ear attaches to the head oval.

For the left ear, do a backwards "S" for the ear fold from the top edge of the left ear down to the middle, where the edges of the ear meet the head oval.

Draw the tail, creating a petal-like shape at the left end of the main body. Continue the curve of the left end of the body downwards to create the left edge of the tail shape. The left tail line should be an extension of the back of the animal and appear continuous in one smooth line. Draw the left line down until the end is level with where the left line of the upper portion of the near-side hind leg meets the main body shape. To finish the tail shape, draw the right side in an opposite curve until you meet the main body shape halfway between where the left tail line meets the body and the left line of the upper portion of the near-side hind leg meets the body.

Add the lower portions of the legs starting with the far-side foreleg. Add a narrow "U" shape to the bottom end of the upper portion of the leg. This "U" should be only a little shorter than the upper "U" and half the width. Point the lower "U" in the same direction as the upper "U." At the end of the lower "U," draw the hoof "U" shape. The hoof "U" should be the same width as the lower leg "U" and one-third the height. Point the hoof "U" more to the right ever so slightly. The hoof "U" will be the same for all four legs.

For the near-side foreleg, add the lower leg "U" by repeating the same size "U" drawn for the far-side leg. Have this "U" pointing in the same direction as the upper portion. Add the hoof "U," pointing a little to the right of the lower leg "U."

Add the lower portion of the near-side hind leg. The "U" shape will start wider at the top. It will then taper down the same width as the lower portions of the forelegs. Aim this "U" down towards the five o'clock direction and end level with the bottom of the "U"s drawn for the forelegs. Attach the hoof "U," pointing in the same direction as the lower "U" for the near-side hind leg.

Draw the lower leg for the far-side hind leg. This "U" will start at the bottom end of the far-side upper hind leg and continue down until level with the bottom of the lower portions of the previous three legs. It will be similar to the "U" drawn for the near-side hind leg. Add the hoof "U," pointing a little more to the right.

Step 5: Add some extra details.

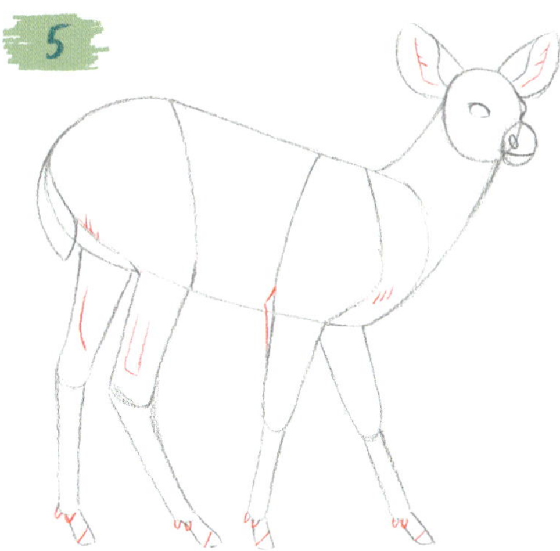

Add the inner ear fluff to the ears. Draw an "L" shape that runs centrally in the space, left of the ear fold. Then, draw little ticks off the long edge of the "L" pointing towards the ear fold. This creates fur definition. Do the mirror image for the right ear.

Add some fur just right of the reverse "L" drawn for the shoulder shape. Just below where the "L" bends, draw three small ticks side by side.

Add the elbow on the near-side foreleg by drawing an upside-down backward "L" to the left of where the upper portion of the near-side foreleg meets the left shoulder line. Draw the short edge of the "L" ⅛ inch (3 mm) up from the bottom edge of the main body shape, pointing in an eight o'clock direction. Then draw the long edge of the "L" down in a six o'clock direction until you meet the middle of the left edge on the upper portion of the near-side foreleg.

Draw some definition for the muscles and tendons on the hind legs. Add an angular "U" within the upper portion of the near-side hind leg. This "U" should be a smaller version of the upper portion of the near-side hind leg. It should be half the height and one-quarter the width, with twice as much space on the right of the small "U" as the left. The same distance on the left of the "U" should be below it too. For the far-side hind leg, draw a curved line. Position it similarly to the "U" within the near-side hind leg.

Add some fur to the near-side rump. Just below where the right edge of the tail meets the main body, add three small ticks along the line for the near-side rump.

At the bottom of the lower portions of the legs, draw the dewclaws and toe sections. Repeat this process for all four legs. Attach two tiny "U" shapes at the bottom of the lower leg "U" shapes: one on the very bottom of the left edge of the "U" and the second in the middle of the curved bottom of the "U." For the toes, draw a diagonal line across the hoof "U"s. Draw from two-thirds of the way down the right edge of the hoof "U" to the bottom left of the hoof "U."

Step 6: Draw the outline of the doe with a thicker pen.

Start with the head by going over the right eye curve and around the muzzle oval. Then when you meet the top of the throat line, draw a horizontal line along the bottom edge of the main head oval. This creates the doe's jaw.

Draw over the ear shapes, and then connect the two top edges of the ear by drawing over the section of the head oval between them. Carry on from the bottom of the left ear by drawing over the left line of the neck, over the back and down towards the tail. At the points where the tail meets the body, draw a few tick marks to indicate fur. Draw over the rest of the tail.

Draw over the outside lines of the far-side hind leg. Make sure to draw over the dewclaws. Then do the same for the near-side hind leg, making sure to draw over the ticks drawn for the fur definition. Where the right edge of the near-side hind leg meets the main body, draw only slightly over the bottom of the thigh guideline. One-eighth of the line should be enough to show where the knee of the doe is.

Draw over the tummy and elbow, adding a couple of tick marks to the long edge of the "L" added in step 5 to indicate fur. Continue down and over the near-side foreleg. Where the right of the near-side foreleg meets the shoulder shape, draw partially over the short edge of the backwards "L" added in step 2 (page 143). Draw the far-side foreleg.

Add the lower right end of the main body shape, drawing a couple of ticks where the lower neck line meets the main body. Then draw the lower neck line.

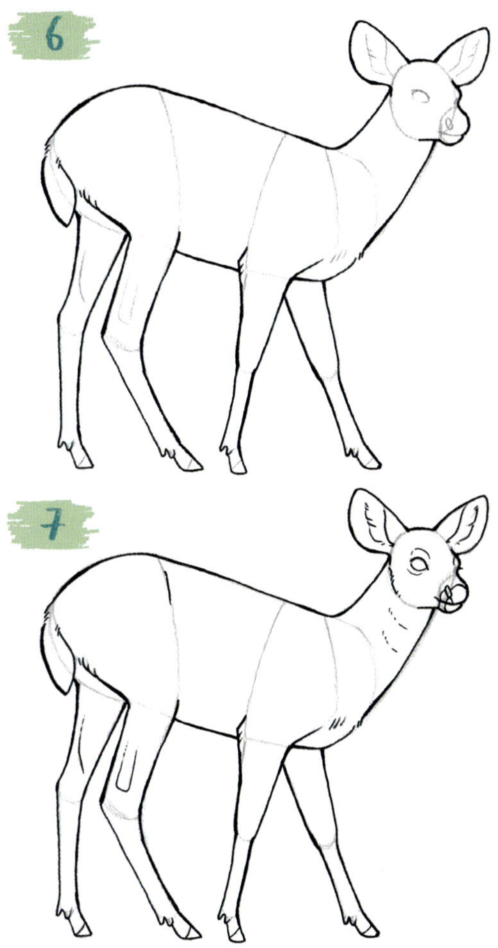

Step 7: With a thinner pen, add the details.

Draw the inner ear fur and ear folds by drawing over the ear fold "S" shapes. Then go over the inner ear fur.

Draw over the eye almond shape, and add a short line in the middle of the far-side eye curve, creating eyelashes.

Over the top and below the bottom of the eye almond, add two opposite curved lines. This emphasizes the structure of the eye. Do a similar small curve at the top of the far-side eye curve.

Along the left edge of the head oval, draw a series of ticks and apostrophes. This adds fur along the jawline.

Draw over the nostril and the mouth line. Also, add detail for the muzzle. To the left of the nostril, draw two parallel lines that run through the mouth line until they meet the lower part of the muzzle oval. Then draw a curve from the middle of the right edge of the nostril oval until you meet the right edge of the muzzle oval. Draw a little line from the bottom end of the oval to the mouth line. This forms the nose.

Along the throat, do two parallel rows of ticks and dashes for fur. They should be below the bottom left of the head oval and equally spaced. Draw over the three short ticks for the fur to the right of the shoulder curve.

Draw the toes for all of the hoof "U" shapes. Then, go over the smaller "U" and curved lines in the upper portions of the hind legs. At the tops of these shapes, make the line broken into dots to soften the look.

Erase all your pencil guidelines.

Step 8: Shade your doe (optional).

Fill in the doe with a lighter pencil. Make her slightly lighter along the bottom edge of the neck and tummy section.

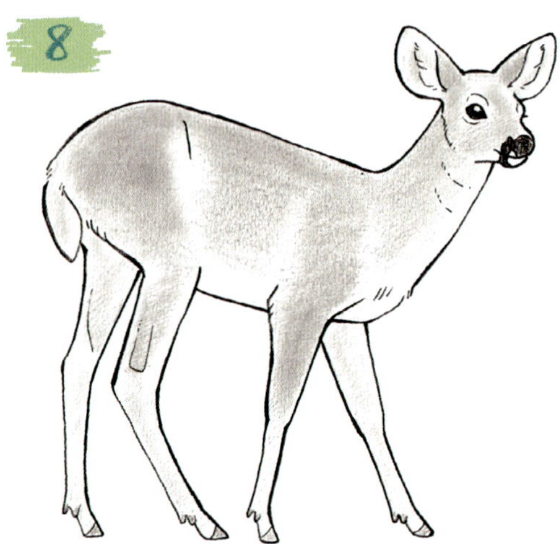

With a darker pencil, fill in the eye. Leave a small white circle at the top of the eye almond for the shine in her eyes. Again, with the darker pencil, fill in the nose structure. The doe's nose is typically completely black. Leave the section below the nostril and along the chin white.

Add some darker areas to the body. Good places to shade are the ear folds, a little within the face area and down the back of the neck. Leave the space around the eye where the curves are as lighter fur. Continue the shading along the doe's back, within the middle of the shoulder shape and down the upper portion of the near-side foreleg. Shade the middle of the animal and within the middle of the thigh shape, down the upper portion of the near-side hind leg. Leave bands of lighter fur along where the shoulder and thigh guidelines were placed. Shade the toes and dewclaws a little darker than the main body.

For a smoother finish, take your finger or a tissue and blend together the pencil shading.

The Next Stages

ADDING COLOR

A great way of expanding on your animal drawings is by adding color. In art, there are so many ways to do this, each with its own benefit and results. Typically, they each require additional skillsets, but there's nothing that cannot be learned with a bit of play and exploration. Here are a few of my favorite ways of adding color. At the beginning of this book, I highlighted the brands I like to use (page 10). Again though, using those exact brands isn't necessary if you have access to something different.

WATERCOLOR

The lovely thing about watercolor is how versatile it is. You can fill large areas with color or use a finer brush to add detail. It's a very diverse medium that can take a while to get used to, but when you've nailed some of the techniques, it's an exquisite way of adding color to your animal drawings. Here are a few things to bear in mind to make using watercolor enjoyable.

- **Make sure your drawing is waterproof if the drawing is done before the paint is added.** There are two ways of creating a watercolor illustration: Paint before or after. Painting before can be quite liberating, and you can always draw over it once the paint is dry. If you decide to add color after you've done the drawing, it's important to make sure the drawing is waterproof; otherwise, everything will bleed together and could be unsightly. Graphite is waterproof, so you can sketch as much as you like in pencil before adding watercolor paint. If you've added an outline to your animal drawing, make sure the pen you've used has waterproof ink. Some fineliners will say if they are, so that's something to bear in mind when picking your supplies.
- **The paper matters.** Some paper is better designed for the application of wet media. Thicker paper tends to cope better. So, bear in mind whether the paper you use will cope with adding watercolor. Also, some paper will get damaged if it's overworked (i.e. with lots of repetitive brush strokes while the page is wet). A good paperweight to look for is 140lb (300gsm).
- **Lots of layers are better** (unless you want the colors to bleed together). When using watercolor, patience is important. If you're adding a lot of detail and color to your illustration, it's good practice to let each layer dry before adding another one. Of course, there is the technique where you add water to the entire illustration and keep adding color so that they blend and merge together, but this is better for bases.

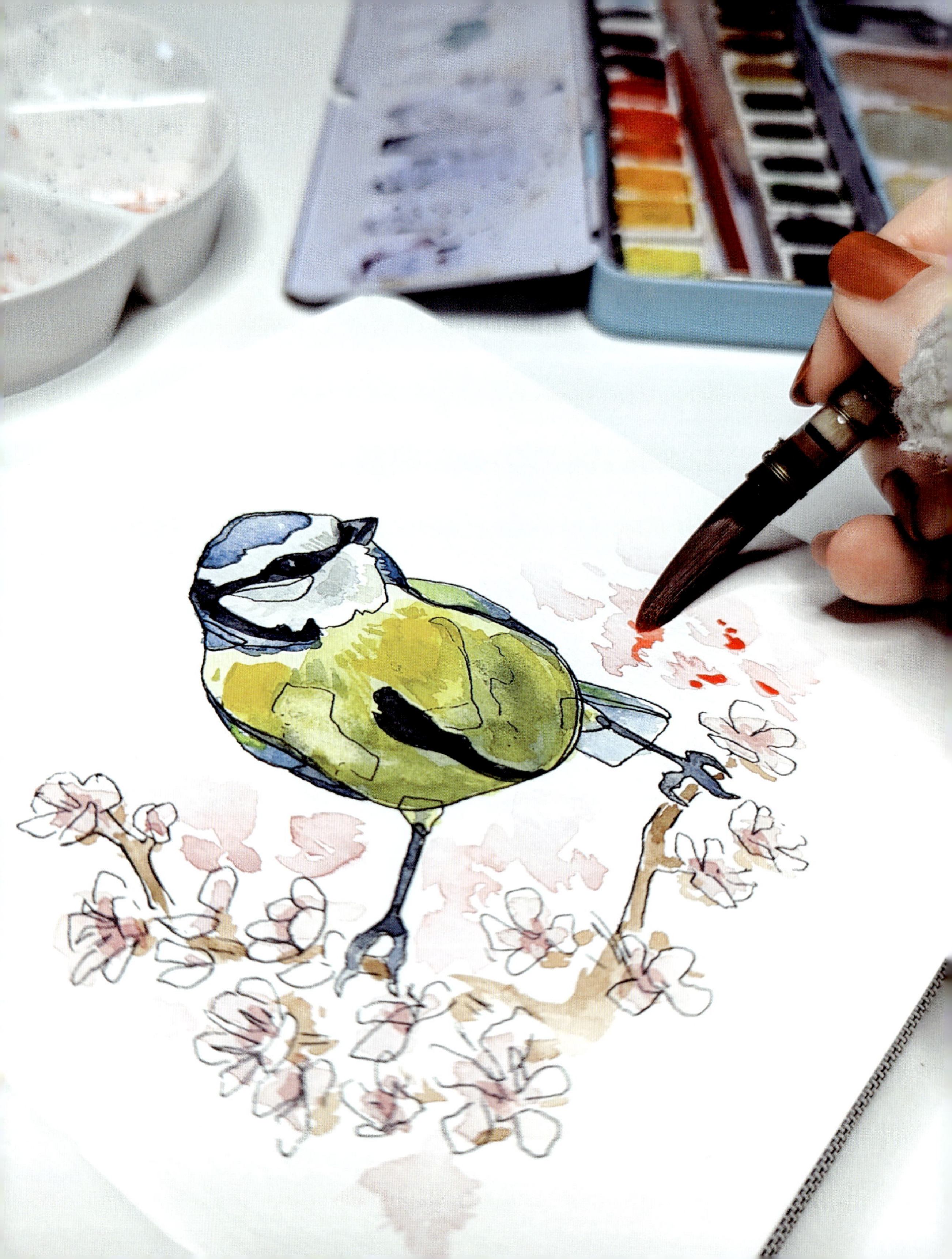

- **Less is more when it comes to water.** Water dilutes pigments into a more usable format, and the amount of water you use determines how opaque or transparent the pigment is. If you want a faint pigment, adding more water will make this happen. Just make sure to dab off the excess on a tissue so that not too much water is added to your page. This will make the paint smoother too and less runny or blotchy.

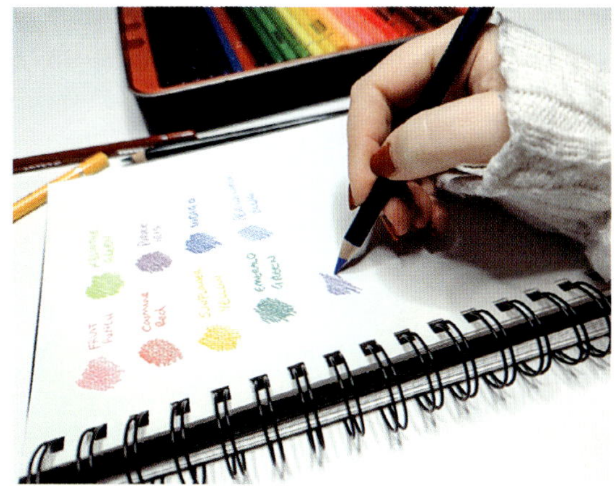

ALCOHOL MARKERS

Using alcohol markers is a really fun way of filling in large areas with flat colors. They also blend really well together, especially if they haven't completely dried when adding a new layer. Here are some tips to get the most out of alcohol markers.

- **Protect the next page of your sketchbook or the surface below the paper.** Alcohol markers have a strong tendency to bleed through paper, especially if you go over the same area a lot. It's a good habit to protect your surfaces or follow pages in a sketchbook with either extra paper or magazine pages.
- **Look out for different pen nib types.** They can come in fine points, chisels or brushes. I love using brushes because they can be used for details or large areas.
- **If adding details using an alcohol marker, make sure the previous layers have dried.** If the previous layer is still wet, it can cause other layers to blend and the edges to soften. If this is what you're after, then go ahead!
- **Store alcohol marker pens horizontally.** This keeps the nips nicely saturated and stops them from drying out.
- **Try to color in sections, allowing sections next to each other to dry so they don't bleed.** This may be handy for animals like birds that have a wide array of colors and markings. If there are different colors right next to each other, adding them separately and letting them dry before you add the other is the best way to make sure the colors don't mix and bleed.

COLORED PENCILS

Colored pencils are incredibly versatile. They can blend, be used precisely or fill in large areas. They can be used in so many ways to complement your drawings and add color. Here are some tips on using them for your animal illustrations.

- **Keep them sharp.** Sharp pencils help create a smoother application of color, especially if the paper you are using is on the rough side. The fine pencil point will get into all the small nooks and crannies to make the appearance of color nice and smooth. Also, use a manual sharpener. This will give you better control, and there will be less risk of lead breakage.

- **Take your time and add layers slowly.** Pencils have the amazing ability to be built up in layers, especially if you work from light to dark. It's a medium that can require precision, so patience is important.
- **Blend or burnish colored pencil for a smooth finish.** It is possible to get pencils that are colorless, which can be used for blending colored pencils without affecting the pigment. You can also use a paper stump tool to smooth them out and reduce the pencil strokes from being visible.

Why stick to just one type of medium? It's possible to combine the types of media I have mentioned here in wonderful ways. Perhaps you could layer large areas of color in watercolor and shade over the top in colored pencil. Or if you're creating characters, perhaps a flat layer of alcohol marker with an outline in dark pencil would look nice. It's all about playing around and finding what you like!

Tip: Test all of your colors on spare bits of paper before using them for a final illustration. One of the most disheartening things is using the wrong color on a drawing and feeling like it's been ruined. Plus, how the colors appear may not be completely accurate. At least if you've tested them, you know which one will be right for you.

SKETCH WHAT YOU SEE

A great way of taking your animal drawing skills to the next level is learning to draw from life or images. Doing this will help build up a library of poses in your head and really help with understanding how shapes fit together. The enormous benefit of drawing from animals that are right in front of you, such as your own pet dog or the cows in the field nearby, is that it helps you understand perspective and volume. These are the things that give drawings depth and 3D-like qualities.

One thing you'll probably realize is that unless an animal is asleep, they tend to move a lot. So, you might ask, "How do I draw a pose if it's constantly moving?" It's a good question, and especially pertinent when you're learning to draw. This is where techniques called sketching and gesture drawings come in. The point of sketching and gesturing is not about creating finished illustrations but rather getting the basic structures. So, this means drawing quickly, which will probably seem scary at first. If you want to try gesture drawing and sketching, here are a few tips.

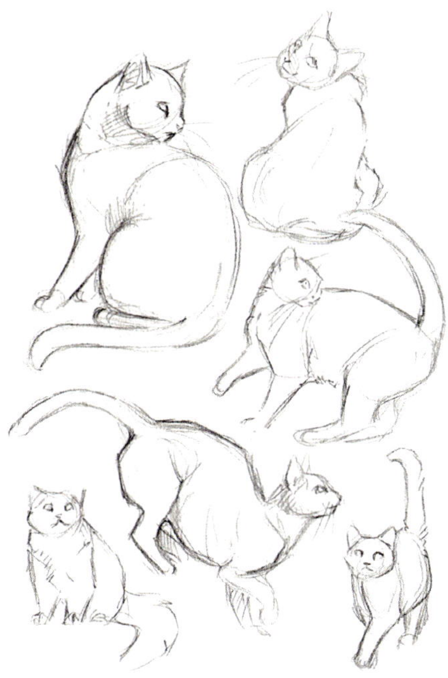

- **Keep your drawing tool loose in your hand.** It's all about being quick and going with the flow. Tension can lead to rigid drawings as well as causing you physical discomfort.
- **Draw from the shoulder and elbow, not the wrist.** This might feel tricky, especially if you're standing up. Support your sketchpad in your non-drawing arm and try to stick to just moving the upper parts of your arms while keeping your wrist relaxed but still. This creates much more fluid movement in your drawings.
- **Focus on the main shapes first, such as the head, body and direction of the legs.** It's okay if you're drawing so quickly that the legs just look like lines. It's more about getting the general gist of the animal.
- **Try to focus on the bigger picture and not the finer details.** If the animal is moving a lot, there won't be time for the details. This is about capturing the animal in its entirety and learning how to create dynamism in your drawings.
- **Flit your eyes between the animal and your drawing.** This takes a bit of practice and will involve learning how to sketch without constantly looking at your page. But, by doing this, you build up hand-eye coordination, which is an excellent drawing skill to have.
- **Be accurate, but don't worry if the lines don't go exactly where you intended.** Remember this is about learning, and there are no such things as mistakes when you're working on a new skill. Plus, try not to erase. Just re-sketch a line if you need to move it.

Even if the animals in this book are not ones that you can easily find, or going out looking for them isn't easy for you, there are many other resources you can use. The internet is an impressive source of reference photos. You can type a few words into a search engine, and before you know it, you'll have tens, hundreds or even thousands of images to draw from. Or if the internet isn't quite your thing, nature documentaries or books can be excellent references. Nature documentaries, for example, can be paused to create still images you then can draw.

The more you find time to sketch what you see either in real life or from images, the better your drawing skills will become.

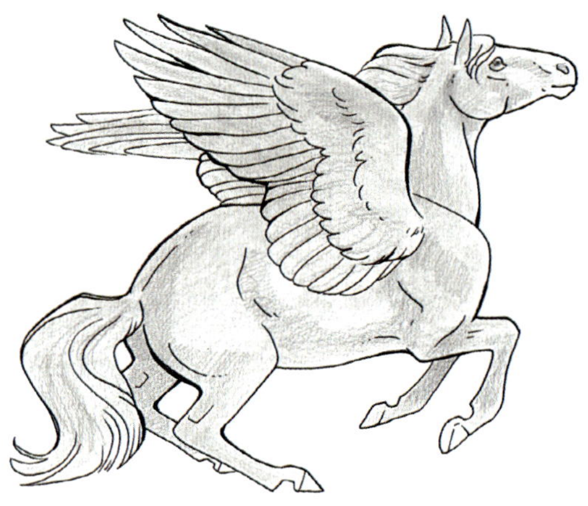

IMAGINATION IS ENDLESS

Why stop at drawing only what you see? Sometimes the most fun can come when you draw from your imagination. This can come in so many different forms, but there are a few great ways to turn to your imagination to create new and exciting drawings.

FANTASY ILLUSTRATIONS

How about creating fictional creatures such as a Pegasus? You could do this either by remembering what you've learned in this book or even simply going back and combining two tutorials. Add wing shapes from the flying bird tutorials to one of the horse tutorials, and there you have it! You could also try combining other animals to create weird and wonderful new creatures.

POSES FROM MEMORY

Once you've become comfortable drawing animals, and you've spent time drawing from life or images, your memory bank of animals will grow. Then, in time and with practice, you should be able to recall those poses and create your own drawings by heart.

STYLIZED CREATURES AND CHARACTERS

When you think of classic animated films, many of the animal characters look like the animal they are intended to be, only they're not very realistic. Typically, this will involve the exaggeration of features to stylize the animals so they're unique and distinct, but still intrinsically the animal they're supposed to be. You might like to try this and create your own characters. For example, you could make their eyes larger or their legs thinner. The beauty of this is that you can do exactly what you want to create your own perspective on animals.

Being artistically inclined and having the desire to create should never be limited. Sure, there are boundaries when drawing realistically. A realistic illustration of an animal should be based on how that animal looks in real life to make it believable. But there is beauty and fun in going off on a tangent and playing around. Let yourself be free to enjoy that.

FINAL WORD OF ENCOURAGEMENT

Learning a new skill is always admirable. At times, it can also be a challenge. We might find that things don't always go to plan, or it feels too difficult. Drawing is one of those things that can feel challenging from time to time, but remember that it's okay to find it difficult. When we are new to something, it's unlikely we are going to be good right away. If this book is the first time you've ever tried drawing animals, well done for making that decision! No matter how you're finding it right now, it will get easier. So keep going.

One thing I want you to remember is not to worry if the drawings you make don't look exactly like the ones in this book. For one, you're learning, and that's okay. In addition, that may just be your style coming through as you learn from these tutorials. You may well be putting your own unique spin on it, and that can only be a good thing.

I said at the beginning of this book that there was a key to making improvements in your drawings: Practice. Practice as often as you can. Whether that's daily, a few times a week or a couple of times a month, with practice, improvement will come. Give yourself time and be patient. The more you work at it, the easier it will feel, and before you know it, you'll be drawing with ease.

A big part of who I am as an artist is that I want creativity to be encouraged and enjoyed. It's important to me that people who want to draw, do. I hope this book has brought you inspiration and made drawing animals accessible, especially if they seemed to be intimidating before. Well done for making the choice to learn new skills too! For that I am glad and proud of you.

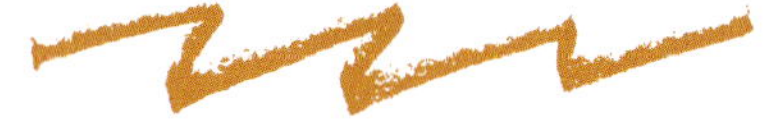

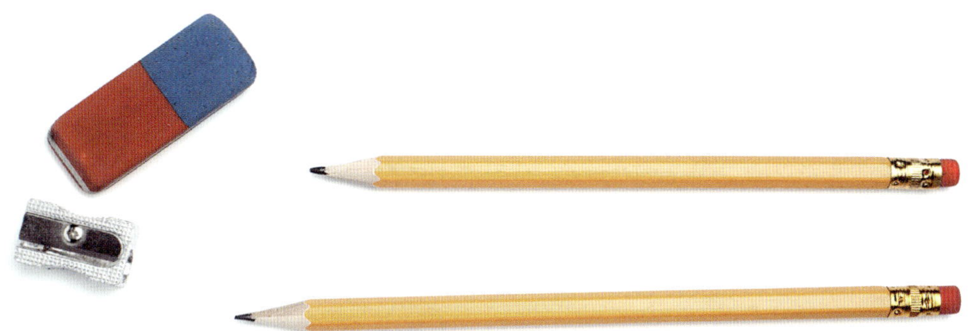

Acknowledgments

Thank you Page Street Publishing Co., without whom this endeavor wouldn't have even been a figment of my imagination, let alone a fully fledged book at the fingertips of aspiring artists wishing to draw animals. To Katherine Lima, who approached me and helped my vision become reality, to Sarah Monroe who guided me down the right path to making this book what it became and to Alexandra Murphy, who joined me seamlessly on this journey. My heartfelt thanks goes to the wonderful design team, namely Rosie Stewart, for making this book so beautiful. I, of course, mustn't forget the editors, proofreaders, marketing team and all of those who've had a say in what *The Animal Drawing Primer* has become. You are all awesome.

Thanks also go to my immediate family, Stephanie, Richard and Robyn. I had the most incredible fortune to be surrounded by people who never told me that I couldn't do what would make me happy. They allowed me to make the decisions I did with compassion, care and love, and for that, I am truly grateful.

Thank you to the rest of my family too. I'm so grateful to have been surrounded by such smart, kind and loving people. And to my departed grandfathers, John and Graham. Neither of you got to see where the creative genes I inherited from you took me. I feel robbed of your guidance and presence as I grew and took on the desire to be artistic. I hope I have made you proud.

Thank you to Katharine and Hartwig Gomme, for giving me a home to live in while I braved an unknown future as an artist. If I didn't have that security, I'm not sure I'd ever have taken on the opportunity to create for a living. This book is possible because of your generosity.

To my dearest Hype Girls: Niki Benney and Chrissy Rapsey, your positivity and empowerment have been infectious, and I wouldn't be here without it.

Thank you to each one of my social media supporters too. Again, I quite literally wouldn't have been able to create this book if you weren't there encouraging me.

Of course, to my dearest Olly. Perhaps the most important and heartfelt thanks go to you. My biggest supporter. To be able to love you is an honor, and to call you my sidekick in life brings me pride beyond measure. You help me see that opportunities are to be taken, and you hold me up when I feel I am out of my depth. You are my hero.

Oh, and Dusty, the three-legged emotional support cat. You're the best.

About the Author

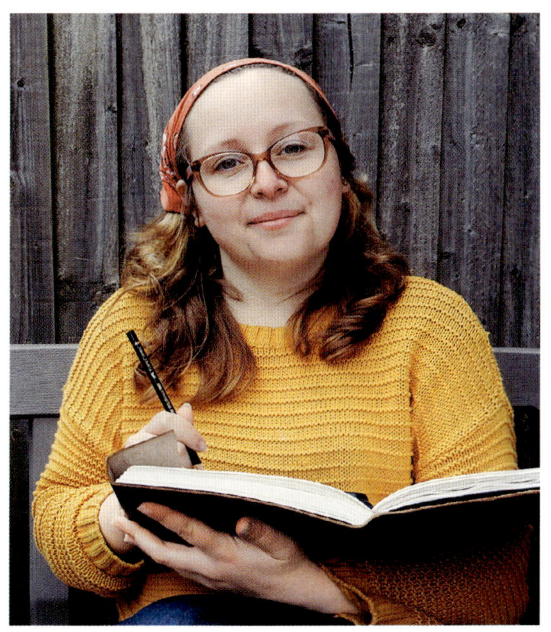

Jen is a self-taught animal artist, originally from the UK, who is now based in Germany. She has spent her life dedicated to animals, having studied animal care and behavior. With a creative upbringing, it was only natural that her love for animals merged with her passion for creating.

She has taught animal illustration on Domestika and regularly produces educational and inspirational content for all of those who follow her on social media.

You can follow Jen's work on Instagram and YouTube (@JenRaeArt) or via her website (www.jenrae.art).

The Animal Drawing Primer is Jen's first book.

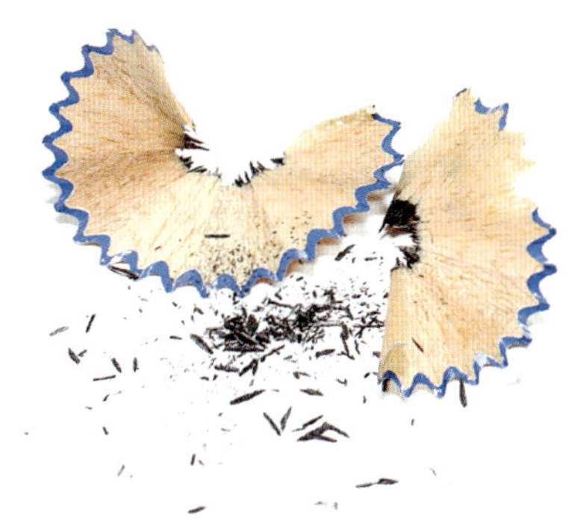

Index